Understanding
ROBERT BURNS

Understanding
ROBERT BURNS
VERSE, EXPLANATION AND GLOSSARY

George Scott Wilkie

NEIL WILSON PUBLISHING LIMITED • GLASGOW

Thanks to my son, Stuart, for his help on the computer front,
and to Diana Peacock for pushing me into the first edition.

First published by
Neil Wilson Publishing
303a The Pentagon Centre
36 Washington Street
GLASGOW
G3 8AZ
Tel: 0141-221-1117
Fax: 0141-221-5363
E-mail: info@nwp.sol.co.uk
www.nwp.co.uk

A catalogue record for this book is available
from the British Library.

ISBN 1-903238-48-X
Typeset in Jenson
Designed by Mark Blackadder
Printed by WS Bookwell, Finland

Contents

Foreword

In the forerunner to this book, *Select Works of Robert Burns*, George Wilkie displayed his comprehensive knowledge of the bard's works and his understanding of Burns as both man and poet.

Understanding Robert Burns develops this idea, bringing the reader an easily accessible glossary with an interpretation of those verses that may be difficult to understand. For the newcomer to Burns, George will give invaluable insight into the works. The aficionado, too, will gain from the excellence of George's research.

It gives me great pleasure to commend George Wilkie's book, *Understanding Robert Burns*, and I hope it brings you as much enjoyment as it has to me.

James Cosmo
January, 2002

James Cosmo is one of Scotland's most celebrated actors, and has starred in many film and television productions over the years, including the Inspector Rebus TV series and the Oscar-winning Braveheart. He is also passionate about the works of Robert Burns.

Introduction

As January 25 approaches each year, thousands of people in countries all over the globe prepare to celebrate the life of Scotland's most famous son. The kilts are brought out and the sporrans and skean-dhus are given a polish. The speeches are rehearsed, the haggis is prepared along with the tatties and the neeps, and, of course, a few wee drams will be consumed during the evening.

The Bard's most popular works will be brought out, given an airing, and we'll hear what a lad he was for the lassies, and what a terrible fellow he was for fathering so many children by so many women. There'll be all sorts of scandalous stories regarding his private life that will be dressed up as the 'Immortal Memory', his life-style seemingly more important than his life's work.

Then, at the end of the evening, everyone will go home feeling that they've had a great night and promptly forget about Robert Burns until the same time next year.

They don't know what they're missing!

Burns, in common with many other great figures in history, did indeed have a colourful and eventful life during his 37 short years upon this earth, his early demise due in no small part to the doctors of the time who believed that standing immersed in the freezing waters of the Solway Firth would benefit his failing health.

But his lifestyle is not the reason for his everlasting fame. That is due simply to the wonderful legacy of poems and songs that he left to the world, and which most certainly deserve to be read more than once a year.

Robert Burns was a man of vision. He believed absolutely in the equality of man, irrespective of privilege of rank or title. He detested cruelty and loved the gifts of nature.

It is undeniable that Burns liked the company of women, but what is not generally recognised is that he was a strong advocate of women's rights, at a time when few men were.

He despised false piety and consequently was unpopular with the church as he mocked their preachers mercilessly.

I have, however, heard an eloquent Church of Scotland minister describe some lines from the Bard's works as being no less than modern proverbs, and it is difficult to disagree with that statement when one considers the depth of meaning in some of the words that Burns wrote.

'The best laid schemes o' mice and men gang aft agley!'

'Man's inhumanity to man makes countless thousands mourn!'

'O wad some Power the giftie gie us to see oursels as ithers see us!'

'An honest man's the noblest work of God!"

The works of Robert Burns are indeed full of wisdom!

Burns' poems and songs are wonderful to read, but as many are composed in what is virtually a foreign language to the bulk of English speakers, they can be heavy going to the non-Scot, or non-Scots speaker.

This book contains a varied selection of Burns' works, some well known, others less so. It is designed to make the understanding of the verses simpler than constantly having to refer to the glossary, but without interfering in any way with the original. Burns' words remain sacrosanct! Where necessary, each verse is annotated with a simple explanation that allows the reader to follow the poem without constant interruption, and hopefully to appreciate with ease what the Bard is saying.

Let me stress that the explanations are merely my own thoughts as to the meaning of the works. If you would prefer to work them out for yourself I would recommend sitting down and writing out or typing each verse. This is essential if you are a student with exams to sit on Burns, and will ensure that your eyes do not skate across the lines, missing out much of what is contained in them.

Read and enjoy the words of Robert Burns and you will join the many millions who have fallen under his spell.

George Scott Wilkie
Hemingford Grey

Handsome Nell

O Once I Lov'd

This particular poem merits attention simply because it was the Bard's first venture into verse, written when he was merely 15. During the gathering of the harvest, it was the custom at that time to pair off male and female workers, probably to combine physical strength with nimbleness of finger. Young Robert's co-worker that year was a 14-year-old lass, Nelly Kilpatrick, daughter of a local farmer.

The following lines are a precursor to many others written by Burns in honour of the countless young ladies who caught his eye.

O once I lov'd a bonie lass	
Ay, and I love her still!	*ay*=yes
An' while that virtue warms my breast,	
I'll love my handsome Nell.	
As bonie lasses I hae seen,	*hae*=have
And mony full as braw,	*mony*=many
But for a modest gracefu' mien	*mien*=look/demeanour
The like I never saw.	
A bonie lass, I will confess,	
Is pleasant to the e'e;	*e'e*=eye
But without some better qualities	
She's no' a lass for me.	
But Nelly's looks are blythe and sweet,	
And what is best of a'–	
Her reputation is compleat,	
And fair without a flaw.	
She dresses ay sae clean and neat,	
Both decent and genteel:	
And then there's something in her gait	
Gars ony dress look weel,	*gars*=makes

A gaudy dress and gentle air
May slightly touch the heart;
But it's innocence and modesty
That polishes the dart.

'Tis this in Nelly pleases me,
'Tis this enchants my soul!
For absolutely in my breast
She reigns without controul.

O Tibbie, I Hae Seen The Day

Robert Burns was 17 when he composed this song. It relates to Isabella Steven, daughter of a wealthy local farmer. The sense of injustice that young Rab felt at the class divisions between the rich and the poor, which was to be the source of so many of his later works, comes pouring out in these verses.

CHORUS

O Tibbie, I hae seen the day,
Ye wadna been sae shy!
For laik o' gear ye lightly me,   *laik o' gear* = lack
But, trowth, I care na by.

Yestreen I met you on the moor,   *spak' na but gaed by like stoure* = didn't speak
Ye spak' na but gaed by like stoure!   but went by like blowing dust, *geck* = toss
Ye geck at me because I'm poor—   the head, *fient a* = not a
But fient a hair care I!

When comin' hame on Sunday last,   *snufft* = sniffed; *trowth* = truth;
Upon the road as I cam' past,   *caretna* = cared not
Ye snufft an' gae your head a cast—
But trowth, I care'tna by!

I doubt na lass, but ye may think,   *clink* = wealth
Because ye hae the name o' clink,
That ye can please me at a wink,
When'er ye like to try.

But sorrow tak' him that's sae mean,   No matter how poor a boy is, only misery
Altho' his pouch o' coin were clean,   will become of marrying a girl for money.
Wha follows ony saucy Quean,
That looks sae proud and high!

Altho' a lad were e'er sae smart,   Even if he were very smart, you would
If that he want the yellow dirt,   still scorn him for being poor.
Ye'll cast your head anither airt,   *anither* = another; *airt* = direction; *fu'* =
An' answer him fu' dry.   full/completely

But if he hae the name o' gear,   However, if he were wealthy, you wouldn't
Ye'll fasten to him like a breer,   care how stupid he was.
Tho' hardly he for sense or lear,   *gear* = money; *breer* = briar, *lear* =
Be better than the kye.   learning, *kye* = cattle

But, Tibbie, lass, tak' my advice;
Your daddie's gear maks you sae nice.
The Deil a ane wad spier your price,
Were ye as poor as I.

Without her father's money she would
soon sell her soul to the devil.
gear = money, *spier* = ask

There lives a lass beside yon park,
I'd rather hae her in her sark
Than you wi' a' your thousand mark,
That gars you look sae high.

There's another girl with nothing who I'd
rather have than you with all your money.
sark = shift, *gars* = makes

The Rigs O' Barley

Burns composed this verse in 1782. One of his early tales of love and romance, it is still very popular now.

It is obvious that the Bard has lost his early innocence and that shy modesty in a girl is no longer a prime factor in his estimation of her.

CHORUS
Corn rigs. an' barley rigs,   rigs = the ridges and furrows in the fields
An' corn rigs are bonie;
I'll ne'er forget that happy night
Amang the rigs wi' Annie.

It was upon a Lammas night,   *Lammas* = the night of August 1st;
When corn rigs are bonie,   *bonie* = pretty
Beneath the moon's unclouded light,
I held awa to Annie;
The time flew by, wi' tentless heed;
Till, 'tween the late and early,   *tentless heed* = undue haste
Wi' sma' persuasion she agreed
 To see me thro' the barley.

The sky was blue, the wind was still,
The moon was shining clearly;
I set her down, wi' right good will,
Amang the rigs o' barley;
I ken't her heart was a' my ain;   *ken't* = knew
I lov'd her most sincerely;
I kissed her owre and owre again,   *owre* = over
Amang the rigs o' barley.

I lock'd her in my fond embrace;
Her heart was beating rarely:
My blessings on that happy place,
Amang the rigs o' barley!   *amang* = among
But by the moon and stars so bright,
That shone that hour so clearly!
She ay shall bless that happy night   *ay* = always
Amang the rigs o' barley.

I hae been blythe wi' comrades dear;
I hae been merry drinking;
I hae been joyfu' gath'rin gear;
I hae been happy thinking:
But a' the pleasures e'er I saw,
Tho' three times doubl'd fairly—
That happy night was worth them a'.
Amang the rigs o' barley.

Nothing he has experienced in life could compare to the joy of that night.

blythe = cheerful; *gath'rin gear* = gathering possessions; *e'er* = ever

The Lass of Cessnock Banks

Burns was so smitten by the subject of this poem, Alison Begbie, that he sent her a formal proposal of marriage which she rejected. The compliments that he pays her in the following lines need no explanation as his feelings towards Alison are abundantly clear.

On Cessnock banks a lassie dwells,
Could I describe her shape and mien! *mien* = demeanour;
Our lasses a' she far excels,
An' she has twa sparkling, rogueish een! *twa* = two; *een* = eyes

She's sweeter than the morning dawn *Phoebus* = the sun (after Apollo, the
When rising Phoebus first is seen, Greek sun god)
And dew-drops twinkle o'er the lawn;
An' she has twa sparkling, rogueish een!

She's stately, like yon youthful ash *yon* = yonder; *braes* = hillsides
That grows the cowslip braes between,
And drinks the stream with vigour fresh;
An' she has twa sparkling, rogueish een!

She's spotless, like the flow'ring thorn,
With flow'rs so white and leaves so green,
When purest in the dewy morn;
An' she has twa sparkling, rogueish een!

Her looks are like the vernal May, *vernal* = spring tide
When ev'ning Phoebus shines serene,
While birds rejoice on every spray;
An' she has twa sparkling, rogueish een!

Her hair is like the curling mist
That climbs the mountain-sides at e'en, *e'en* = evening
When flow'r-reviving rains are past;
An' she has twa sparkling, rogueish een!

Her forehead's like the show'ry bow
When gleaming sunbeams intervene,
And gild the distant mountain's brow;
An' she has twa sparkling, rogueish een!

Her cheeks are like yon crimson gem,
The pride of all the flowery scene,
Just opening on its thorny stem;
An' she has twa sparkling, rogueish een!

Her teeth are like the nightly snow
When pale the morning rises keen,
While hid the murm'ring streamlets flow-
An' she has twa sparkling, rogueish een!

Her lips are like yon cherries ripe
Which sunny walls from Boreas screen;
They tempt the taste and charm the sight;
An' she has twa sparkling, rogueish een.

Her breath is like the fragrant breeze
That gently stirs the blossom'd bean,
When Phoebus sinks beneath the seas;
An' she has twa sparkling, rogueish een!

Her voice is like the ev'ning thrush,
That sings on Cessnock banks unseen,
While his mate sits nestling in the bush;
An she has twa sparkling, rogueish een!

But it's not her air, her form, her face,
Tho' matching Beauty's fabled Queen:
'Tis the mind that shines in ev'ry grace—
An' chiefly in her rogueish een!

A Prayer In The Prospect of Death

There were many occasions for Burns when life itself was nothing but intolerable hardship, and death offered release and eternal peace. This short poem shows how Burns had no fear of death and trusted God to forgive him for his transgressions.

O Thou unknown, Almighty Cause
Of all my hope and fear!
In whose dread presence, ere an hour,   *ere = ever*
Perhaps I must appear!

If I have wandered in those paths
Of life I ought to shun;
As *Something*, loudly, in my breast,
Remonstrates I have done—

Thou know'st that Thou hast formed me
With passions wild and strong;
And list'ning to their witching voice
Has often led me wrong.

Where human weakness has come short,
Or frailty stept aside,
Do Thou, All-Good, — for such Thou art—
In shades of darkness hide.

Where with intention I have err'd,   *err'd = errored*
No other plea I have,
But, Thou art good; and Goodness still
Delighteth to forgive.

I'll Go and be a Sodger

At 23, ruin was staring Burns in the face. His business partner in a flax-dressing shop had defrauded him, and on top of that, while indulging in the New Year festivities, his shop burned down. Little wonder he contemplated a career in the army.

O why the deuce should I repine,
And be an ill-foreboder ?
I'm twenty-three and five feet nine,
I'll go and be a sodger!

deuce = devil; *repine* = feel discontent;
ill-foreboder = forecaster of misfortune;

sodger = soldier

I gat some gear wi' meikle care,
I held it weel thegither;
But now it's gane, and something mair;
I'll go and be a sodger!

gear = wealth, *meikle* = much,
weel thegither = well together,
gane = gone; *mair* = more

John Barleycorn: A Ballad

Barley has always held a position of great importance in the farming economy of Scotland, not least for its contribution to the worlds of brewing and distilling. John Barleycorn describes the process.

There was three kings into the east,
Three kings both great and high,
And they hae sworn a solemn oath
John Barleycorn should die.

They took a plough and plough'd him down,
Put clods upon his head,
And they hae sworn a solemn oath   *hae* = have
John Barleycorn was dead.

But the cheerful Spring came kindly on,
And show'rs began to fall,
John Barleycorn got up again,
And sore surpris'd them all.

The sultry suns of Summer came,
And he grew thick and strong;
His head weel arm'd wi' pointed spears,
That no one should him wrong.

The sober Autumn enter'd mild,
When he grew wan and pale;
His bending joints and drooping head,
Show'd he began to fail.

His colour sicken'd more and more,
He faded into age;
And then his enemies began,
To show their deadly rage.

They've ta'en a weapon, long and sharp,
And cut him by the knee;
They ty'd him fast upon a cart,
Like a rogue for forgerie.

They laid him down upon his back,
And cudgell'd him full sore.   *cudgell'd* = clubbed
They hung him up before the storm,
And turn'd him o'er and o'er.

They filled up a darksome pit
With water to the brim,
They heav'd in John Barleycorn—
There let him sink or swim!

They laid him upon the floor,
To work him further woe;
And still, as signs of life appear'd,
They toss'd him to and fro,

They wasted, o'er a scorching flame,
The marrow of his bones;
But a miller us'd him worst of all
For he crush'd him between two stones.

And they hae ta'en his very heart's blood,
And drank it round and round;
And still the more and more they drank,
Their joy did more abound.

John Barleycorn was a hero bold,
Of noble enterprise;
For if you do but taste his blood,
'Twill make your courage rise.

'Twill make a man forget his woe;
'Twill heighten all his joy;
'Twill make the widow's heart to sing,
Tho' the tear were in her eye.

Then let us toast John Barleycorn,
Each man a glass in hand;
And may his great posterity
Ne'er fail in old Scotland!   *ne'er* = never

The Death and Dying Words of Poor Mailie

THE AUTHOR'S ONLY PET YOWE;

AN UNCO MOURNFU' TALE

Burns had bought a ewe and her two lambs from a neighbouring farmer, really just to keep as pets. The ewe was kept tethered in a field adjacent to his house.

Unfortunately, the ewe managed to entangle herself in her rope and fell into a ditch where she lay, apparently dying. The poem tells the story of the poor old ewe's dying wishes which she related to a passerby who happened upon her as she lay there, but who was unable to be of any assistance to her.

This poem is one of the Bard's earliest works, if not his first, to be written in the Auld Scots tongue, and here the glossary is essential to the understanding of the poem.

As Mailie, an' her lambs thegither,
Was ae day nibblin' on the tether
Upon her cloot she coost a hitch,
An' owre she warsl'd in the ditch;
There, groanin', dyin', she did lie,
When Hughoc he cam doytin by.

Mailie the ewe gets herself tangled in her tether and falls into the ditch where she is found by Hughoc, a farm labourer.
thegither = together; *ae* = one; *cloot* = hoof; *coost a hitch* = caught in a loop; *owre* = over; *warsl'd* = wrestled; *cam doyting by* = came doddering by

Wi glowrin een, an' lifted han's,
Poor Hughoc like a statue stan's
He saw her days were near-hand ended
But, waes my heart!!
He could na mend it!
He gaped wide, but naething spak–
At length poor Mailie silence brak.

Hughoc can only stand and stare, unable to move and speechless until Mailie breaks the silence.
wi' glowrin een = with staring eyes; *han's* = hands; *near-hand* = close-by; *wae* = woe, *could na mend it* = could not help it; *naething spak* = said nothing; *brak* = broke

'O thou, whase lamentable face
Appears to mourn my woefu' case!
My dying words attentive hear,
An' bear them to my Master dear,

She instructs him to listen to her dying words and make certain that he relates them to her master.
whase = whose; *lamentable* = sad; *woefu'case* = deplorable state

'Tell him, if e'er again he keep
As muckle gear as buy a sheep,
O, bid him never tie them mair,
Wi' wicked strings o' hemp or hair!
But ca' them out to park or hill,
An' let them wander at their will;
So, may his flock increase an' grow
To scores of lambs and packs o' woo!

Should her master ever be able to afford more sheep, then he is to let them roam freely and nature will increase the size of his flock and produce more wool.
muckle gear = much wealth; *mair* = anymore; *woo* = wool

'Tell him he was a Master kin',
An' ay was guid to me an' mine;
An' now my dying charge I gie him,
My helpless lambs, I trust them wi' him.

Her dying wish is that her master be responsible for the upbringing of her lambs.
kin' = kind; *ay* = always

'O, bid him save their harmless lives,
Frae dogs, an' tods, an' butcher's knives!
But gie them guid cow-milk their fill,
'Till they be fit to fend themsel';
An' tent them duly, e'en an' morn,
Wi' taets o' hay an' ripps o' corn.

The master should ensure that the lambs are not savaged by dogs or foxes. He must not allow them to be butchered but must see that they are fed carefully both morning and night.
tods = foxes; *taets* = small quantities; *ripps* =handfuls

'An may they never learn the gaets,
Of other vile, wanrestfu' pets!
To slink thro' slaps, an' reave an' steal
At stacks o' pease, or stocks o' kail!
So may they, like their great forbears,
For monie a year come thro' the sheers:
So wives will give them bits o' bread,
An' bairns greet for them when they're dead.

They must not become thieving wastrels. With pride in their ancestry they will supply wool for years to come, and when they die they will be sadly missed.
gaets = manners; *wanrestfu'* = restless; *thro' slaps* = through gaps in hedges; *come thro' the sheers* = be sheared; *greet* = cry

'My poor toop-lamb, my son an' heir,
O, bid him breed him up wi' care!
An' if he lives to be a beast,
To put some havins in his breast!

The eldest child must learn good behaviour and grow up to be a proud ram.
toop= tup; *put some havins* = put some good manners

'An' warn him, what I winna name,
To stay content wi' yowes at hame;
An' no' to rin an' wear his cloots,
Like ither menseless, graceless brutes.

'An' niest, my yowie, silly thing,
Gude keep thee frae a tether string!
O, may thou ne'er forgather up,
Wi' onie blastit, moorland toop;
But ay keep mind to moop an' mell,.
Wi' sheep o' credit like thysel'

'And now, my bairns, wi' my last breath,
I lea'e my blessin wi' you baith;
An' when you think upo' your Mither,
Mind to be kind to ane anither

'Now, honest Hughoc, dinna fail,
To tell my master a' my tale;
An' bid him burn this curs'd tether
An' for thy pains thou's got my blather.'

This said, poor Mailie turn'd her head,
An' clos'd her een amang the dead!

He must stay with the flock, unlike other ill-behaved oafs.
no to rin = not to run; *wear his cloots* = wear out his hoofs; *menseless* = stupid.

The silly baby ewe must be told to watch out for tethers, and to save herself for sheep of her own class and not to get involved with the wild rams that wander the moorlands.
niest = next; *moop an' mell* = nibble and mix

Maillie blesses her children and reminds them to be kind to each other.
baith = both

Hughoc must tell the master of her wishes And see to it that the tether is burned. His reward has been to hear her speak.

All this said, Maillie closes her eyes and dies.

Poor Mailie's Elegy

Following the death of his pet sheep and his poem of her dying wishes, Burns shows his own feelings for Mailie the ewe, and expresses his deep sorrow for her departure from this earth.

Lament in rhyme, lament in prose,
Wi' saut tears trickling down your nose;
Our Bardie's fate is at a close,
Past a' remead!
The last, sad cape-stane of his woes;
Poor Mailie's dead.

saut = salt; *past a' remead* = is incurable;
cape-stane = cope stone

It's no' the loss o' warl's gear,
That could sae bitter draw the tear,
Or mak our bardie, dowie, wear
The mourning weed;
He's lost a friend and neebor dear,
In Mailie dead.

He does not regard her simply as a piece of property he has lost, but believes her to have been a true friend.
warl's gear = wordly wealth; *dowie* = sad;
mourning weed = mourning clothes

Thro' a' the town she trotted by him;
A lang half-mile she could descry him;
Wi' kindly bleat, when she did spy him,
She ran wi' speed:
A friend mair faithfu' ne'er came nigh him,
Than Mailie dead.

She'd trot by him, recognising him at a distance, running to him when she did.
descry = recognise; *ne'er came nigh* = never came close

I wat she was a sheep o' sense,
An' could behave hersel' wi' mense;
I'll say 't, she never brak a fence,
Thro' thievish greed,
Our Bardie, lanely keeps the Spence
Sin' Mailie's dead.

She really was a sensible and graceful sheep who never attempted to break through into other fields to steal food.
wat = know; *mense* = good manners; *brak* = break; *lanely* = lonely; *keeps the spence* = stays in the parlour

Or, if he wanders up the howe,
Her living image in her yowe,
Comes bleating to him, owre the knowe,
For bits o' bread;
An' down the briny pearls rowe
For Mailie dead.

The ewe lamb is so like Mailie that the Bard is reduced to tears when she comes looking for bread, just as her mother did.
howe = dell; *owre the knowe* = over the hills; *briny pearls* = salt tears; *rowe* = roll

She was nae get o' moorlan tips,
Wi' tauted ket, an' hairy hips;
For her forbears were brought in ships,.
Frae 'yont the Tweed;
A bonier fleesh ne'er cross'd the clips
Than Mailie's dead.

Mailie had good ancestry, unlike the sheep that roamed the moors. She came from foreign parts and gave the finest wool.
fae get o' moorland tips = not the offspring of moorland rams; *wi' tauted ket* = with matted fleece; *a bonnier fleesh ne'e cross'd the clips* = a better fleece was never sheared

Wae worth the man wha first did shape,
That vile wanchancie thing – a rape!
It maks guid fellows girn and gape
Wi' chokin dread;
An' Robin's bonnet wave wi' crape
For Mailie dead

He curses the first man to shape a rope. Good men dread it and Burns is mourning Mailie because of it.
wae worth = woe befall; *wanchancie* = unlucky; *rape* = rope; *girn and gape* = whimper and stare; *bonnet* = hat; *ave wi' crape* = adorned with black crepe

O, a' ye Bards on bonie Doon!
An' wha on Aire your chanters tune!
Come, join the melancholious croon
O' Robin's reed!
His heart will never get aboon!
His Mailie's dead!

Finally he calls on all poets and pipers to join in a lament for Mailie. He, Robert Burns, is himself heart-broken – His Mailie is dead.
a' ye = all you; *chanter* = bagpipes; *melancholious croon* = lament; *reed* = music pipe; *aboon* = above

Remorse

Burns was in full agreement with the philosopher, Adam Smith, in his *Theory of Moral Sentiments*, that remorse is the most painful of sentiments. Rab had great experience of remorse in his life and these words are written with deep feeling.

Of all the numerous ills that hurt our peace,
That press the soul, or wring the mind with anguish,
Beyond comparison the worst are those
That to our Folly, or our Guilt we owe.
In ev'ry other circumstance, the mind
Has this to say,' It was no deed of mine.'
But, when to all the evil of misfortune
The sting is added, 'Blame thy foolish self!'
Or, worser far, the pangs of keen remorse,
The torturing, gnawing consciousness of guilt,
Of guilt, perhaps, where we've involved others;
The young, the innocent, who fondly lov'd us;
Nay, more that very love their cause of ruin!
O! burning Hell! in all thy store of torments
There's not a keener lash!
Lives there a man so firm, who, while his heart
Feels all the bitter horrors of his crime,
Can reason down its agonizing throbs,
And, after proper purpose of amendment,
Can firmly force his jarring thoughts to peace?
O happy, happy, enviable man!
O glorious magnamity of soul!

The Ruined Farmer

The following verses were doubtless inspired by the death of the poet's father, William Burnes, whose Calvinistic attitude towards learning ensured that Robert was well-schooled in many subjects. Sadly, Burnes' move to Ayrshire led him into a life of toil and hardship, ending with a court appearance because of rent arrears. Although he won on appeal, he died shortly afterwards through 'physical consumption aggravated by hardship and worry.'

The sun he is sunk in the west,
All creatures retired to rest,
While here I sit, all sore beset,
With sorrow, grief, and woe;
And it's O, fickle Fortune, O!

The prosperous man is asleep,
Nor hears how the whirlwinds sweep;
But Misery and I must watch
The surly tempest blow:
And it's O, fickle Fortune, O!

There lies the dear Partner of my breast;
Her cares for a moment at rest:
Must I see thee, my youthful pride,
Thus brought so very low!
And it's O, fickle Fortune, O!

There lie my sweet babies in her arms;
No anxious fear their little hearts alarms;
But for their sake my heart does ache,
With many a bitter throe:
And it's O, fickle Fortune, O!

I once was by Fortune carest,
I once could relieve the distrest,
Now life's poor support, hardly earn'd,
My fate will scarce bestow:
And it's O, fickle Fortune, O!

No comfort, no comfort I have!
How welcome to me were the grave!
But then my wife and children dear —
O, whither would they go!
And it's O, fickle Fortune, O!

O, whither, O, whither shall I turn!
All friendless, forsaken, forlorn!
For, in this world, Rest or Peace
I never more shall know:
And it's O, fickle Fortune, O!

Mary Morrison

This poem is one of the Bard's earlier works, written in praise of one of the countless young ladies who happened to catch his eye. It is generally thought to be dedicated to a lass of that name who died from consumption at the age of 20, and whose tombstone can be seen in Mauchline churchyard. This is possible, but is not certain, as she would have only been 13 or 14 when the poem was written.

O Mary, at thy window be,
It is the wish'd, the trysted hour.
Those smiles and glances let me see,
That make the miser's treasure poor.
How blythely wad I bide the stoure,   *bide the stoure* = bear the struggle
A weary slave frae sun to sun,   *frae* = from
Could I the rich reward secure—
The lovely Mary Morrison!

Yestreen, when to the trembling string   *yestreen* = yesterday
The dance ga'ed thro' the lighted ha',   *ha'* = hall
To thee my fancy took its wing,
I sat, but neither heard, nor saw;
Tho' this was fair, and that was braw,   *braw* = good
And yon the toast of a' the town,   *yon* = those
I sigh'd, and said amang them a',
"Ye are na Mary Morrison!"

O, Mary, canst thou wreck his peace
Wha for thy sake wad gladly die?
Or canst thou break that heart of his
Whase only faute is loving thee?   *whase* = whose; *faute* = fault;
If love for love thou wilt na gie,   *gie* = give
At least be pity to me shown:
A thought ungentle canna be
The thought o' Mary Morrison.

Address to The Unco Guid
or The Rigidly Righteous

My son, these maxims make a rule
An' bump them a' thegither;
The Rigid Righteous *is a fool,*
The Rigid Wise *anither;*
The cleanest corn that e'er was dight
May have some piles o' caff in ;
So ne'er a fellow creature slight
For random fits o' daffin,
SOLOMON ——Eccles Ch vii verse 16

Robert Burns was never one to tolerate the 'Holier Than Thou' attitude held by others.

O ye, wha are sae guid yoursel'.
Sae pious and sae holy,
Ye've naught to do but mark and tell
Your neebour's fauts and folly!
Whase life is like a weel-gaun mill,
Supply'd wi' store o' water;
The heapet happer's ebbing still,
An' still the clap plays clatter!

Self righteous people believe their orderly lives permit them to criticise others who they believe to have inferior standards of behaviour. *wha are sae guid* = who are so good; *naught* = nothing; *neebor* = neighbour/friend; *fauts and folly* = faults and foolishness; *whase* = whose; *weel-gaun* = good going; *heapit happer* = heaped hopper; *ebbing* = sinking; *plays clatter* = acts noisily

Hear me, ye venerable core,
As counsel for poor mortals
That frequent pass douce Wisdom's door
For glaikit Folly's portals;
I, for their thoughtless, careless sakes,
Would here propone defences—
Their donsie tricks, their black mistakes,
Their failings and mischances.

Burns offers a defence for those who might have been foolish in their lives, whose sexual adventures may have caused them some regret, and who are generally regarded as failures by society. *venerable core* = revered company; *douce* = grave; *glaikit* = foolish; *propone* = propose; *gonsie tricks* = stupid pranks; *mischance* = ill-luck

Ye see your state wi' theirs compared,
And shudder at the niffer;
But cast a moment's fair regard,
What maks the mighty differ ?
Discount what scant occasion gave;
The purity ye pride in;
And (what's aft mair than a' the lave)
Your better art o' hidin'.

The self-righteous may shudder at being compared with such people, but often the only difference is that they may never have been put to the test.
niffer = comparison; *scant occasion* = slight opportunity; *aft mair* = often more; *a' the lave* = all the rest

Think, when your castigated pulse
Gies now and then a wallop,
What ragings must his veins convulse,
That still eternal gallop!
Wi' wind and tide fair i' your tail,
Right on ye scud your sea-way,
But in the teeth o' baith to sail,
It maks an unco lee-way.

Remember how it feels when your pulses race. All may may be fine when all is going their way, but it may be different when faced with adversity.
castigated = chastised; scud = drive before the wind; baith = both; an unco lee-way = uncommonly hard-going

See Social-life and Glee sit down,
All joyous and unthinking,
Till, quite transmugrify'd, they're grown
Debauchery and Drinking:
O would they stay to calculate
Th' eternal consequences,
Or, your more dreaded hell to state –
Damnation of expenses!

While ordinary people regard socialising as an occasion for enjoyment, the self-righteous tend to see such events as deeply sinful, and therefore a direct path to hell.
transmugrify'd = transformed

Ye high, exalted, virtuous dames,
Ty'd up in godly laces,
Before ye gie poor Frailty names,
Suppose a change o' cases;
A dear-lov'd lad, convenience snug.
A treach'rous inclination –
But let me whisper i' your lug,.
Ye're aiblins nae temptation.

Burns then questions how the good ladies, all tied up in their corsets, would react if offered the opportunity for pleasure with someone they deeply admired, but then cuttingly doubts if they would be capable of attracting any man.
snug = sheltered; aiblins = perhaps

Then gently scan your brother Man,
Still gentler sister Woman;
Tho' they may gang a kennin wrang,
To step aside is human:
One point must still be greatly dark,
The moving *Why* they do it;
And just as lamely can ye mark,.
How far perhaps they rue it.

He asks that consideration and forgiveness be given to one's fellow man and woman who may have erred in life. Without knowing what prompted them to have sinned in the first place, there is no knowing the sorrow and regret that a person may now be suffering.
a kennin = a little bit; wrang = wrong

Who made the heart, 'tis He alone
Decidedly can try us;
He knows each chord, its various tone,
Each spring its various bias;
Then at the balance let's be mute,
We never can adjust it;
What's done we partly may compute,
But know not what's resisted.

Only God has the ability to judge us. Only He knows the full story. Although we may have witnessed some transgressions, we have no way of knowing how many others have been resisted.

The Ronalds of the Bennals

This poem refers to a family, the Ronalds, who farmed the Bennals, a prosperous 200-acre farm close to where the Burns family were desperately scraping a living from their under-nourished land. One can feel a strong touch of resentment, and possibly a little spite, on the part of Robert as both he and brother Gilbert were considered to be unlikely suitors for the daughters of such a well-to-do family.

In Tarbolton, ye ken, there are proper
    young men,
And proper young lasses and a', man;
But ken ye the Ronalds that live
    in the Bennals?
They carry the gree frae them a', man.

There may be plenty young ladies and gentlemen in the area, but the Ronalds are a cut above the rest.
ken = know; *carry the gree* = bear the bell

Their father's a laird, and weel he can spare't,
Braid money to tocher them a', man;
To proper young men, he'll clink in the hand
Gowd guineas a hunder or twa, man.

The father is wealthy enough to offer a good dowry to the correct suitor.
braid = broad; *tocher* = dowry; *gowd* = gold; *hunder* = hundred

There's ane they ca' Jean, I'll warrant ye've seen
As bonie a lass or as braw, man;
But for sense and guid taste she'll
    vie wi' the best,
And a conduct that beautifies a', man.

You may well have seen others as lovely as Jean, but her sense and good taste set her apart.

The charms o' the min', the langer they shine
The mair admiration they draw, man;
While peaches and cherries, and
    roses and lilies,
They fade and they wither awa', man.

Better an intelligent woman than one whose beauty is merely skin-deep.

If ye be for Miss Jean, tak this frae a frien',
A hint o' a rival or twa, man
The Laird o' Blackbyre wad gang through
    the fire,
If that wad entice her awa, man.

Jean is a very popular young lady who is already being pursued by some wealthy suitors.

The Laird o' Braehead has been on his speed,
For mair than a towmond or twa, man;
The Laird o' the Ford will straught
    on a board,
If he canna get her at a', man

towmond = twelve months;

straught = stretch

Then Anna comes in, the pride o' her kin,
The boast of our bachelors a', man;
Sae sonsy and sweet, sae fully complete,
She steals our affections awa, man.

Anna is the one that the local swains really admire.

If I should detail the pick and the wale
O' lasses that live here awa, man
The faut would be mine, if she didna shine
The sweetest and best o' them a', man.

She is positively the pick of the bunch.
wale = choice; *faut* = fault.

I lo'e her mysel', but darena weel tell,
My poverty keeps me in awe, man;
For making o' rhymes, and working at times,
Does little or naething at a', man.

The poet loves Anna but dare not tell her as he has no wealth to offer. His poetry and his farm work earn him very little.

Yet I wadna choose to let her refuse
Nor ha'et in her power to say na, man;
For though I be poor, unnoticed, obscure,
My stomach's as proud as them a', man.

He would never confess his love to her.

Though I canna ride in weel-booted pride,
And flee o'er the hills like a craw, man,
I can haud up my head wi' the best
    o' the breed,
Though fluttering ever so braw, man.

He may not be able to afford a fine steed to carry him over the hills, but he can hold his head high in any company.

My coat and my vest, they are Scotch o'
    the best;
O' pairs o' good breeks I hae twa, man,
And stockings and pumps to put
    on my stumps,
And ne'er a wrang steek in them a', man.

His clothes are of good quality, he owns two pairs of breeches, and his stockings are whole and undarned.
breeks = breeches; *steek* = stitch

My sarks they are few, but five o' them new,
Twal'-hundred, as white as the snaw, man!
A ten-shillings hat, a Holland cravat—
There are no monie poets sae braw, man!

He owns five new shirts of top quality linen, and with his fine hat and cravat believes few poets can equal him for elegance. *sarks* = shirts; *twal'-hundred* = a grade of linen

I never had freen's weel stockit in means,
To leave me a hundred or twa, man;
Nae weel-tocher'd aunts, to wait on
    their drants,
And wish them in hell for it a', man;

No friends nor relatives have ever left him money in their wills.
weel stockit = wealthy; *tocher'd* = doweried; *drants* = sulks, moods

I never was cannie for hoarding o' money,
Or claughtin 't together at a', man;
I've little to spend and naething to lend,
But devil a shilling I awe, man.

He'd never been good at saving money, but in spite of having so little, owes nothing to anyone.
claughtin = grasoing

The Belles of Mauchline

Robert has by now got over the earlier rejection of his marriage proposal to Alison Begbie, and his eye is now taken by the girl who was to eventually become his wife, Jean Armour. Here he compares her favourably with the other young girls in the village.

In Mauchline there dwells six proper young belles,
The pride of the place and its neighbourhood a',
Their carriage and dress, a stranger would guess,
In Lon'on or Paris they'd gotten it a'.

Miss Miller is fine, Miss Murkland's divine,
Miss Smith she has wit, and Miss Morton is braw,
There's beauty and fortune to get wi' Miss Morton;
But Armour's the jewel for me o' them a'.

Epistle to John Rankine

John Rankine was a local tenant-farmer who was a close friend of Robert Burns. On discovering that Elizabeth Paton was pregnant by Burns, Rankine joshed him mercilessly. Burns retaliated with the following verses which hardly show remorse for the situation in which he had found himself. The church adopted a very hard attitude towards anyone found indulging in sex outside marriage. The culprits were publicly chastised and had fines imposed upon them.

O rough, rude, ready-witted Rankine,
The wale o' cocks for fun an' drinkin!
There's mony godly folks are thinkin,
Your dreams and tricks
Will send you, Korah-like, a-sinkin,
Straught to auld Nick's.

Rankine may be a popular fellow with the drinking fraternity, but some people think that his actions will send him to Hell.
wale = pick; *mony* = many; *Korah–like* = Numbers xvi verses 29-33, his soul will be cut off forever; *straught* = straight

Ye hae sae mony cracks an' cants,
And in your wicked druken rants,
Ye mak a devil o' the saunts,
An' fill them fou;
And then their failings, flaws an' wants,
Are a' seen thro'.

You have so many stories to tell, but in your drunkenness you make fools of the good people, revealing all their failings.
cracks and cants = anecdotes; *saunts* = saints; *fou* = full

Hypocrisy, in mercy spare it!
That holy robe, O, dinna tear it!
Spare't for their sakes, wha aften wear it—
The lads in black;
But your curst wit, when it comes near it,
Rives't aff their back.

Don't be a hypocrite. Leave the preaching to the priests.
rives't = rips

Think, wicked sinner, wha ye're skaithing;
It's just the Blue-gown badge an' claithing,
O saunts; tak that, ye lea'e them naething,
To ken them by,
Frae onie unregenerate heathen,
Like you or I.

He points out that without their badges and gowns, the priests would be just like everyone else.
skaithing = wounding; *Blue-gown badge* = a badge given to beggars on the king's birthday; *claithing* = clothin

I've sent you here, some rhymin' ware,
A' that I bargain'd for, an' mair;
Sae, when ye hae an hour to spare,
I will expect,
Yon sang ye'll sen't, wi' cannie care,
And no neglect.

He has enclosed some songs and poems for Rankine to look over.

Tho faith, sma' heart hae I to sing:
My Muse dow scarcely spread her wing!
I've play'd mysel' a bonie spring,
And danc'd my fill!
I'd better gaen an' sair't the King
At Bunker's Hill.

He has little to sing about at the moment, and might have been better off fighting for the King in America.
dow = scarcely; *sair't* = served; *Bunker's Hill* = a battle-field in the American war

'Twas ae night lately, in my fun,
I gaed a rovin' wi' the gun,
An' brought a paitrick to the grun'—
A bonie hen;
And, as the twilight was begun,
Thought nane wad ken.

His sexual exploits are disguised by using the analogy of the hunter in pursuit of game, and explains that as it was dusk, he did not expect to be discovered.
paitrick = partridge; *grun'* = ground.

The poor wee thing was little hurt;
I straikit it a wee for sport,
Ne'er thinkin' they wad fash me for't;
But Deil-ma-care!
Somebody tells the Poacher-Court
The hale affair.

Nobody was hurt by the encounter and he was very surprised to be reported to the Kirk Session for his misdemeanours.
straikit it a wee = stroked it a little, *fash* = worry; *Poacher- Court* = Kirk Session, *hale* = whole.

Some auld, us'd hands hae ta'en a note,
That sic a hen had got a shot;
I was suspected for the plot;
I scorn'd to lie;
So gat the whissle o' my groat,
An' pay't the fee.

Someone has reported that the girl is pregnant and he is the main suspect. Rather than try to lie his way out, he accepts responsibility and pays the fine.
gat the whissle o' my groat = lost my money

But by my gun, o' guns the wale,
An' by my pouther an' my hail,
An' by my hen an' by her tail,
I vow an' swear!
The game shall pay, owre moor an' dale,
For this, niest year!

He feels aggrieved and is determined that he will get full value for his money in the following year.
wale = pick; *pouther an' hail* = powder and shot; *niest* = next

As soon's the clockin-time is by,
An' the wee powts begun to cry,
Lord, I'se hae sportin' by an' by
For my gowd guinea;
Tho' I should herd the buckskin kye
For't, in Virginia

As soon as the mother is able, he intends to pursue her again even although he might have to flee to America to herd cattle.
clockin-time = incubation period; *powts* = chicks; *buckskin kye* = longhorn cattle

Trowth, they had muckle for to blame!
'Twas neither broken wing nor limb,
But twa-three chaps about the wame,
Scarce thro' the feathers;
An' baith a yellow George to claim,
An' thole their blethers!

There were many others who could have been blamed, and it's not as if she had been injured, merely lightly touched, and it's cost him a guinea to shut them up.
chaps = knocks; *wame* = belly; *yellow George* = golden guinea; *thole* = tolerate

It pits me ay as mad's a hare;
So I can rhyme nor write nae mair;
But pennyworths again is fair,
When time's expedient:
Meanwhile, I am, respected Sir,
Your most obedient.

He is so angry about the situation that he cannot concentrate on his writing, but he will get his own back in due course.

The Twa Herds; or, The Holy Tulzie
An Unco Mournfu Tale

Blockheads with reason, wicked wits abhor,
But fool with fool is barborous civil war.— Pope

A quarrel over parish boundaries between two ministers, Alexander Moodie of Riccarton, and John Russell of Kilmarnock came to a head at a meeting of the presbytery, resulting in loud and abusive altercations between the two men.

Burns was never one to let such an opportunity slip, and wrote the following satire about the occasion. The Auld–Light preachers were the fire and brimstone brigade, threatening their congregations with eternal damnation, while the New–Lights were the moderates who preached with understanding and compassion.

O a' ye pious godly flocks,
Weel fed on pastures orthodox,
Wha now will keep you frae the fox,
Or worrying tykes?
Or wha will tent the waifs and crocks.
About the dykes?

This division means that the regular churchgoers will have no minister to turn to and the sick and elderly will be left without assistance. *wha* = who; *frae* = *from*; *tykes* = dogs; *tent the waifs an' crocks* = tend to the stragglers and the elderly

The twa best herds in a' the wast,
That e'er gae gospel horns a blast
These five an' twenty simmers past—
O dool to tell!
Hae had a bitter, black outcast
Atween themsel.

The two ministers who have long been friends have fallen out.
herd = shepherd; *wast* = west; *dool* = sad; *simmers* = summers

O Moodie, man, an' wordy Russell,
How could you breed sae vile a bustle?
Ye'll see how New–Light herds will whistle,
An' think it fine!
The Lord's cause gat na sic a twissle
Sin' I hae min'.

While the two are at loggerheads, the others will benefit. He cannot recall such a carry-on in the Church.
gat na sic a twissle = got into such a twist; *sin I hae min'* = since I can recall

O Sirs! whae'er wad hae expeckit
Your duty ye wad sae negleckit?
Ye wha was ne'er by lairds respeckit
To wear the plaid,
But by the vera brutes eleckit,
To be their guide!

This refers to the choosing of ministers by the lairds in the expectation that they would be their spiritual guides. The plaid was the clothing worn by shepherds which was the dress at that time for ministers.

What flock wi' Moodie's flock could rank
Sae hale an' hearty every shank?
Nae poison'd, soor Ariminian stank
He let them taste;
But Calvin's fountain-head they drank,—
O, sic a feast!

Moodie's congregation had always been the most pious and righteous, and were extremely Calvinistic in their lives.
hale = whole; *shank* = leg; *soor Ariminian stank* = stagnant pool; *sic* = such

The fulmart, wil-cat, brock, an' tod
Weel kend his voice thro' a' the wood;
He smell'd their ilka hole an' road,
Baith out an' in;
An' weel he lik'd to shed their bluid,
An' sell their skin.

Moodie's voice was well known to the furry creatures in the woods as he loved to trap and kill them and sell their skins.
fulmart = polecat; *wil-cat* = wildcat; *brock* = badger; *tod* = fox; *ilka* = every; *baith* = both; *bluid* = blood

What herd like Russell tell'd his tale?
His voice was heard o'er muir and dale;
He ken'd the Lord's sheep, ilka tail,
O'er a' the height;
An' tell'd gin they were sick or hale,
At the first sight.

Burns compares Russell's congregation to a flock of sheep which he knew intimately. He knew if they were genuinely ill or merely evading him.
muir = moor; *gin* = if

He fine a maingy sheep could scrub;
And nobly fling the gospel club;
Or New-Light herds could nicely drub
And pay their skin;
Or hing them o'er the burning dub,
Or shute them in.

He knew how to purify any poor sinner by threats about hell. As for the New-Lights, he would hang them over the fires of hell or simply throw them in to roast.
hing = hang; *the burning dub* = the lake of hell

Sic twa – O! do I live to see 't?—
Sic famous twa sud disagree 't,
An' names like, 'Villain, Hypocrite,'
Each ither gi'en
While enemies wi' laughing spite,
Say 'neither's liein!'

While the two are busy insulting each other with abusive name-calling, the moderates are laughing and stating that they are both telling the truth about each other.

sud = should; *liein* = lying.

A' ye wha tent the Gospel fauld,
Thee Duncan deep, an' Peebles shaul',
But chiefly great Apostle Auld,
We trust in thee,
That thou wilt work them, het an' cauld,
To gar them gree.

Burns now uses deep sarcasm as he pleads with those preachers who have made his life a misery over the years to resolve the quarrel between their fellows.

tent = tend; *fauld* = fold; *shaul* = shallow; *het* = hot; *cauld* = cold

Consider, sirs, how we're beset!
There's scarce a new herd that we get
But comes frae 'mang that cursed set,
I winna name:
I trust in Heav'n to see them het
Yet in a flame!

He mockingly tells how concerned he is that any new preacher is from the moderate camp and that he would like to see them burn in hell.

Dalrymple has been lang our fae,
M'Gill has wrought us meikle wae,
An' that curs'd rascal ca'd M'Quhae,
An' baith the Shaws,
That aft hae made us black an' blae,
Wi' vengeful paws.

He goes on to relate the fear that has been generated by various preachers.

fae = foe; *meikle wae* = much woe

Auld Wodrow lang has wrought mischief,
We trusted death wad bring relief,
But he has gotten, to our grief,
Ane to succeed him,
A chield wha'll soundly buff our beef—
I meikle dread him.

They thought that when Wodrow died that they would have some relief, but his successor is just as brutal in his ministry.

chield = fellow; *buff our beef* = strike us

And monie mae that I could tell,
Wha fain would openly rebel,
Forby turn-coats amang oursel:
There's Smith for ane—
I doubt he's but a greyneck still,
An' that ye'll fin'!

There's lots more that he could tell. One
of the preachers is still a gambler, as they
will find out.

fain = gladly; *forby* = besides; *greyneck* =
gambler

O! a' ye flocks o'er a' the hills,
By mosses, meadows, moors, an' fells,
Come, join your counsels and your skills
To cowe the lairds,
And get the brutes the power themsels
To chuse their herds!

He then suggests that all the congrega-
tions should rally against the lairds and let
the preachers choose their own parishes.

Then Orthodoxy yet may prance,
An' Learning in a woody dance,
An' that curst cur ca'd Common-sense,
Wha bites sae rair,
Be banished o'er the sea to France—
Let him bark there!

The old-style will flourish while that
whipper-snapper called the New-Light
will be banished from these shores.

woody dance = hanging

Then Shaw's an' Dalrymple's eloquence,
McGill's close, nervous excellence,
M'Qhae's pathetic, manly sense,
An' Guid M'math,
Wha thro the heart can brawly glance,
May a' pack aff!

His biting sarcasm closes with the
comments that the excellent, sensible
preachers can then all be got rid off if the
old lot get their way.

Holy Willie's Prayer

And send the godly in a pet to pray – Pope

The church, or Kirk, was obviously a source for much of Burns' verse. *Holy Willie's Prayer* is a classic example of how he could see through hypocrisy and false piety as if he was looking through glass.

This time his target was an elder (an office-bearer in the Presbyterian Church) of Mauchline Parish. An old bachelor who, although not adverse to sexual encounters with certain ladies of the Parish, still considered himself to be far superior to the other lesser mortals who attended the Kirk, and who really believed that the Good Lord should send them all to Hell, but of course, he and his kinsfolk should go straight to Heaven.

Should you ever have an opportunity to listen to this poem being recited by a true exponent of Burns, then grasp the opportunity – it will be a delight to be savoured for a long, long time.

O Thou that in the Heavens does dwell!
Wha, as it pleases best Thysel,
Sends ane to Heaven, an' ten to Hell,
A' for Thy glory,
And no' for onie guid or ill
They've done before Thee!

In the first three verses, Holy Willie is concentrating on ingratiating himself with the Lord by pointing out just how great and mighty He is.
ane = one, onie guid = any good

I bless and praise Thy matchless might,
When thousands Thou hast left in night,
That I am here before Thy sight,
For gifts an' grace
A burning and a shining light
To a' this place.

What was I, or my generation
That I should get sic exaltation?
I, wha deserv'd most just damnation
For broken laws,
Sax thousand years ere my creation,
Thro' Adam's cause!

sic = such; wha = who

sax = six; ere = before

When from my mither's womb I fell,
Thou might hae plung'd me deep in Hell,
To gnash my gooms, and weep and wail
In burning lakes
Whare damned devils roar and yell,
Chain'd to their stakes.

The next two verses show us Willie at his best as a groveller, but one whose opinion of his own standing knows no bounds.

mither = mother

Yet I am here, a chosen sample,
To show Thy grace is great and ample;
I'm here a pillar o' Thy temple,
Strong as a rock,
A guide, a buckler, and example,
To a' Thy flock!

buckler = shield

(O Lord Thou kens what zeal I bear,
When drinkers drink, and swearers swear,
And singin' there, and dancin' here,
Wi' great an' sma';
For I am keepet by Thy fear,
Free frae them a'.)

But yet, O Lord, confess I must
At times I'm fash'd wi' fleshly lust;
An' sometimes, too, in wardly trust,
Vile self gets in;
But Thou remembers we are dust,
Defil'd wi' sin.

Next he confesses to his sexual transgressions, but they were all mistakes and not really his fault, because, as he reminds the Lord, we are only made of dust and are susceptible to sin.

fash'd = troubled

O Lord! yestreen, Thou kens, wi' Meg –
Thy pardon I sincerely beg—
O, may 't ne'er be a living plague
To my dishonour!
An' I'll ne'er lift a lawless leg
Again upon her

yestreen = last night; *Thou kens, wi' Meg* = You know, with Meg

Besides, I farther maun avow –
Wi' Leezie's lass, three times I trow –
But, Lord, that Friday I was fou
When I cam near her,
Or else, Thou kens, Thy servant true
Wad never steer her

In fact, it had only happened with Lizzie's daughter because he had too much to drink, otherwise he would never have touched her.

maun avow = must say; *trow* = believe;
fou = drunk; *steer* = molest

Maybe Thou lets this fleshly thorn
Buffet Thy servant e'en and morn,
Lest he owre proud and high should turn,
That he's sae gifted:
If sae, thy han' maun e'en be borne,
Until Thou lift it.

Now he starts to wonder if perhaps the Lord might have given him this earthly problem to prevent him from becoming too high and mighty, even although he is obviously very gifted.

e'en and morn = night and day; *owre* = over; *Thy han' maun e'en be borne* = the weight of Your hand must always be felt

Lord, bless Thy chosen in this place,
For here Thou hast a chosen race!
But God, confound their stubborn face
An' blast their name,
Wha bring Thy elders to disgrace
An' open shame!

Finally, we discover that the real purpose of Willie's praying is to have Holy retribution brought upon one who Willie insists is a disgrace to the community.

Lord, mind Gau'n Hamilton's deserts;
He drinks, an' swears, an' plays at cartes.
Yet has sae monie takin arts,
Wi' great an' sma',
Frae God's ain Priest the people's hearts
He steals awa'.

Now he complains to the Lord that his enemy, Gavin Hamilton, is a man who drinks and swears and gambles, but is so popular that he is turning people away from the kirk.

cartes = cards; *so monie takin' arts* = is so popular; *wi' great and sma'* = with all classes of people; *frae* = from, *ain* = own

And when we chasten'd him therefore,
Thou kens how he bred sic a splore,
An' set the warld in a roar
O' laughin' at us;
Curse Thou his basket and his store,
Kail an' potatoes!

Here, Willie complains that when he attempted to punish Hamilton, he caused such an uproar that everyone finished up by laughing at Willie.

sic a splore = such a fuss; *kail* = cabbage

Lord, hear my earnest cry and pray'r
Against that Presbt'ry of Ayr!
Thy strong right hand, Lord, mak it bare
Upo' their heads!
Lord, visit them, and dinna spare,
For their misdeeds!

While he is at it, Willie decides to tackle the Lord on another area giving him problems, the Presbytery of Ayr. He asks that the Lord really makes these people suffer for their wrong-doings.
hard mak' it bare = hit them hard

O Lord, my God! that glib-tongu'd Aiken,
My vera heart and flesh are quaking
To think how I sat, sweatin, shakin,
An' pish'd wi' dread,
While Auld wi' hingin lip gaed sneakin,
And hid his head.

The particular culprit is one Robert Aiken, who had apparently given Willie a tongue-lashing which had left him sweating and shaking with fear and almost wetting himself.

Lord, in Thy day o' vengeance try him!
Lord, visit him wha did employ him!
And pass not in Thy mercy by them
Nor hear their pray'r,
But for Thy people's sake destroy them,
An' dinna spare!

Not only does Willie want the Lord to make Aiken suffer, he wants anyone for whom Aiken had ever worked to suffer the same fate with no mercy.

But, Lord, remember me and mine
Wi' mercies temporal and divine,
That I for grace an' gear may shine,
Excelled by nane;
And a' the glory shall be Thine –
Amen, Amen!

The final verse is a wonderful example of sanctimonious grovelling, as Willie points out to the Lord, that he, Willie, is such a wonderful person, of such grace, that he and his family should be treated mercifully by the Lord.
gear = wealth

Epistle to J Lapraik

The poems, songs and letters of Robert Burns give a remarkable insight into the various lifestyles of the period. John Lapraik was an elderly farmer, forced into bankruptcy through the collapse of the Ayr Bank, and subsequently jailed for debt. Although he had already built himself a reputation as a poet, his period of incarceration provided him with time to concentrate on his verse and his works were eventually published in 1788. Burns was very impressed by Lapraik's writings, as the following verses show.

While briers an' woodbines budding green,
And paitricks scraitchin' loud at e'en,
An' morning poussie whiddin seen,
Inspire my Muse,
This freedom, in an *unknown* frien'
I pray excuse.

Burns explains to his new friend that he finds his inspiration in the fields, and hopes that Lapraik will excuse his presumptions.
paitricks = partridges; *scraitchin'* = screeching; *poussie whiddin* = running hares

On Fasten-e'en we had a rockin',
To ca' the crack and weave our stockin';
And there was muckle fun and jokin',
Ye need na doubt;
At length we had a hearty yokin',
At 'sang about.'

On the evening before Lent he had enjoyed the fellowship of his neighbours with lots of merriment and singing.
Fasten-e'en = the eve of Lent; *rockin'* = party, *ca' the crack* = chat; *weave our stockin'* = dancing; *yokin'* = a stretch; *sang about* = sing-song

There was ae sang amang the rest,
Aboon them a' it pleas'd me best,
That some kind husband had address't,
To some sweet wife;
It thirl'd the heart-strings thro' the breast,
A' to the life.

One particular song told of the love of a man for his wife, and this one really appealed to Burns.
aboon = above; *thirl'd* = thrilled

I've scarce heard ought describ'd sae weel,
What gen'rous, manly bosoms feel;
Thought I, 'Can this be Pope, or Steele,
Or Beatties wark?'
They told me 'twas an odd kind chiel
About Muirkirk.

He had seldom heard the feelings of a man described with such tenderness, and thought it must be by one of the famous writers of the time, until told it was by the man from Muirkirk.

chiel = fellow

It pat me fidgin-fain to hear't,
An' sae about him there I spier't;
Then a' that kent him round declar'd
He had ingine;
That nane excell'd it, few cam near 't,
It was sae fine:

He was so excited about the song that he had to find out about the writer, who was described as a genius whose work could not be bettered.

pat me fidgin-fain = got me excited; *spier't* = enquired; *kent* = knew; *ingine* = genius

That, set him to a pint of ale,
An' either douce or merry tale,
Or rhymes an' sangs he'd made himsel',
Or witty catches,
'Tween Inverness and Teviotdale,
He had few matches.

Put a pint of ale in front of him and, whether drunk or sober, he will entertain you with his own songs and verses which nobody in Scotland can equal.

douce = grave; sober

Then up I gat, an' swoor an aith,
Tho' I should pawn my pleugh an' graith,
Or die a cadger pownie's death,
At some dyke-back,
A pint an' gill, I'd gie them baith
To hear your crack.

Burns swears that he would give anything to meet with Lapraik to hear him for himself.

swoor an aith = swore an oath; *pleugh an' graith* = plough and equipment; *cadger pownie* = tinker's pony; *dyke-back* = behind a fence; *crack* = cha

But, first an' foremost, I should tell,
Amaist as soon as I could spell,
I to the crambo-jingle fell;
Tho' rude an' rough—
Yet croonin' to a body's sel'.
Does weel enough.

He explains that he started rhyming almost as soon as he could spell, and although it was rough and ready, he enjoyed singing to himself.

amaist = almost; *crambo-jingle* = rhymes; *croonin'* = humming; *a body's sel'* = oneself

I am nae poet, in a sense;
But just a rhymer like by chance,
An' hae to learning nae pretence;
Yet, what the matter?
Whene'er my Muse does on me glance,
I jingle at her.

He makes no claim to being a proper poet,
merely a rhymer, and has no pretences
about his education. He writes about
what inspires him at the time.
Muse = an inspiring goddess; *I jingle at her*
= I recite my verses to her

Your critic-folk may cock their nose,
And say 'How can you e'er propose,
You wha ken hardly verse frae prose,
To mak a sang?'
But, by your leaves, my learned foes,
Ye're maybe wrang.

His critics may look down their nose at
his efforts, but he is not dismayed for they
may well be wrong.
wha ken hardly = who hardly know

What's a' your jargon o' your schools.
Your Latin names for horns an' stools?
If honest Nature made you fools,
What sairs your grammars?
Ye'd better ta'en up spades and shools,
Or knappin-hammers.

What good is their education if they
remain fools? Better to work as labourers.
a' your jargon = all your chatter; *sairs* =
serves; *shools* = shovels; *knappin-hammers* =
sledge-hammers

A set o' dull conceited hashes
Confuse their brains in college-classes,
They gang in stirks, and come out asses,
Plain truth to speak;
An' syne they think to climb Parnassus
By dint o' Greek

Many who attend college become conceited
fools. They go in like bullocks but come out
like asses, believing that a scant knowledge
of Greek will lead them to greatness.
hashes = useless fellows; *stirks* = bullocks;
syne = then; *by dint o'* = on the strength of

Gie me ae spark o' Nature's fire,
That's a' the learning I desire;
Then tho' I drudge thro' dub an' mire
At pleugh or cart,
My Muse, tho' hamely in attire,
May touch the heart.

Burns needs only Nature to inspire him
and, although his writing may be simple,
he hopes it will touch the hearts of those
who read it.
dub an' mire = puddles and mud; *hamely in*
attire = simply dressed; *pleugh* = plough

O for a spunk o' Allan's glee,
Or Ferguson's, the bauld an' slee,
Or bright Lapraik's, my friend to be,
If I can hit it!
That would be lear eneugh for me,
If I could get it.

He would like to have a spark of the talent of other poets, and would be content to be as good as Lapraik.
spunk = spark; *bauld an' slee* = bold and sly; *lear* = learning

Now, sir, if ye hae friends enow,
Tho' real friends I b'lieve are few,
Yet, if your catalogue be fow,
I'se no insist;
But, gif ye want a friend that's true,
I'm on your list.

Should Lapraik already have enough friends, then Burns will not pursue the matter, but if he is looking for one who will be true, then he is the man.
enow = enough; *fow* = full; *gif* = if

I winna blaw about mysel',
As ill I like my fauts to tell;
But friends an' folk that wish me well,
They sometimes roose me;
Tho' I maun own, as monie still
As far abuse me.

He does not wish to boast, neither does he want to relate his faults. While some praise comes from his friends he also gets abuse from others.
winna blaw = won't boast; *ill* = little; *roose* = praise; *maun own* = must admit

There's ae wee faut they whiles lay to me,
I like the lasses – Gude forgie me!
For monie a plack they wheedle frae me
At dance or fair;
Maybe some ither thing they gie me,
They weel can spare.

He does have one little fault in that he has a weakness for the girls. Often he's been coaxed into giving them some money, but it would probably be repaid through some sexual favour.
Gude forgie = God forgive; *plack* = coin.

But Mauchline Race or Mauchline Fair,
I should be proud to meet you there;
We'se gie ae night's discharge to care,
If we forgather;
An hae a swap o' rhymin-ware
Wi' ane anither.

Burns would love to meet Lapraik at the races or the fair. He is sure that they will have a wonderful time drinking and exchanging songs and verses

The four-gill chap, we'se gar him clatter,
An' kirsen him wi' reekin' water;
Syne we'll sit down an' tak our whitter
To cheer our heart;
An' faith, we'se be acquainted better
Before we part.

The four-gill whisky cup will be well used,
then they will settle down with their ale. By
the end of the evening they will be old
friends.
chap = cup; *kirsen* = christen; *reekin'* =
steaming; *whitter* = a hearty draught

Awa ye selfish, warly race,
Wha think that havins, sense an' grace,
Ev'n love an' friendship should give place
To Catch-the-Plack!
I dinna like to see your face,
Nor hear your crack.

Burns scorns the wordly people who cast
aside manners, and even love and
friendship, in the pursuit of money. He
has no wish to associate with them.
warly = wordly; *havins* = manners; *Catch-the- Plack* = making money; *crack* = chat

But ye whom social pleasure charms,
Whose hearts the tide of kindness warms,
Who hold your being on the terms,
'Each aid the others,'
Come to my bowl, come to my arms,
My friends and brothers!

Kind, convivial people are the sort that
Burns wishes to have around him. People
who support their friends in times of
hardship.

But, to conclude my lang epistle,
As my auld pen's worn to the grissle,
Twa lines frae you would gar me fissle,
Who am most fervent,
While I can either sing or whistle,
Your friend and servant.

His pen is finally wearing out, but even
just two lines from his fellow poet would
thrill him.
grissle = gristle; *would gar me fissle* = would
make me tingle

Death and Doctor Hornbook

Betty Davidson, an old friend of Burns' mother, loved to tell the children tales of the supernatural, much of which is evident in the Bard's works, and no more so than in this ghostly tale.

A hornbook was a learning-aid used extensively in schools. It was a sheet of paper on which was written the letters of the alphabet, numbers, the rules of spelling and the words of the Lord's prayer, mounted upon a piece of board and covered by a very thin sheet of transparent horn.

Schoolmasters were commonly referred to as hornbooks, and Burns' inspiration for this poem was one John Wilson, who was appointed to Tarbolton School in 1781, and who Burns came to know through his Masonic activities. To Burns' alarm, Wilson enjoyed flouting his limited knowledge of medicine, and during a time when practising medicine was uncontrolled, quacks such as Wilson were in abundance.

Some books are lies frae end to end,
And some great lies were never penn'd:
Ev'n ministers, they hae been kend,
In holy rapture,
A rousing whid at times, to vend,
And nail 't wi Scripture.

All that is written is not always true, and even ministers have been known to embellish the Scriptures.
penn'd = written; *hae been kend* = have been known; *whid* = lie; *vend and nail't wi' Scripture* = insist it is true because it is in the Bible

But this that I am gaun to tell,
Which lately on a night befel,
Is just as true's the Deil's in Hell,
Or Dublin city:
That e'er he nearer comes oursel
'S a muckle pity!

This is going to be the honest truth. It seems that Dublin was considered the equivalent of Hell by Presbyterians at that time.
gaun = going; *Deil* = Devil; *muckle* = great

The clachan yill had made me canty,
I was na fou, but just had plenty;
I stacher'd whyles, but yet took tent ay
To free the ditches;
An' hillocks, stanes, and bushes, kend ay
Frae ghaists an' witches.

He'd drunk enough to be jolly, but not full, and although staggering, was careful to avoid places that might conceal ghosts and witches.
clachan yill = village ale; *canty* = jolly; *fou* = drunk; *stacher'd whyles* = sometimes staggered; *took tent* = took care

The rising moon began to glowr
The distant Cumnock Hills out-owre;
To count her horns, wi' a' my pow'r,
I set mysel';
But whether she had three or four,
I cou'd na tell.

As the moon rose, he concentrated on trying to count the peaks on the distant hills, but was unable to focus clearly.
glowr = stare; *out-owre* = above; *horns* = peaks

I was come round about the hill,
And todlin' down on Willie's mill,
Setting my staff wi' a' my skill,
To keep me sicker;
Tho' leeward whyles, against my will,
I took a bicker.

Coming down towards the mill he needed his stick to keep steady, but against his will, his legs just kept running away with him.
todlin' = tottering; *sicker* = balance; *leeward whiles* = at times; *bicker* = run

I there wi' *Something* does forgather,
That pat me in an eerie swither;
An awfu' scythe, out-owre ae shouther,
Clear-dangling, hang;
A three-tae'd leister on the ither
Lay, large and lang.

He panicked when he realised he was not alone. There was a figure with a scythe on one shoulder and a large trident on the other.
eerie swither = terrified panic; *ae shouther* = one shoulder; *three-tae'd-leister* = trident

Its stature seem'd lang Scotch ells twa,
The queerest shape that e'er I saw,
For fient a wame it had ava;
And then its shanks,
They were as thin, as sharp an' sma'
As cheeks o' branks.

The creature was tall and seemed to have no stomach, but had very thin, small legs.
lang Scotch ells twa = about two metres; *fient a wame it had ava* = it had no belly at all; *cheeks o' branks* = horse bridle bits

'Guid-e'en,' quo I: 'Friend! hae ye
    been mawin',
When ither folk are busy sawin'?'
It seem'd to mak a kind o' stan',
But naething spak.
At length says I, 'Friend! whare ye gaun?
Will ye go back?'

In terror, the poet attempted to speak to the creature by inquiring if it had been mowing, but although it stopped, it said nothing.
mawin' = mowing; *sawin'* = sewing; *whare ye gaun* = where are you going

It spak right howe, -'My name is *Death*,
But be na fley'd'— Quoth I, 'Guid faith,
Ye're may be here to stap my breath;
But tent me billie:
I red ye weel, tak care o' skaith,
See, there's a gully!'

In a hollow voice, it said its name was Death,
but not to be afraid. The terrified poet said
he was armed with a knife and would fight.
howe = hollow; *fley'd* = afraid; *stap* = stop; *tent
me* = heed me; *billie* = brother; *red ye weel* =
advise you; *skaith* = injury; *gully* = large knife

'Gudeman,' quo he, 'put up your whittle,
I'm no design'd to try its mettle;
But if I did, I wad be kittle
To be mislear'd;
I wad na mind it, no that spittle
Out-owre my beard.'

The creature told him to put the knife away
as it would be useless against him, although
he might find it amusing it to shave his
beard with it.
whittle = whittle; *wad be kittle* = would be
amused; *mislear'd* = mischievous

'Weel, weel!' says I, 'a bargain be't;
Come, gies your hand, an' sae we're gree't;
We'll ease our shanks, an' tak a seat;
Come, gie's your news:
This while ye hae been monie a gate,
At monie a house.'

They agreed to shake hands and sit down
for a chat, as the poet was curious to know
about the many visits Death had made over
the years.
weel = well'; *gie's* = give me; *gree't* = agreed;
ease our shanks = rest our legs; *monie* = many

'Ay, ay!' quo he, an' shook his head,
'It's e'en a lang, lang time indeed
Sin' I began to nick the thread,
An' choke the breath;
Folk maun do something for their bread,
An' sae maun *Death*.'

Death agreed that he had been a long time
on his journey, but everyone must earn their
keep, and he was no different in that respect.
nick the thread an' choke the breath = take away
life; *an' sae maun* = and so must

'Sax thousand years are near-hand fled
Sin' I was to the butching bred,
An monie a scheme in vain's been laid,
To stap or scar me;
Till ane Hornbook's ta'en up the trade,
And faith! he'll waur me.'

In the six thousand years he had been
working he had no competition, but
Hornbook was now killing off his customers
at a very rapid rate, much to his disgust.
near-hand fled = nearly passed; *butching bred* =
learning to bring death; *stap* = stop; *waur* =
wear

'Ye ken Jock Hornbook i' the clachan?
Deil mak his kings-hood in a spleuchan!
He's grown sae weel acquaint wi' Buchan
And ither chaps,
The weans haud out their fingers laughin'
An' pouk my hips.'

He is so upset by Hornbook that he hopes the Devil will take his scrotum and turn it into a tobacco pouch. Hornbook even has children mocking Death.
i' the clachan = of the village; *king's-hood* = scrotum; *spleuchan* = tobacco pouch; *weans* = children; *haud* = hold; *pouk* = poke

'See, here's a scythe, an' there's a dart,
They hae pierc'd monie a gallant heart;
But Doctor Hornbook, wi' his art
An' cursed skill,
Has made them baith no worth a fart,
Damn'd haet they'll kill!'

Death's trident and scythe have taken many lives over the years, but Hornbook's medicines are killing people much faster, Death's tools are almost useless.
dart = trident; *baith* = both; *no' worth a fart* = useless; *damn'd haet they'll kill* = there's little they can kill

'Twas but yestreen, nae further gane,
I threw a noble throw at ane;
Wi' less, I'm sure, I've hundreds slain;
But Deil-ma-'care!
It just play'd dirl on the bane,
But did nae mair.'

Only yesterday Death had thrown his trident at someone, and it simply bounced off a bone doing no serious damage.
yestreen = yesterday; *gane* = gone; *Deil-ma'-care* = Devil-may-care; *dirl on the bane* = tinkled off the bone; *nae mair* = no more

'Hornbook was by, wi' ready art,
An' had sae fortify'd the part,
That when I looked to my dart,
It was sae blunt.
Fient haet o't wad hae pierc'd the heart
Of a kail-runt.'

Hornbook's influence was so strong that it had blunted the trident so badly, it couldn't even penetrate a cabbage-stalk.
fient haet o't wad hae = would hardly; *kail-runt* = cabbage stalk

'I drew my scythe in sic a fury,
I near-hand cowpit wi' my hurry,
But yet the bauld Apothecary
Withstood the shock;
I might as weel hae try'd a quarry
O' hard whin-rock.'

Death was so furious that he almost fell over in his haste to attack Hornbook with his scythe, but he might as well have attacked a lump of granite.
sic = such; *near-hand cowpit* = almost fell over; *bauld Apothecary* = bold doctor; *whin rock* = very hard rock

'Ev'n them he canna get attended,
Altho' their face he ne'er had kend it,
Just shite in a kail-blade, and send it,
As soon's he smells 't,
Baith their disease, and what will mend it,
At once he tells 't.'

Hornbook's powers are such that he doesn't need to see a patient. All he needs is their faeces wrapped in a cabbage leaf and he will diagnose the problem simply by the smell. *canna get attended* = cannot see; *ne'er had kend it* = never knew; *kail-blade* = cabbage-leaf; *baith* = both

'And then a' doctors saws and whittles,
Of a' dimensions, shapes and mettles,
A' kinds o' boxes, mugs, and bottles,
He's sure to hae;
Their Latin names as fast he rattles
As A B C.'

He has at hand all sorts of medical paraphernalia and knows the Latin names of the various potions that he keeps. *whittles* = knives

'Calces o' fossils, earths, and trees;
True *sal-marinum* o' the seas;
The *farina* o' beans an' pease,
He has 't in plenty;
Aqua-fontis, what you please,
He can content ye.'

Death believes that the potions that Hornbook dispenses will make everyone feel that he knows his medicine, but will simply kill them off rapidly. *calces* = powders; *pease* = peas

'Forbye some new, uncommon weapons,
Urinus spiritus of capons;
Or mite-horn shavings, filings, scrapings,
Distill'd *per se*,
Sal-alkali o' midge-tail clippings
And monie mae.'

He goes on to describe some of the more revolting potions which might seem more at home in the hut of a witch-doctor. *monie mae* = many more

'Waes me for Johnie Ged's-Hole now,'
Quoth I, 'if that thae news be true!
His braw calf-ward whare gowans grew,
Sae white an' bonie,
Nae doubt they'll rive it wi' the plew;
They'll ruin Johnie!'

If Death is correct, the gravedigger's beautiful pasture will have to be dug up to accommodate all the bodies. *waes me* = woe is me; *Johnie Ged's-Hole* = gravedigger; *braw calf-ward* = lovely grazing plot; *gowans* = daisies; *rive* = tear; *sheugh* = ditch

The creature grain'd an eldritch laugh,
And says; 'Ye needna yoke the pleugh,
Kirkyards will soon be till'd eneugh,
Tak ye nae fear;
They'll a' be trench'd wi' monie a sheugh
In twa - three year.'

Death laughed and declared that within a year or two there would be a need for ditches, not graves in the churchyards.

grain'd = groaned; eldritch = unearthly; pleugh = plough; eneugh = enough; sheugh = ditch

'Whare I kill'd ane, a fair strae death,
By loss o' blood or want o' breath,
This night I'm free to tak my aith,
That Hornbook's skill
Has clad a score i' their last claith,
By drap an' pill.'

Hornbook's skill is so lethal that he is killing twenty to every one that Death can manage.

a fair strae death = died in bed; aith = oath; clad a score i' their last claith = put twenty in their burial shrouds; drap = drop of medicine

'An honest wabster to his trade,
Whase wife's twa nieves were scarce
     weel-bred,
Gat tippence-worth to mend her head,
When it was sair;
The wife slade cannie to her bed,
But ne'er spake mair.'

A weaver's wife had paid twopence for a cure for a headache, and although she had been a strong lady, she went to bed never to rise again.

wabster = weaver; twa nieves = two fists; tippence = twopence; sair = sore; slade cannie = crept quietly; ne'er spake mair = never spoke again/died

'A countra Laird had ta'en the batts,
Or some curmurring in his guts,
His only son for Hornbook sets,
An' pays him well,
The lad, for twa guid gimmer-pets
Was Laird himself.'

A country laird had colic, or some other stomach upset. His son took two ewes along to Hornbook to pay for a cure, only to become laird himself when his father died.

batts = colic; curmurring = commotion; guid gimmer-pets = good pet ewes

'A bonie lass, ye kend her name,
Some ill-brewn drink had hov'd her wame;
She trusts hersel, to hide the shame,
In Hornbook's care;
Horn sets her aff to her lang hame,
To hide it there.'

A young girl had drank something which caused her stomach to swell, probably making her look pregnant. Hornbook's remedy was to send her home to hide herself.

kend = knew; hov'd her wame = swollen her stomach

'That's just a swatch o' Hornbook's way;
Thus goes he on from day to day,
Thus does he poison, kill, an' slay,
An's weel paid for 't;
Yet stop me o' my lawfu' prey,
Wi' his damn'd dirt.'

These are just some examples of Hornbook's work, yet he continues to get well paid for poisoning and killing people while Death cannot get on with his legitimate business.

swatch = sample

'But hark! I'll tell you of a plot
Tho' dinna you be speakin' o't!
I'll nail the self-conceited sot,
As dead's a herrin';
Niest time we meet, I'll wad a groat,
He gets his fairin.!'

Death confides his intention to kill the doctor, and will wager that it will be done by their next meeting.

sot = drunkard; *niest* = next; *wad a groat* = wager small amount; *fairin'* = just desserts

But just as he began to tell,
The auld kirk-hammer strak the bell
Some wee, short hour ayont the twal,
Which rais'd us baith;
I took the way that pleas'd mysel',
And sae did *Death*.

However, before he could tell of his plan, the church -bell rang out telling them it was past midnight, so they both rose to their feet and took their separate ways.

auld kirk-hammer strak the bell = church bell rang; *ayont the twal* = after midnight

Second Epistle to J Lapraik

APRIL 21, 1785

Lapraik had responded to the first epistle from Burns in similar vein, which prompted Rab to write a second epistle to Lapraik, lamenting the lot of the two poets. The opening verses give some insight into the long hours of toil that Burns endured as a young man.

While new-ca'd kye rowte the stake,
An' pownies reek in pleugh or braik,
This hour on e'enin's edge I take,
To own I'm debtor
To honest-hearted, auld Lapraik,
For his kind letter.

It's the end of the working day and he is grateful to Lapraik for his letter.
new-ca'd kye = newly driven cattle; *rowte* = low; *reek* = steam; *braik* = harrow

Forjesket sair, with weary legs,
Rattlin the corn out-owre the rigs,
Or dealing thro' amang the naigs,
Their ten-hours bite;
My awkwart Muse sair pleads and begs,
I would na write.

He is exhausted after a day of ploughing and feeding the horses, and sense tells him not to attempt the reply.
forjesket sair = tired and sore; *rattlin* = spreading; *dealing thro amang the naigs* = feeding the horses

The tapetless, ramfeezl'd hizzie,
She's saft at best an' something lazy;
Quo she, 'Ye ken we've been sae busy
This month an' mair,'
That trowth, my head is grown right dizzie,
An' something sair.

His girl helper is complaining at how hard they are having to work.
tapetless = foolish; *ramfeezl'd* = exhausted; *hizzie* = girl

Her dowf excuses pat me mad,
'Conscience,' says I, ' ye thowless jad!
I'll write, an' that a hearty blaud,
This vera night;
So dinna ye affront your trade,
But rhyme it right.'

He is so incensed by her laziness that he resolves to write a long letter to show her up.
dowf = witless; *thowless* = lacking in spirit; *jad* = hussy; *blaud* = screed

'Shall bauld Lapraik, the king o' hearts,
Tho' mankind were a pack o' cartes,
Roose ye sae weel for your deserts,
In terms sae friendly;
Yet ye'll neglect to shaw your parts
An' thank him kindly?'

He feels an obligation to Lapraik to thank him for his words of praise and friendship, and he must do it promptly.
cartes = cards; *roose* = praise

Sae I gat paper in a blink,
An' doon gaed stumpie in the ink:
Quoth I, 'Before I sleep a wink,
I vow I'll close it;
An' if ye winna mak it clink,
By Jove, I'll prose it!'

He promised himself that he would finish it that same night even if he had to use prose.
stumpie = quill; *mak it clink* = make it rhyme

Sae I've begun to scrawl, but whether
In rhyme, or prose, or baith thegither,
Or some hotch-potch that's rightly neither,
Let time mak proof;
But I shall scribble down some blether
Just clean aff-loof.

The letter is begun, but will it be rhyme or prose, or both? He is writing straight off the cuff as the words come to him.
aff-loof = off the cuff

My worthy friend, ne'er grudge an' carp,
Tho' Fortune use you hard an' sharp;
Come, kittle up your moorlan harp
Wi' gleesome touch!
Ne'er mind how Fortune waft an' warp;
She's but a bitch.

His advice is to ignore the misfortunes that nature throws at one, but to keep happy at all time.
kittle = tickle; *waft* = weave

She's gien me monie a jirt an' fleg,
Sin' I could striddle o'er a rig;
But, by the Lord, tho' I should beg
Wi' lyart pow,
I'll laugh an' sing, an' shake my leg,
As lang's I dow!

He's had many a shock and scare over the years, but he refuses to bow his head and simply laughs them off.
jirt an' fleg = jerk and fright; *striddle* = straddle; *lyart pow* = grey head; *dow* = can

Now comes the Sax-and-twentieth simmer
I've seen the bud upo' the timmer,
Still persecuted by the limmer
Frae year to year;
But yet, despite the kittle kimmer,
I, Rob, am here.

Now aged 26, Rab is still persecuted because of his many affairs, but he carries on despite the gossip.
timmer = branches; *limmer* = hussies; *kittle kimmer* = idle gossip

Do you envy the city-gent,
Behind a kist to lie and sklent;
Or purse-proud, big wi' cent, per cent;
An' muckle wame,
In some bit brugh to represent
A bailie's name?

He has no envy of the city gent who spends his life behind a counter with his fat belly and who might even become a magistrate.
kist = counter/chest; *sklent* = squint greedily; *muckle wame* = fat belly; *brugh* = borough; *bailie* = magistrate

Or is 't the paughty feudal thane,
Wi' ruffl'd sark an' glancin cane,
Wha thinks himself nae sheep-shank bane,
But lordly stalks;
While caps an' bonnets aff are taen,
As by he walks?

Or what about he haughty fellow, dressed in his fancy shirt and carrying a cane, who considers himself to be lordly and expects lesser people to raise their caps to him.
paughty = haughty; *ruffled sark* = shirt with ruffs

'O Thou wha gies us each guid gift!
Gie me o' wit an' sense a lift,
Then turn me, if Thou please adrift,
Thro' Scotland wide;
Wi' cits nor lairds I wadna shift,
In a' their pride!'

He then suggests to God that he might turn him loose to wander Scotland, but would not associate with city people or lairds. (A promise to be forgotten later in his life.)
lift = load; *cits* = city people

Were this the charter of our state,
'On pain o' hell be rich an' great,'
Damnation then would be our fate,
Beyond remead;
But, thanks to Heaven, that's no' the gate
We learn our creed.

If gaining wealth and fame was the reason for living then both he and Lapraik would be destined to eternal damnation.
remead = remedy

For thus the Royal mandate ran,
When first the human race began,
The social, friendly, honest man,
Whate'er he be,
'Tis *he* fulfils great Nature's plan,
An' none but *he*.'

However, since man was born, only honest men count for anything at the end of their lives.

O mandate, glorious and divine!
The followers o' the ragged Nine—-
Poor, thoughtless devils! yet may shine
In glorious light;
While sordid sons o' Mammon's line
Are dark as night!

The true followers of the Muses will find their way into Heaven, while those who have led dishonest lives are condemned to darkness

Tho' here they scrape, an' squeeze, an' growl,
Their worthless nievefu' of a soul,
May in some future carcase howl,
The forest's fright;
Or in some day-detesting owl
May shun the light.

Their greed might find them in a future existence reborn as wild animals or some night creature who fears the daylight.
nievefu' = fistful

Then may Lapraik and Burns arise,
To reach their native, kindred skies,
And sing their pleasures, hopes an' joys
In some mild sphere;
Still closer knit in friendship's ties,
Each passing year!

Burns and Lapraik will rise to the heavens and sing their songs forever and they will become close friends in the coming years.

Welcome to a Bastart Wean

Elizabeth Paton, a servant of the Burns family became pregnant by Robert Burns. Burns' family, with the exception of his mother, considered Elizabeth to be much too uncouth to be a suitable partner for him. Burns too must have considered her as being little more than a willing sexual partner, as the poem he wrote about her, 'My Girl She's Airy', could hardly be considered to be an epistle of love and respect. However, the following lines, dedicated to his illegimate daughter display a true paternal fondness for the child.

Thou's welcome wean! mischanter fa' me,
If thoughts o' thee, or yet thy mammie.
Shall ever daunton me or awe me,
My bonie lady,
Or if I blush when thou shalt ca' me
Tyta, or daddie!

In the opening verse, Burns welcomes the arrival of his child and asks that misfortune fall upon him should he ever have ill-thoughts about the child or her mother, or if he should be embarrassed when his child calls him daddy. *wean* = child; *mischanter* = misfortune; *fa'* = fall; *daunton* = subdue; *awe* = owe; *Tyta* = father

Tho' now they ca' me fornicator,
An' tease my name in kintra clatter,
The mair they talk, I'm kend the better,
E'en let them clash!
An auld wife's tongue's a feckless matter
To gie ane fash.

He knows that people will call him unkind names and will gossip about him, but that by their talk he will become better known. One should not let gossips worry you. *kintra-clatter* = country gossip; *mair* = more, *kend* = known; *clash* = idle talk; *auld wife* = old woman; *feckless* = powerless; *gie ane fash* = give one trouble

Welcome! my bonie, sweet, wee dochter!
Tho' ye came here a wee unsought for;
And tho' your coming I hae fought for
Baith kirk and queir;
Yet by my faith, ye're no unwrought for—
That I shall swear!

He tells his daughter that even although her arrival was unplanned, she is no less welcome, and that he fought both the church and the courts to ensure her well-being, and that she must never think she was unwanted. *dochter* = daughter; *kirk and queir* = church and court; *unwrought* = unwanted

Sweet fruit o' monie a merry dint,
My funny toil is no' a' tint,
Tho' thou cam to the warl' asklent,
In my last plack thy part's be in it
The better half o't.

Although the result of many a happy liaison between her parents, some people may mock her for being illegimate, but he will spend his last penny to ensure her well-being. *monie* = many; *dint* = liaison; *a' tint* = all lost; *warl* = world; *asklent* = obliquely; *plack* = small coin; *o't* = of

Tho' I should be the waur bestead,
Thou's be as braw and bienly clad,
And thy young years as nicely bred,
Wi' education,
As onie brat o' wedlock's bed,
In a' thy station

Although it will make him poorer, he will see that she is as well-dressed, well-brought up, and well-educated as any child born to married parents.
waur = worse; *bestead* = position; *braw* = beautiful; *bienly* = comfortably; *onie brat o' wedlock's bed* = legitimate child

Wee image o' my bonie Betty,
As fatherly I kiss and daut thee,
As dear, and near my heart I set thee
Wi' as guid will,
As a' the priests had seen me get thee
That's out o' Hell.

He sees in her a miniature of her lovely mother, and as he kisses her, he promises to love and cherish her, despite the terrible disapproval of the church.
daut = dote

Gude grant that thou may ay inherit
Thy mither's looks an' gracefu' merit,
An' thy poor, worthless daddie's spirit,
Without his failin's!
'Twill please me mair to see thee heir it,
Than stockit mailins.

He asks that God grants her her mother's beauty and graceful demeanour, and that she be given his spirit but without his faults. She will be better off with these gifts than having been left a well-stocked farm.
gude = God; *ay* = always; *mither* = mother; *stockit-mailin* = well-stocked farm

And if thou be what I wad hae thee
I'll never rue my trouble wi' thee—
The cost nor shame o't,
But be a loving father to thee,
And brag the name o't.

Finally he tells her that if she takes his advice and grows up as he would wish, then he will never regret the shame that he brought upon himself, but that he will be a truly loving father who boasts about his child.

The Fornicator

This is a rather defiant poem which appears to relate to the affair he had with Elizabeth Paton. Whereas the outcome of that relationship was the baby Elizabeth, Burns refers in this poem to a son.

Ye jovial boys who love the joys,
The blissful joys of Lovers;
Yet dare avow with dauntless brow,
When th' bony lass discovers;
I pray draw near and lend an ear,
And welcome in a Frater,
For I've lately been on quarantine,
A proven Fornicator.

He scorns the men who bear no responsibility when their lover becomes pregnant and tells how he has stood up to accept his punishment publicly.
th' bony lass discovers = finds herself pregnant; *Frater* = brother

Before the Congregation wide
I pass'd the muster fairly,
My handsome Betsey by my side,
We gat our ditty rarely;
But my downcast eye by chance did spy
What made my lips to water,
Those limbs so clean where I, between,
Commenc'd a Fornicator.

The kirk paraded defaulters publicly and the ministers chastised them verbally.
Burns does not appear to be unduly concerned as he admits to having lecherous thoughts during the sermon.
ditty = sermon

With rueful face and signs of grace
I pay'd the buttock-hire,
The night was dark and thro' the park
I could not but convoy her;
A parting kiss, what could I less,
My vows began to scatter,
My Betsey fell-lal de del lal lal,
I am a Fornicator.

He payed his fine with pious expression but all his vows of penitence disappeared as soon as Betsey and he were alone in the dark.
buttock-hire = a fine imposed by the kirk upon fornicators; *convoy* = accompany

But for her sake this vow I make,
And solemnly I swear it,
That while I own a single crown,
She's welcome for to share it;
And my roguish boy, his Mother's joy,
And the darling of his Pater,
For him I boast my pains and cost
Although a Fornicator.

He swears that half of what money he has shall be hers.

Ye wenching blades whose hireling jades
Have tipt ye off blue-boram,
I tell ye plain, I do disdain
To rank ye in the Quorum;
But a bony lass upon the grass
To teach her esse Mater,
And no reward but for regard,
O that's a Fornicator.

He scorns those who use prostitutes and become stricken with venereal disease. Far better to make love to an honest lass and pay for the consequences.
hireling jades = prostitutes; *tipt ye off blue-boram* = passed on pox (believed to refer to the infamous Blue Boar tavern in London); *esse Mater* = be a mother

Your warlike Kings and Heros bold,
Great Captains and Commanders;
Your mighty Caesars fam'd of old,
And Conquering Alexanders;
In fields they fought and laurels bought,
And bulwarks strong did batter,
But still they grac'd our noble list
And ranked Fornicator!!!

He finally equates himself with famous figures in history who have also been fornicators.

The Vision

Following his venture into the supernatural with Death and Doctor Hornbook, Burns returns to the theme. It commences with the Bard looking back over his life and lamenting how his rhyming has failed to augment his income. The Vision, naturally in the shape of a beautiful young woman, extols the beauty of the Scottish countryside and the virtues of Scotland's writers and heroes. Written and amended over a period of three or four years, it is interesting to note the change in style from the Auld Scots to pure English as the poem develops. Apart from a few glossary references in the opening verses, the poem is lucid in its meaning throughout.

The sun had clos'd the winter day,
The curlers quat their roaring play,
And hunger'd maukin taen her way,
To kail-yards green,
While faithless snaws ilk step betray
Whare she has been.

quat = quit; *roaring play* = curling; *maukin* = hare; *ilk* = each

The thresher's weary flingin-tree,
The lee-lang day had tired me;
And when the day had clos'd his e'e,
Far i' the west,
Ben i' the spence, right pensivelie,
I gaed to rest.

flingin tree = flail; *lee-lang* = full length; *ben* = through; *spence* = back parlour; *gaed* = went

There, lanely by the ingle-cheek,
I sat an' ey'd the spewing reek,
That fill'd, wi' hoast-provoking smeek,
The auld, clay-biggin;
An' heard the restless rattons squeak
About the riggin'.

ingle-cheek = fireplace; *spewing reek* = fire; *hoast-provoking smeek* = cough making smoke; *clay–biggin* = primitive cottage; *rattons* = rats; *riggin'* = boughs that made the roof

All in this mottie, misty clime,
I backward mus'd on wasted time:
How I had spent my youthfu prime,
An' done nae-thing,
But stringing blethers up in rhyme,
For fools to sing.

mottie = spotty; *mus'd* = mused; *blethers* = chatters

Had I to guid advice but harket,
I might, by this, hae led a market,
Or strutted in a bank and clarket
My cash-account:
While here, half-mad, half-fed, half-sarket,
Is a' th' amount.

harket = listened; *clarket* = clerked; *half-sarket* = half-clothed

I started, muttr'ing 'blockhead! coof!'
An' heav'd on high my wauket loof,
To swear by a' yon starry roof,
Or some rash aith,
That I, henceforth, would be rhyme-proof
Till my last breath—

coof = fool; *wauket loof* = calloused palm; *aith* = oath

When click! the string the snick did draw;
And jee! the door gaed to the wa';
And by my ingle-lowe I saw,
Now bleezin bright,
A tight, outlandish hizzie, braw,
Come full in sight.

snick = door-latch; *ingle-lowe* = flame from fire; *hizzie* = young woman; *bleezin* = blazing

Ye need na doubt, I held my whisht;
The infant aith, half-formed, was crush't;
I glowr'd as eerie's I'd been dush't,
In some wild glen;
When sweet, like modest Worth, she blush't,
And stepped ben.

held my whisht = kept quiet; *glowr'd* = stared; *dush't* = touched; *ben* = through

Green, slender, leaf-clad holly boughs
Were twisted, graceful, round her brows;
I took her for some Scottish Muse,
By that same token;
And come to stop those reckless vows,
Would soon be broken.

A 'hair-brain'd, sentimental trace'
Was strongly marked in her face;
A wildly-witty, rustic grace
Shone full upon her;
Her eye, ev'n turned on empty space,
Beam'd keen with honor.

Down flow'd her robe, a tartan sheen,
Till half a leg was scrimply seen;   *scrimply* = barely; *peer* =equal
And such a leg! my bonie Jean
Could only peer it;
Sae straught, sae taper, tight an' clean
Nane else came near it.

Her mantle large, of greenish hue,   *mantle* = cloak
My gazing wonder chiefly drew;
Deep lights and shades, bold-mingling,
threw,
A lustre grand;
And seem'd, to my astonish'd view,
A well-known land.

Here, rivers in the sea were lost;
There, mountains to the sky were toss't;
Here, tumbling billows mark'd the coast,
With surging foam;
There, distant shone, Art's lofty boast,
The lordly dome.

Here, Doon pour'd down his far-fetch'd
    floods;
There, well-fed Irvine stately thuds:
Auld hermit Ayr staw thro' his woods,   *staw* = stole
On to the shore;
An' many a lesser torrent scuds,   *scuds* = whips
With seeming roar.

Low, in a sandy valley spread,
An ancient borough rear'd her head;
Still, as in Scottish story read,
She boasts a race,
To ev'ry nobler virtue bred,
An' polish'd grace.

By stately tow'r, or palace fair,
Or ruins pendent in the air,
Bold stems of heroes, here and there,
I could discern;
Some seem'd to muse, some seem'd to dare,
With feature stern.

My heart did glowing transport feel,
To see a race heroic wheel,
And brandish round the deep-dy'd steel,
In sturdy blows;
While, back-recoiling, seem'd to reel
Their Suthron foes.   *Suthron* = southern

His Country's Saviour, mark him well!   William Wallace, and others who fought
Bold Richardson's heroic swell!   for Scotland.
The chief, on Sark, who gloriously fell
In high command;
And he whom ruthless fates expel
His native land.

There, where a sceptr'd Pictish shade
Stalk'd round his ashes lowly laid,
I mark'd a martial race, pourtray'd
In colours strong:
Bold, soldier-featur'd, undismay'd,
They strode along.

Thro' many a wild, romantic grove,
Near many a hermit fancy'd cove
(Fit haunts for friendship or for love,
In musing mood),
An aged Judge, I saw him rove,
Dispensing good.

With deep-struck, reverential awe,
The learned Sire and Son I saw:
To Nature's God, and Nature's law,   Some of Scotland's famous scholars.
They gave their lore;
This, all its source and end to draw,
That, to adore.

Brydon's brave Ward I well could spy,
Beneath old Scotia's smiling eye;
Who call'd on Fame, low standing by,
To hand him on,
Where many a patriot-name on high,
And hero shone.

DUAN THE SECOND

With musing-deep, astonish'd stare,
I view'd the heavenly-seeming Fair;
A whisp'ring throb did witness bear
Of kindred sweet,
When with an elder sister's air
She did me greet.

'All hail! my own inspired Bard!
In me thy native Muse regard!
Nor longer mourn thy fate is hard,
Thus poorly low!
I come to give thee such reward,
As we bestow!

'Know, the great Genius of this land
Has many a light, aerial band,
Who, all beneath his high command
Harmoniously,
As arts or arms they understand,
Their labours ply.

'They Scotia's race among them share:
Some fire the sodger on to dare;
Some rouse the patriot up to bare
Corruption's heart;
Some teach the bard, a darling care,
The tuneful art.

'Mong swelling floods of reeking gore,
They, ardent, kindling spirits pour;
Or, 'mid the venal Senate's roar,
They sightless, stand,
To mend the honest patriot-lore,
And grace the hand.

'And when the bard, or hoary sage,
Charm or instruct the future age,
They bind the wild, poetic rage
In energy,
Or point the inconclusive page
Full on the eye.

'Hence, Fullarton, the brave and young;
Hence, Dempster's truth prevailing tongue;
Hence, sweet harmonious Beattie sung
His 'Minstrel lays;'
Or tore, with noble ardour stung,
The sceptic's bays.

'To lower orders are assign'd
The humbler ranks of human-kind,
The rustic bard, the labouring hind,
The artisan;
All chuse, as various they're inclin'd,
The various man.

'When yellow waves the heavy grain,
The threat'ning storm some strongly rein;
Some teach to meliorate the plain,
With tillage-skill;
And some instruct the shepherd-train,
Blythe o'er the hill.

'Some hint the lover's harmless wile;
Some grace the maiden's artless smile;
Some soothe the lab'rer's weary toil
For humble gains,
And make his cottage-scenes beguile
His cares and pains.

'Some, bounded to a district-space,
Explore at large man's infant race,
To mark the embryotic trace
Of rustic bard;
And careful note each op'ning grace,
A guide and guard.

'Of these am I - Coila my name:
And this district as mine I claim,
Where once the Campbells, chiefs of fame,
Held ruling pow'r:
I mark'd thy embryo-tuneful flame,
Thy natal hour.

'With future hope, I oft would gaze
Fond, on thy little early ways:
Thy rudely caroll'd, chiming phrase,
In uncouth rhymes
Fir'd at the simple, artless lays
Of other times.

'I saw thee seek the sounding shore,
Delighted with the dashing roar;
Or when the North his fleecy store
Drove thro' the sky,
I saw grim Nature's visage hoar
Struck thy young eye.

'Or when the deep green-mantled earth,
Warm cherish'd ev'ry flow'rets birth,
And joy and music pouring forth,
In ev'ry grove;
I saw thee eye the gen'ral mirth
With boundless love.

When ripen'd fields and azure skies,
Call'd forth the reapers rustling noise,
I saw thee leave their ev'ning joys,
And lonely stalk,
To vent thy bosom's swelling rise,
In pensive walk.

'When youthful Love, warm-blushing, strong,
Keen-shivering, shot thy nerves along,
Those accents, grateful to thy tongue,
Th' adored *Name*,
I taught thee how to pour in song,
To soothe thy flame.

'I saw thy pulses maddening play,
Wild-send thee Pleasure's devious way,
Misled by Fancy's meteor-ray,
By passion driven;
But yet the light that led astray
Was light from Heaven.

'I taught thy manners-painting strains,
The loves, the ways of simple swains,
'Till now, o'er all my wide domains,
Thy fame extends;
And some, the pride of Coila's plains,
Become thy friends.

Thou canst not learn, nor can I show,
To paint with Thomson's landscape glow;
Or wake the bosom-melting throe,
With Shenstones art;
Or pour, with Gray, the moving flow,
Warm on the heart.

'Yet, all beneath th' unrivall'd rose,
The lowly daisy sweetly blows;
Tho' large the forest's monarch throws
His army-shade,
Yet green the juicy hawthorn grows,
Adown the glade.

'Then never murmur nor repine;
Strive in thy humble sphere to shine;
And trust me, not Potosi's mine,
Nor king's regard,
Can give a bliss o'er matching thine,
A rustic Bard.

'To give my counsels all in one,
Thy tuneful flame still careful fan;
Preserve the dignity of Man,
With soul erect:
And trust the Universal Plan
Will all protect.

'And wear thou *this*'—She solemn said,
And bound the holly round my head;
The polish'd leaves and berries red
Did rustling play;
And, like a passing thought, she fled,
In light away.

Man Was Made to Mourn – A Dirge

This cheerless poem is yet another version of the Bard's loathing of the class differences between the workers and the land-owners. It shows again his deep compassion for the man trying to find work in order to feed and house his family.

As is the case with many of Burns' works, two lines raise it to the level of a modern proverb.

'Man's inhumanity to man
Makes countless thousands mourn!'

How sadly appropriate the words are long after the death of Robert Burns.

When chill November's surly blast
Made field and forests bare,
One ev'ning, as I wander'd forth
Along the banks of Ayr,
I spied a man, whose aged step
Seem'd weary, worn with care;
His face was furrow'd o'er with years,
And hoary was his hair.

When out walking, the poet met a man who was carrying the strain of life's toils engraved upon his face.

hoary = white or grey with age

'Young stranger, whither wand'rest thou?'
Began the rev'rend Sage;
'Does thirst of wealth thy step constrain,
Or youthful pleasures rage?
Or haply, prest with cares and woes,
Too soon thou hast began,
To wander forth, with me to mourn
The miseries of Man.

The stranger wanted to know if Burns was constrained by poverty, and if he was already cast down by care with no future except one of misery and toil.

haply = perhaps

'The sun that overhangs yon moors,
Out-spreading far and wide,
Where hundreds labour to support
A haughty lordling's pride;
I've seen yon weary winter-sun
Twice forty times return;
And ev'ry time has added proofs,
That Man was made to mourn.'

For eighty years he has toiled in order that some aristocratic land-owner might live a life of sustained luxury.

O man! while in thy early years,
How prodigal of time!
Mis-spending all thy precious hours,
Thy glorious, youthful prime!
Alternate follies take the sway,
Licentious passions burn;
Which tenfold force gives Nature's law,
That Man was made to mourn.

When one is young and carefree, there is little thought given to what life has in store in the years to come.

'Look not alone on youthful prime,
Or manhood's active might;
Man then is useful to his kind,
Supported is his right;
But see him on the edge of life,
With cares and sorrows worn,
Then Age and Want – oh! ill-matched pair!-
Shew Man was made to mourn.

When one is young, the problems are a long way off, but as one grows old and work becomes more and more difficult to obtain, then life is harsh and survival is difficult.

'A few seem favourites of Fate,
In pleasure's lap carest;
Yet, think not all the rich and great,
Are likewise truly blest;
But oh! what crowds in ev'ry land,
All wretched and forlorn,
Thro' weary life this lesson learn,
That Man was made to mourn!

Although it appears that some are greatly favoured by being born into wealth and care-free existence, this is not always the case, for all over the world people are bowed down under the harshness of their existence.

'Many and sharp the num'rous ills
Inwoven with our frame!
More pointed still we make ourseves,
Regret, remorse, and shame!
And Man, whose heav'n-erected face
The smiles of love adorn,
Man's inhumanity to man
Makes countless thousands mourn!'

The Bard's amazing perception of mankind is abundantly clear here as he explains that although man was born of God with the ability to love, he is also capable of inflicting cruelty and misery upon his fellows.

'See yonder poor, o'er labour'd wight,
So abject, mean and vile,
Who begs a brother of the earth
To give him leave to toil;
And see his lordly fellow-worm,
The poor petition spurn,
Unmindful, tho' a weeping wife,
And hapless offspring mourn.'

The employer will casually refuse work to a fellow man with no thought at all of the consequences which will befall his starving family.

'If I'm design'd yon lordling's slave,
By Nature's law design'd,
Why was an independent wish
E'er planted in my mind?
If not, why am I subject to
His cruelty, or scorn?
Or why has Man the will and pow'r
To make his fellow mourn?"

If his destiny was to be no more than a slave, then why was he given an independent mind, and why should he be considered a less worthy person than his employer, and what is it in some men that makes them seek power over others?

'Yet, let not this too much, my son,
Disturb thy youthful breast;
This partial view of human-kind
Is surely not the last!
The poor, oppressed, honest man
Had never, sure, been born,
Had there not been some recompense
To comfort those that mourn!'

The old man tries to reassure the poet by explaining that there must be a reason for his poverty, and that his suffering will be rewarded in a future existence.

'O Death! the poor man's dearest friend,
The kindest and the best!
Welcome the hour my aged limbs
Are laid with thee at rest!
The great, the wealthy fear thy blow,
From pomp and pleasure torn;
But Oh! a blest relief to those
That weary-laden mourn!'

Death may be a source of fear to the rich, but it is a welcome relief from the strain of a lifetime of hard toil to those who have had no respite during their lifetime.

Young Peggy

The story of Young Peggy, or Margaret Kennedy, to give her full name, is one that is sadly familiar throughout the ages, and in all levels of society. She was a good-looking girl who was seduced by an army captain, resulting in the birth of a daughter. The unchivalrous captain denied all responsibility for the child and the case was subsequently taken to court where it was decided that a secret marriage had indeed taken place, and that the child was the legitimate offspring of wedded parents. The court also awarded a very substantial sum of money to Peggy, but sadly, by the time the award was finally made, she had died at the tender age of twenty-nine.

Burns' verses concerning Peggy were written some ten years earlier, but Young Peggy's destiny was far removed from the Bard's wishes for her future life.

Young Peggy blooms our boniest lass,
Her blush is like the morning,
The rosy dawn, the springing grass,
With early gems adorning.
Her eyes outshine the radiant beams
That gild the passing shower,
And glitter o'er the crystal streams,
And cheer each fresh'ning flower.

Her lips, more than the cherries bright,
A richer dye has graced them;
They charm th' admiring gazer's sight,
And sweetly tempt to taste them.
Her smile is as the ev'ning mild,
When feather'd pairs are courting,
And little lambkins wanton wild,
In playful bands disporting.

Were Fortune lovely Peggy's foe,
Such sweetness would relent her,
As blooming Spring unbends the brow
Of surly, savage Winter.
Detraction's eye no aim can gain
Her winning powers to lessen,
And fretful Envy grins in vain,
The poison'd tooth to fasten.

Ye Pow'rs of Honour, Love, and Truth,
From ev'ry ill defend her!
Inspire the highly-favour'd youth
The destinies intend her!
Still fan the sweet connubial flame
Responsive in each bosom;
And bless the dear parental name
With many a filial blossom.

To a Mouse

ON TURNING UP THE NEST OF A FIELDMOUSE
WITH HIS PLOUGH, NOVEMBER, 1785

Surely one of the finest poems written by Burns, containing some of the most famous and memorable lines ever written. It is not fully understood by the mass of English-speaking poetry lovers, however, as it is written in Scots.

All readers of Burns know of the 'Wee sleekit cow'rin tim'rous beastie' but how many understand the sadness and despair contained within the lines of this poem. What was the Bard saying when he was inspired by turning up a fieldmouse in her nest one day while out ploughing?

Wee, sleekit, cow'rin, tim'rous beastie,
Oh, what a panic's in thy breastie!
Thou need na start awa' sae hasty.
Wi' bickerin' brattle!
I wad be laith to rin an' chase thee
Wi' murdering pattle!

The poet is doing his utmost to assure this terrified little creature that he has no intention of causing it any harm.
bickerin' brattle = scurry/run; *laith* = loath; *pattle* = a small spade for cleaning a plough

I'm truly sorry Man's dominion
Has broken Nature's social union,
An' justifies that ill opinion,
Which makes thee startle,
At me, thy poor, earth-born companion
An' fellow mortal!

He then goes on to apologise to the mouse for the behaviour of mankind. This gives some understanding as to what made Burns such a greatly loved man.

I doubt na, whyles, but though may thieve;
What then? Poor beastie, thou maun live!
A daimen icker in a thrave
'S a sma' request
I'll get a blessin' wi' the lave
An' never miss 't !

He tells the mouse that he understands its need to steal the odd ear of corn, and he does not mind. He'll get by with the remainder and never miss it.
daimen = occasional; *icker* = an ear of corn; *thrave* = twenty-four sheaves; *lav* = remainder

Thy wee-bit housie, too, in ruin!
Its silly wa's the win's are strewin'!
An' naething, now, to big a new ane
O' foggage green!
An' bleak December win's ensuing',
Baith snell an' keen!

Dismay at the enormity of the problems he has brought upon the mouse causes him to reflect on what he has done – destroyed her home at a time when it is impossible to rebuild. There is no grass to build a new home and the December winds are cold and sharp. Her preparations for winter are gone!
big = build; *foggage* = moss; *baith* = both

Thou saw the fields laid bare an' waste
An' weary winter comin' fast,
An' cozie here, beneath the blast,
Thou thought to dwell,
Till crash!
The cruel coulter past
Out thro' thy cell.

Where the mouse thought that she was prepared for winter in her comfortable little nest in the ground, she is now faced with trying to survive in a most unfriendly climate, with little or no hope in sight.
cosie = comfortable; *coulter* = iron cutter in front of a ploughshare

That wee bit heap o' leaves an' stibble,
Hast cost thee monie a weary nibble!
Now thou's turn'd out, for a' thy trouble
But house or hald,
To thole the Winter's sleety dribble,
An' cranreuch cauld!

It seems probable that here the poet is really comparing his own hard times with that of the mouse. A life of harsh struggle with little or no reward at the end.
monie =many; *thole* = to endure; *dribble* = drizzle; *cranreuch* = hoar-frost; *cauld* = cold

But Mousie, thou art no' thy lane,
In proving foresight may be vain:
The best-laid schemes o' Mice an' Men,
Gang aft agley,
An' lea'e us nought but grief an' pain
For promis'd joy!

How many times have people glibly trotted out 'The best laid schemes' without realising that they were quoting Burns? The sadness, the despair, the insight contained within this verse are truly remarkable and deeply moving.
no thy lane = not alone; *gang aft agley* = often go awry

Still, thou art blest, compar'd wi' me!
The present only toucheth thee;
But Och! I backward cast my e'e
On prospects drear!
An' forward, tho' I canna see,
I guess an' fear!

The final verse reveals the absolute despondency that Burns was feeling at this stage in his life. Not at all what one would expect from a young man of twenty-six, supposedly so popular with the lassies, and with his whole life ahead of him, but nevertheless expressing sentiments with which many of us can easily relate.

Epistle to the Rev John McMath

INCLOSING A COPY OF *HOLY WILLIE'S PRAYER*,

WHICH HE HAD REQUESTED. SEPT. 17, 1785

John McMath had been educated at Glasgow University and joined the ministry as one of the New-Licht liberal preachers. His liking for drink was the cause of his downfall as a minister and this failing appears to have been seized upon by the old brigade, forcing his resignation. Burns had huge sympathy with his plight as the following lines show.

While at the stook the shearers cow'r
To shun the bitter blaudin' show'r,
Or, in gulravage rinnin, scowr:
To pass the time,
To you I dedicate the hour
In idle rhyme.

While others are sheltering from the wind and rain, or indulging in horseplay, he decided to write this epistle.
stook = *corn-stack*; *blaudin'* = teeming; *gulravage* = romp; *rennin* = running; scowr = a shower/squall

My Musie, tir'd wi' monie a sonnet
On gown an' ban', an' douse black-bonnet,
Is grown right eerie now she's done it,
Lest they should blame her,
An' rouse their holy thunder on it
And anathem her.

His Muse, who is responsible for so many of his sober poems, thinks that perhaps she will be cursed for this letter.
douse = sober; *anathem* = curse; *monie* = many; *eerie* = scary

I own 'twas rash, an' rather hardy,
That I, a simple, countra Bardie,
Should meddle wi' a pack sae sturdy,
Wha, if they ken me,
Can easy, wi' a single wordie,
Louse Hell upon me.

It is foolhardy of such a lowly person to criticise such a powerful bunch of people, as they can cause him great hardship.

But I gae mad at their grimaces,
Their sighin, cantin, grace-proud faces,
Their three-mile prayers, and hauf-mile graces,
Their raxin conscience,
Whase greed, revenge, an' pride disgraces
Waur nor their nonsense.

But he finds them totally aggravating with their hypocritical attitude and falseness.
cantin = furious; *raxin* = elastic; *waur* = worse than; *gae* = go; *raxin* = growing

There's Gau'n, misca'd waur than a beast,
Wha has mair honour in his breast
Than monie scores as guid's the priest
Wha sae abus't him:
An' may a Bard no' crack his jest
What way they've use't him?

Gavin Hamilton has been verbally abused by them, yet he has more honour than any of them, so why should Burns not make a joke of them.

See him, the poor man's friend in need,
The gentleman in word and deed,
An' shall his fame an' honor bleed
By worthless skellums,
An' not a Muse erect her head
To cowe the blellums?

skellums = scoundrels;

blellums = blusterings; *cowe* = surpass

O Pope, had I thy satire's darts
To gie the rascals their deserts,
I'd rip their rotten, hollow hearts,
An' tell aloud
Their jugglin', hocus-pocus arts
To cheat the crowd!

He wishes that he had the talent of Alexander Pope to satirise them properly.

God knows, I'm no' the thing I shou'd be,
Nor am I even the thing I cou'd be,
But twenty times I rather wou'd be
An atheist clean,
Than under gospel colors hid be
Just for a screen.

He knows that he is no saint, but would prefer to be an atheist with a clear conscience than one who uses religion as a cover-up for their own faults.

An honest man may like a glass,
An honest man may like a lass;
But mean revenge, an' malice fause
He'll still disdain,
An' then cry zeal for gospel laws,
Like some we ken.

An honest man may like drinking and women but would not resort to the meanness and spite that those people adopt.
fause = false

They take religion in their mouth;
They talk of Mercy, Grace an' Truth;
For what? to gie their malice skouth
On some puir wight;
An' hunt him down, o'er right an' ruth,
To ruin streight.

They use religion as a weapon to beat some defenceless fellow with.

skouth = liberty; wight = fellow; ruth = pity; *puir* = poor; *streight* = straight

All hail, Religion! maid divine!
Pardon a Muse sae mean as mine,
Who in her rough imperfect line
Thus daurs to name thee;
To stigmatize false friends of thine
Can ne'er defame thee.

daurs = dares

Tho' bloch't an' foul wi' monie a stain,
An' far unworthy of thy train,
With trembling voice I tune my strain,
To join with those,
Who boldly dare thy cause maintain
In spite of foes:

He may be imperfect but he knows that true religion is worth fighting for.

In spite o' crowds, in spite of mobs,
In spite of undermining jobs,
In spite o' dark banditti stabs,
At worth an' merit,
By scroundrels, even wi' holy robes,
But hellish spirit!

He will not be be put off by the priests who have no souls.

O Ayr! my dear, my native ground,
Within thy presbyterial bound
A candid lib'ral band is found
Of public teachers,
As men, as Christians too, renown'd,
An' manly preachers.

He is thankful that Ayr is a centre for those who are true teachers of religion, and of liberal disposition.

Sir, in that circle you are nam'd;
Sir, in that circle you are fam'd;
An, some, by whom your doctrine's blam'd
(Which gies ye honor),
Even Sir, by them your heart's esteem'd,
An' winning manner.

Pardon this freedom I have ta'en,
An' if impertinent I've been,
Impute it not, good Sir, in ane
Whase heart ne'er wrang'd ye,
But to his utmost would befriend
Ought that belang'd ye.

He is pleased to assure McMath that he
is considered to be one of that group.

Finally, an apology in case he has been
too forward with his comments.

The Holy Fair

The original Holy Fairs were the gathering of several parishes to join in communal worship over a period of several days. However, by the time of Robert Burns they had transformed into an excuse for revelry with the holy part largely disregarded. Burns made good use of this poem to criticise several of the local clergy for whom he had little respect. This is a truly colourful and descriptive piece that brings the Fair vividly to life.

Upon a simmer Sunday morn,
When Nature's face is fair,
I walked forth to view the corn,
An' snuff the caller air,
The rising sun, owre Galston Muirs
Wi' glorious light was glintin',
The hares were hirplin' down the furrs,
The lav'rocks they were chantin'
Fu' sweet that day.

The story opens on a beautiful Sunday morning with the poet out for an early-morning stroll, enjoying the beauties of nature.

simmer = summer; *snuff the caller air* = smell the fresh air; *owre* = over; *hirplin'* = hopping; *furrs* = furrows; *lav'rocks* = larks

As lightsomely I glowr'd abroad,
To see a scene sae gay,
Three hizzies, early at the road,
Cam skelpin' up the way.
Twa had manteeles o' dolefu' black,
But ane wi' lyart lining;
The third, that gaed a wee a-back,
Was in the fashion shining,
Fu' gay that day.

As he admired the view, three young women came hurrying up the road. Two were dressed in sombre clothes, but the third was brightly clad in the fashion of the day.

glowr'd = gazed; *hizzies* = girls; *cam skelpin'* = came hurrying; *manteeles o' dolefu' black* = sombre black cloaks; *lyart* = grey; *gaed a wee a–back* = was a little to the rear

The twa appear'd like sisters twin,
In feature, form an' claes;
Their visage wither'd, lang an' thin,
An' sour as onie slaes:
The third cam up, hap-step-an-lowp,
As light as onie lambie,
An' wi' a curchie low did stoop,
As soon as e'er she saw me,
Fu' kind that day.

Two were like twins with miserable, sour faces. The third one skipped up to him and curtsied.

claes = clothes; *visage* = face; *onie slaes* = any sloes; *hap–step–an–lowp* = hop; skip and jump; *onie lambie* = any lamb; *curchie* = curtsy

Wi' bonnet aff, quoth I, 'Sweet lass,
I think ye seem to ken me;
I'm sure I've seen that bonie face,
But yet I canna name ye.'
Quo' she, an laughin as she spak,
An' taks me by the hands,
'Ye, for my sake, hae gien the feck
Of a' the Ten Commands
A screed some day.'

Doffing his hat, he apologised to the girl
for being unable to recall her name. She
took him by the hand and laughingly told
him that for her sake he had broken most
of the Ten Commandments.

ken = know; *gien the feck* = given the
greater portion; *a screed* = a tearing–up

'My name is Fun - your cronie dear,
The nearest friend ye hae;
An' this is Superstition here,
An' that's Hypocrisy.
I'm gaun to Mauchline Holy Fair,
To spend an hour in daffin:
Gin ye'll go there, yon runkl'd pair,
We will get famous laughin
At them this day.'

Her name was Fun. She was his best friend
and she was on her way to the Holy Fair.
Her companions, Superstition and
Hypocrisy were also going to be there, but
she and the poet would just laugh at them.

gaun = going; *daffin* = having fun; *gin* = if;
rinkl'd = wrinkled

Quoth I, 'Wi' a' my heart I'll do 't;
I'll get my Sunday's sark on,
An' meet you on the holy spot;
Faith, we'se hae fine remarkin!'
Then I gaed hame at crowdie-time,
An' soon I made me ready;
For roads were clad, frae side to side,
Wi' monie a weary body,
In droves that day.

He dashed home to have his porridge and
put on his best shirt, and was soon back on
the road, which by now was busy with
fellow travellers

sark = shirt; *we'se hae* = we'll have;
crowdie-time = breakfast

Here, farmers gash, in ridin graith,
Gaid hoddin by their cotters;
There, swankies young, in braw braid-claith,
Are springing owre the gutters.
The lasses, skelpin barefit, thrang,
In silks an' scarlets glitter;
Wi' sweet-milk cheese, in monie a whang,
An' farls, bak'd wi' butter,
Fu' crump that day.

Farmers were riding past the labourers.
Young men in their Sunday best, and
bare-footed girls were all making their way,
taking a huge assortment of food with them.
gash = confident; *ridin' graith* = riding gear;
gaid hoddin = rode slowly; *cotters* = labourers;
swankies = youths; *skelpin barefit* = running
barefoot; *thrang* = throng; *whang* = large slice;
farls = oatcakes; *crump* = crisp

When by the plate we set our nose,
Weel heaped up wi' ha'pence,
A greedy glowr black-bonnet throws,
An' we maun draw our tippence.
Then in we go to see the show;
On ev'ry side they're gath'rin,
Some carry dails, some chairs an' stools,
An' some are busy bleth'rin
Right loud that day.

Walking into the gathering they passed a
collection plate already heaped up with
half- pences, but under the stern eye of an
elder they felt obliged to put in twopence.
greedy glowr black-bonnet throws = a
church-elder gives a stern stare; *maun* =
must; *dails* = planks; *tippence* = twopence

Here, stands a shed to fend the show'rs,
An' screen our countra gentry;
There, Racer Jess, an' twa-three whores,
Are blinkin at the entry.
Here sits a row of tittlin jads,
Wi' heavin breasts an' bare neck;
An' there a batch o' wabster lads,
Blackguarding frae Kilmarnock,
For fun this day.

The gentry are concealed behind a shelter,
while a simple lass stands alongside the local
prostitutes to watch people arriving. There is
a row of immodestly dressed young women,
while nearby is a gang of young weavers out
for a day of fun.
fend the show'rs = protect from rain; *blinkin* =
smirking; *tittlin jads* = gossiping hussies;
wabster = weaver; *blackguarding* = roistering

Here, some are thinkin on their sins,
An' some upo' their claes;
Ane curses feet that fyl'd his shins,
Anither sighs an' prays:
On this hand sits a chosen swatch,
Wi' screw'd-up, grace-proud faces;
On that, a set o' chaps, at watch,
Thrang winkin on the lasses
To chairs that day.

Some of the congregation are contemplating their sins while others are more concerned about their attire. The chosen few sit smugly and solemnly while some of the young men are only interested in persuading a girl to sit beside them.
upo' their claes = upon their clothes; *fyl'd* = defiled; *swatch* = sample; *grace–proud* = haughty; *thrang* = busy

O happy is that man, an' blest!
Nae wonder that it prides him!
Whase ane dear lass, that he likes best,
Comes clinkin' down beside him!
Wi' arm repos'd on the chair back,
He sweetly does compose him;
Which, by degrees, slips round her neck,
An's loof upon her bosom,
Unkend that day.

Happiest of all is the man whose sweetheart sits beside him. His arm has slipped around her and he uses the opportunity to take previously unknown liberties.
blest = blessed; *clinkin'* = sitting; *an's loof* = and his palm; *unkend* = unknown

Now a' the congregation o'er,
Is silent expectation;
For Moodie speels the holy door,
Wi' tidings o' damnation:
Should Hornie, as in ancient days,
'Mang sons o' God present him,
The vera sight o' Moodie's face,
To's ain het hame had sent him
Wi' fright that day.

The Rev Moodie is the first to preach, and does so with such vigour that the Devil himself would have retreated home, scared by the preacher's facial expressions.
speels = climbs; *Hornie* = the Devil; *'mang* = among; *to's ain het hame* = to his own hot home

Hear how he clears the points o' Faith
Wi' rattlin an' thumpin!
Now meekly calm, now wild in wrath,
He's stampin, an' he's jumpin!
His lengthen'd chin, his turn'd-up snout,
His eldritch squeal an' gestures,
O how they fire the heart devout,
Like cantharidian plaisters
On sic a day !

His wild rantings and his equally wild
gesturing are so exciting that they have an
aphrodisiac effect of upon the poet.
snout = nose; *eldritch squeals* = unearthly
screams; *cantharidian plaisters* = aphrodisiacs

But hark! the tent has chang'd its voice;
There's peace an' rest nae langer;
For a' the real judges rise,
They canna sit for anger,
Smith opens out his cauld harangues,
On practice and on morals;
An' aff the godly pour in thrangs
To gie the jars an' barrels
A lift that day.

Now it is time for the hierarchy to preach,
and Smith's tone is so full of anger and fury
at their lack of morals, that most of the con-
gregation decide it is time to depart to where
the drink is being served.
cauld = cold; *thrangs* = throngs

What signifies his barren shine,
Of moral powers an' reason?
His English style, an' gesture fine,
Are a' clean out o' season.
Like Socrates or Antonine,
Or some auld pagan heathen,
The moral man he does define,
But ne'er a word o' faith in
That's right that day.

The poet considers that Smith is out of
touch with modern society and that his
sermonising is out of date. What's more, he
expresses no Christian sentiment or
feelings in his preaching.

In guid time comes an antidote
Against sic poison'd nostrum;
For Peebles, frae the water-fit,
Ascends the holy rostrum:
See, up he's got the word o' God,
An' meek an' mim has view'd it,
While common-sense has ta'en the road
An' aff, an' up the Cowgate
Fast, fast that day.

The Rev Peebles apparently was met with
approval. He was not of the hell and
damnation school, but preached with quiet
sincerity and with common sense.
sic poison'd nostrum = such bitter medicine;
frae the water-fit = from the river-mouth;
rostrum = pulpit; *mim* = demure

Wee Miller niest, the guard relieves,
An' Orthodoxy raibles,
Tho' in his heart he weel believes,
An' thinks it auld wives fables:
But faith! the birkie wants a manse,
So, cannilie he hums them;
Altho' his carnal wit an' sense
Like hafflins-wise o'ercomes him
At times that day.

Next on is the Rev Miller. He secretly
regards much of the church's beliefs as no
more than old wives tales. However, he is in
need of a parish so will go along with it.
niest = next; *raibles* = recites; *birkie* = fellow;
cannilie = wordly; *hafflins-wise* = almost half

Now butt an' ben the change-house fills,
Wi' yill-caup commentators;
Here's crying out for bakes and gills,
An' there, the pint-stowp clatters;
While thick an' thrang, an' loud an' lang,
Wi' logic, an' wi' Scripture,
They raise a din, that in the end
Is like to breed a rupture
O' wrath that day.

The crowd becomes rowdy and drunken.
As the cries to be served with food and
drink become more raucous, the preachers
must yell even louder to make themselves
heard, so much so that they are in danger of
giving themselves a hernia.
butt an' ben = out and in; *change-house* = ale
house; *yill-caup* = beer glass; *bakes and gills* =
scones and whisky; *pint-stowp* = beer jug

Leeze me on drink! it gies us mair
Than either school or college;
It kindles wit, it waukens lear,
It pangs us fu' o' knowledge:
Be't whisky-gill or penny wheep,
Or onie stronger potion,
It never fails, on drinkin deep,
To kittle up our notion,
By night or day.

It would appear that the more one drinks, the wittier and more erudite one feels one becomes. Indeed, be it whisky or ale, the result is always the same.

leeze = blessings; *gies us mair* = gives us more; *waukens lear* = wakens learning; *pangs* = crams; *penny wheep* = small ale bought for a penny; *kittle* = tickle

The lads and lasses, blythely bent
To mind baith saul an' body,
Sit round the table, weel content,
An' steer about the toddy:
On this ane's dress, an' that ane's leuk,
They're makin observations;
While some are cozie i' the neuk,
An' forming assignations
To meet some day.

The young people are happy to sit around the table drinking and gossiping. Others take the opportunity to arrange meetings at some other time.

saul = soul; *steer* = stir; *toddy* = spirits, sugar and hot water; *leuk* = appearance; *cozie i' the neuk* = cosy in the corner

But now the Lord's ain trumpet touts,
Till a' the hills are rairin,
An' echoes back return the shouts;
Black Russell is na spairin:
His piercin' words, like Highlan' swords,
Divide the joints an marrow;
His talk o' Hell, whare devils dwell,
Our vera 'sauls does harrow'
Wi' fright that day!

Now you can hear the Rev Russell's words bouncing off the surrounding hills. Here's a man whose words cut through you like a sword and make you fear for your very soul.

touts = sounds; *rairin* = roaring; *sauls* = souls

A vast, unbottom'd, boundless pit,
Fill'd fou o' lowin brunstane;
Whase raging flame, an' scorching heat,
Wad melt the hardest whun-stane!
The half-asleep start up wi' fear,
An' think they hear it roarin';
When presently it does appear,
'Twas but some neebor snorin'
Asleep that day.

He rages on about the fires of hell in such furious manner that some of those who had been enjoying a quiet nap woke up in the belief they could hear the roaring of the flames. Fortunately it was only the sound of a neighbour's snoring they were hearing.

lowin brunstane = blazing brimstone;
whun-stane = granite

'Twad be owre lang a tale to tell,
How monie stories past;
An' how they crouded to the yill,
When they were a' dismist;
How drink gaed round, in cogs an' caups,
Amang the forms an' benches;
An' cheese an' bread, frae women's laps;
Was dealt about in lunches,
An' dawds that day.

It would take too long to relate the many stories of the day, and how everyone crowded into the bar at the end of the proceedings to quench their thirsts and appetites.

yill = ale; *a' dismist* = all dismissed; *cogs an' caups* = wooden dishes and drinking vessels; *dawds* = lumps

In comes a gawsie, gash guidwife,
An' sits down by the fire,
Syne draws her kebbuck an' her knife;
The lasses they are shyer:
The auld guidmen, about the grace,
Frae side to side they bother;
Till some ane by his bonnet lays,
An' gies them't, like a tether
Fu' lang that day.

A very confident woman enters and sits by the fireplace, taking out her cheese and knife. The young girls are much more shy and tend to hang back. As tradition demands some of the older men offer up very long graces until they eventually settle down.

gawsie, gash guidwife = buxom, smart woman;
kebbuck = cheese

Waesucks! for him that gets nae lass,
Or lasses that hae nothing!
Sma' need has he to say a grace,
Or melvie his braw claithing!
O wives, be mindfu', ance yoursel',
How bonie lads ye wanted;
An' dinna, for a kebbuck-heel,
Let lasses be affronted
On sic a day!

Alas for the lad or lass who ends up alone. The lad has little to be thankful for in spite of his smart clothes. The poet pleads with the mothers to remember how they used to feel, so don't embarrass your daughters today.

waesucks = alas; *melvie his braw claithing* = spill food on his good clothes; *kebbuck-heel* = cheese–rind

Now Clinkumbell, wi' rattlin tow,
Begins to jow an' croon;
Some swagger hame, the best they dow,
Some wait the afternoon.
At slaps the billies halt a blink,
Till lasses strip their shoon;
Wi' faith an' hope, an' love an' drink,
They're a' in famous tune
For crack that day.

As the bells tolled, some staggered off, others hung around to socialise. Young men waited by the stiles while the girls removed their little–used shoes from aching feet. All are in good mood after the Fair.

Clinkumbell = bellringer; *rattlin tow* = bell rope; *jow an' croon* = swing and toll; *dow* = can; *slaps* = stiles; *billies* = young men; *shoon* = shoes; *crack* = chat

How monie hearts this day converts
O' sinners and o' lasses!
Their hearts o' stane, gin night are gane
As saft as onie flesh is:
There's some are fou o' love divine;
There's some are fou o' brandy;
An' monie jobs that day begin,
May end in houghmagandie
Some ither day.

This day has been the cause of many romantic meetings. Some have been carried away by the spirit of love, others by the spirit in the brandy bottle.

gin night = by nightfall; *houghmagandie* = love-making

THE TWA DOGS

A TALE OF THOSE WHO HAVE, AND THOSE WHO HAVE NOT,
THE QUESTION IS, WHICH GROUP IS WHICH?

Burns had a dog named Luath that he loved dearly. Sadly, Luath died and the poet resolved to immortalise his old and trusted friend by writing this fine poem. Luath represents the working people of Scotland, while Caesar represents the ruling classes.

'Twas in that place o' Scotland's Isle,
That bears the name o' auld King Coil,
Upon a bonie day in June,
When wearin thro' the afternoon,
Twa dogs, that were na thrang at hame
Forgather'd ance upon a time.

One fine day in June, at Kyle in Scotland, two very dissimiliar dogs who had nothing to do at home, met up with each other.
King Coil = a Pictish monarch; *thro'* = through; *twa* = two; *na thrang at hame* = not busy at home; *for'gather'd* = met; *ance* = once

The first I'll name, they ca'd him Caesar,
Was keepit for his Honour's pleasure,
His hair, his size, his mouth, his lugs,
Shew'd he was nane o' Scotland's dogs;
But whalpit some place far abroad,
Whare sailors gang to fish for cod.

The first was named Caesar, and was purely a pet for his master. His size and shape indicated that he was not native to Scotland, but had probably come from Newfoundland.
ca'd = called; *keepit* = kept; *lugs* = ears; *shew'd* = showed; *nane* = none; *whalpit* = born; *whare* = where; *gang* = go

His locked, letter'd, braw brass collar,
Shew'd him the gentleman an' scholar;
But tho' he was o' high degree,
The fient a pride, nae pride had he,
But wad hae spent an hour caressin',
Ev'n wi' a tinkler-gipsy's messin;
At kirk or market, mill or smiddie,
Nae tawted tyke, tho' e'er sae duddie,
But he wad stan't, as glad to see him,
An' stroant on stanes an' hillocks wi' him.

Despite his fancy collar and high pedigree, he was totally without ambition and was willing to spend his days with any old mongrel willing to spend time with him.
braw = handsome; *the fient* = a fiend; *wad hae* = would have; *messin* = mongrel; *kirk* = church; *smiddy* = blacksmith's; *nae tauted tyke* = no matted dog; *e'er sae duddie* = ever so ragged; *wad stan't* = would stand; *stroant on stanes* = peed on stones

The tither was a ploughman's collie,
A rhyming, ranting, raving billie,
Wha for his friend an' comrade had him,
And in his freaks had Luath ca'd him,
After some dog in Highlan' sang,
Was made lang syne –
Lord knows how lang.

The other was a collie named Luath, owned by a poetic ploughman.

tither = other; *rantin* = joyous; *billie* = comrade; *in his freaks* = in amusement; *lang syne* = long ago

He was a gash an' faithfu' tyke,
As ever lap a sheugh or dyke,
His honest, sonsie, baws'nt face
Ay gat him friends in ilka place;
His breast was white, his towzie back
Weel clad wi' coat o' glossy black;
His gawsie tail, wi' upward curl,
Hung owre his hurdies wi' a swirl.

He was as respectable and faithful a dog as had ever leapt over ditches and walls, and with his friendly face with its white stripe, and his happily wagging tail, he was guaranteed a welcome anywhere.

gash = wise; *lap* = leapt; *sheugh* = ditch; *dyke* = stone wall; *sonsie* = jolly; *bawsn't* = white striped; *gat* = got; *ilka* = every; *towzie* = shaggy; *weel* = well; *gawsie* = handsome; *owre his hurdies* = over his backside

Nae doubt but that they were fain o' ither,
And unco pack an' thick thegither;
Wi' social noses whyles snuff'd an' snowkit;
Whyles mice an' muddieworts they howkit;
Whyles scoure'd awa; in lang excursion
An' worry'd ither in diversion;
'Till tired at last wi' monie a farce,
They set them down upon their arse,
An' there began a lang digression
About the 'lords o' the creation'

There was no doubt that these two dogs enjoyed each other's company as they sniffed out mice and moles and went for long walks. Eventually, however, they would tire of playing and settle down for serious discussion about the meaning of life.

fain o' ither = fond of each other; *unco' pack an' thick thegither* = uncouth and as thick as thieves; *whyles* = sometimes; *snuff' an' snowkit* = sniffed and snuffled; *muddieworts* = moles; *howkit* = dug up; *scour'd* = rushed; *monie a farce* = many a laugh

CAESAR

I've often wonder'd, honest Luath,
What sort o' life poor dogs like you have;
An' when the gentry's life I saw,
What way poor bodies liv'd ava.

Caesar expresses his wonder at the different lifestyles of the rich and poor.
ava = at all

Our laird gets in his racked rents,
His coals, his kain, an' his stents;
He rises when he likes himsel';
His flunkies answer at the bell;
He ca's his coach; he ca's his horse;
He draws a bonie, silken purse,
As lang's my tail, whare thro' the steeks,
The yellow, letter'd Geordie keeks.

Our master gets his money by charging exorbitant rents. His fuel, his food and his taxes are provided by his tenants. His servants rush to get him his coach or his horse. One can see the golden guineas shining through the stitches of his purse.
racked = exorbitant; *kain* = farm produce payed as rent; *stents* = taxes; *flunkies* = servants; *ca's* = calls; *steeks* = stitches; *yellow-letter'd Geordie* = a guinea; *keeks* = peep

Frae morn to e'en it's nought but toiling,
At baking, roasting, frying, boiling;
An' tho' the gentry first are steghan,
Yet e'en the ha' folk fill their peghan
Wi' sauce, ragouts, an' sic like trashtrie
That's little short o' downright wastrie
Our whipper-in, wee blastit wonner,
Poor, worthless elf, it eats a dinner,
Better than onie tenant-man
His Honour has in a' the lan'
An' what poor cot-folk pit their painch in,
I own it's past my comprehension.

Food is prepared all day long. The masters are the first to be served, but the servants get their share. The miserable little kennelman eats better than any of his lordship's tenants.
stechin = completely full; *ha' folk* = house-servants; *pechan* = stomach; *sic* = such; *trashtrie* = rubbish; *wastrie* = extravagance; *whipper-in* = kennelman; *wee blastit wonner* = worthless person; *cot-folk* = cottagers; *pit* = put; *painch* = stomach

LUATH

Trowth, Caesar, whyles they're fash't eneugh;
A cotter howkin in a sheugh,
Wi' dirty stanes biggin' a dyke,
Barin' a quarry, an' sic like.
Himsel', a wife he thus sustains,
A smytrie o' wee duddie weans,
An' nought but his han'darg to keep
Them right an' tight in thack an rape.

Oh, they are worried at times, but they work
hard enough to keep a roof over their heads.
trowth = truth; *fash't enough* = troubled
enough; *cotter* = labourer; *biggin'* = buildin
smytrie o' wee duddie bairns = family of small
ragged children; *han'darg* = hands work; *in
thack an' rape* = with a roof over their heads

An' when they meet wi' sair disasters,
Like loss o' health, or want o' masters,
Ye maist wad think, a wee touch langer,
An' they maun starve o' cauld an' hunger;
But how it comes, I never kend yet,
They're maistly wonderfu' contented;
An' buirdly chiels, an' clever hizzies,
Are bred in sic a way as this is.

When problems arise like ill-health or
unemployment, you would expect them to
die of cold and hunger. I don't know how
they survive, but they usually appear
contented, and they manage to raise
sturdy boys and clever girls.
sair = sor; *ye maist wad think* = you would
believe; *a wee touch langer* = a little longer;
maun = must; *cauld* = cold; *kend* = knew;
maistly = mostly; *buirdly chiels* = sturdy
lads; *hizzies* = young women

CAESAR

But then, to see how you're negleckit,
How huff'd, an' cuff'd, an' disrespeckit!
Lord man, our gentry care as little
For delvers, ditchers, an' sic cattle;
They gang as saucy by poor folk,
As I wad by a stinking brock.

But no one respects you or the cottagers. The gentry pass you as I would pass a stinking old badger.

negleckit = neglected; *huff'd* = bullied; *cuff'd* = beaten; *ditchers* = ditch cleaners; *sic cattle* = such people; *wad* = would; *brock* = badger

I've notic'd, on our laird's court-day,
An' monie a time my heart's been wae,
Poor tenant-bodies, scant o' cash,
How they maun thole a factor's snash;
He'll stamp an' threaten, curse an' swear,
He'll apprehend them, poind their gear
While they maun stan', wi' aspect humble,
An hear it a', an' fear an' tremble!
I see how folk live that hae riches,
But surely poor-folk maun be wretches!

I've been sore-hearted many times on rent-days by the way the landlord's agent abuses tenants who cannot pay their dues. He threatens and curses them and has them arrested, and he impounds their few possessions while all they can do is stand and tremble. I can see how the rich live, but being poor must be terrible.

scant o' cash = short of money; *maun thole* = must endure,; *factor's snash* = agent's abuse; *poind* = seize

LUATH

They're no sae wretched's ane wad think;
Tho' constantly on poortith's brink,
They're sae accustom'd wi' the sight,
The view o't gies them little fright.

They are so used to being close to poverty that they hardly notice it, and it does not worry them unduly.
poortith's brink = edge of poverty

Then chance and fortune are sae guided,
They're ay in less or mair provided,
An' tho' fatigu'd wi' close employment,
A blink o' rest's a sweet enjoyment

They have little control of their own destiny, and as they constantly exhausted, a little nap is a great treat to them.
blink o' rest = a short nap

The dearest comfort o' their lives,
Their grushie weans an' faithfu' wives;
The prattlin' things are just their pride,
That sweeten's a' their fireside.

Their greatest pleasure is simply to be at home with their family.
grushie weans = thriving children; *prattlin'* = chattering

An' whyles twalpennie-worth o' nappy
Can mak the bodies unco happy;
They lay aside their private cares,
To mind the Kirk and State affairs;
They'll talk o' patronage an' priests,
Wi' kindlin' fury in their breasts,
Or tell what new taxation's comin',
An' ferlie at the folk in Lon'on.

While the ale does help them relax, they are serious minded people who discuss in depth the affairs of Church and State. Talking of patronage and priesthood can stir them to anger, and they discuss with amazement these people in London who burden them with yet more taxes.
twalpenny worth o' nappy = small quantity of ale; *wi' kindlin' fury* = with burning anger; *ferlie* = marvel

As bleak-fac'd Hallowmass returns,
They get the jovial, ranting kirns,
When rural life, of ev'ry station,
Unite in common recreation;
Love blinks, Wit slaps, an' social Mirth
Forgets there's care upo' the earth.

When the harvest is in and they are into autumn, they have the most wonderful parties where you would scarce believe they had a care in the world.
rantin' kirns = harvest festivals

That merry day the year begins,
They bar the door on frosty win's;
The nappy reeks wi' mantle ream,
An' sheds a heart-inspiring ream,
The luntin pipe, an' sneeshin mill,
Are handed round wi' right guid-will;
The cantie, auld folks, crackin' crouse,
The young anes rantin' thro' the house.
My heart has been sae fain to see them,
That I for joy hae barkit wi' them.

The arrival of New Year heralds another happy time when the ale flows freely and pipes and snuff are handed around. The elders enjoy a good talk, and the children play so happily that I bark with joy just to be there with them.

win's = winds; *the nappy reeks wi' mantle ream* = the room smells of foaming ale; *luntin'* = smoking; *sneeshin' mill* = snuff box; *cantie auld folks crackin' crouse* = cheerful old people talking merrily; *sae fain* = so glad; *hae barkit* = have barked

Still it's owre true that ye hae said,
Sic game is now owre aften play'd;
There's monie a creditable stock
O' decent, honest, fawsont folk,
Are riven out baith root an' branch,.
Some rascal's pridefu' greed to quench,
Wha thinks to knit himsel' the faster
In favour wi' some gentle master,
Wha aiblins thrang a parliamentin',
For Britain's guid his saul indentin—

Nevertheless, there's a lot of truth in what you say. Many's the family that's been forced out of their home by some unscrupulous agent trying to win favour with his master who is busy with affairs of the state.

fawsont = dignified; *riven* = torn; *gentle* = gentleman; *aiblins thrang a parliamentin'* = perhaps busy in parliament; *his saul identin* = giving his soul

CAESAR

Haith, lad ye little ken about it;
Britain's guid ! guid faith! I doubt it.
Say, rather, gaun as Premiers lead him;
An' saying aye, or no's they bid him
At operas an' plays parading,
Mortgaging, gambling, masquerading;
Or maybe, in a frolic daft,
To Hague or Calais taks a waft,
To mak a tour an' tak a whirl,
To learn *bon-ton* an' see the worl'.

Huh, lad, you don't know the half of it. Working for Britain's good? No, they simply do what their party leaders tell them. Most of the time they're going to the opera or to plays, or they are gambling or going to fancy-dress balls. Or they might decide to go to The Hague or Calais, or even further afield on the Grand Tour.

ye little ken = you little know; *gaun* = going; *taks a waft* = takes a trip

There, at Vienna or Versailles,
He rives his father's auld entails;
Or by Madrid he takes the rout,
To thrum guitars an' fecht wi' nowt;
Or down Italian vista startles,
Whore-hunting amang groves o' myrtles;
Then bowses drumlie German-water,
To mak himsel' look fair an' fatter,
An' clear the consequential sorrows,
Love-gifts of Carnival signoras,
For Britain's guid! for her destruction!
Wi' dissipation, feud an' faction.

They will spend their father's money in Vienna or Versailles, or perhaps in Madrid where they can listen to the music and watch the bull-fights, or go womanizing in Italy before they finish up in some German spa where they drink the muddy mineral ware in order to improve their appearance and hopefully, to clear up the sexual disease picked up from some foreign girl. Forget about them working for Britain's good! They are destroying her with their dissipation and self-indulgence!

rives his auld father's entails = wastes his inheritance; *thrum* = strum; *fecht wi' nowt* = fight bulls; *bowses drumlie German water* = drinks muddy German mineral waters; *consequential sorrows* = venereal diseases

LUATH

Hech man! dear sirs! is that the gate,
They waste sae monie a braw estate!
Are we sae foughten an' harass'd
For gear to gang that gate at last!

We work hard for them while they waste it all away.

gate = way;;*sae monie a braw estate* = many a fine inheritance; *foughten* = troubled

O would they stay aback frae courts,
An' please themsels wi' countra sports,
It wad for ev'ry ane be better.
The laird, the tenant, an' the cotter!
For thae frank, rantin, ramblin billies,
Fient haet o' them's ill-hearted fellows;
Except for breakin' o' their timmer,
Or speakin' lightly o' their limmer,
Or shootin' of a hare or moorcock,
The ne'er a bit they're ill to poor folk.

Why can't they just stay at home and enjoy country pursuits? Everyone would be better off. They really are not such bad fellows you know, although their manners are often poor in the way they discuss their affairs with women so openly, or go shooting hare or moorhens just for the fun of it. They are certainly never nasty to us poor folk.

countra = country; *fient haet* = not one of; *timmer* = timber; *limmer* = mistress

But will ye tell me, master Caesar,
Sure great folks' life's a life o' pleasure?
Nae cauld nor hunger e'er can steer them,
The vera thought o't need na fear them.

But surely Caesar, their life is one of pure pleasure? No worries at all of cold and hunger to upset them.

vera = very

CAESAR

Lord man, were ye but whyles whare I am,
The gentles ye wad ne'er envy 'em!
It's true they need na starve or sweat,
Thro' winter's cauld, or simmer's heat;
They've nae sair-wark to craze their banes,
An' fill auld-age wi' grips an' granes:
But human bodies are sic fools,
For a' their colleges an' schools,
That when nae real ills perplex them,
They mak enow themselves to vex them
An' aye the less they hae to sturt them,
In like proportion, less will hurt them.

If you knew what I knew, you would not envy them. It is true that they neither starve nor sweat, and their bodies are not racked by the pain of toil, but humans are strange creatures and in spite of their education, if they have no real ills to trouble them, they will find something to make them ill for little or no reason.

simmer = summer; *sair work* = sore work; *to craze their banes* = to injure their bones; *wi' grips an' granes* = with aches and groans; *enow* = enough; *sturt* = trouble

A countra fellow at the pleugh,
His acre's till'd, he's right eneugh;
A countra girl at her wheel,
Her dizzen's dune, she's unco weel;
But gentlemen, an' ladies warst,
Wi' ev'n down want o' wark they're curst.
They loiter, lounging, lank an' lazy;
Tho' deil-haet ails them, yet uneasy
Their days, insipid, dull an' tasteless;

When country workers have completed their tasks, they get a feeling of personal satisfaction. But the gentlemen, and even worse, the ladies, have nothing to do but pass the time, lounging around and becoming bored. Their days are long and tedious, and their nights are just as bad.

dizzen's dune = dozen's done; *unco weel* = very well

Their nights, unquiet, lang an' restless.
An' ev'n their sports, their balls an' races,
Their galloping thro' public places,
There's sic parade, sic pomp an' art,
The joy can scarcely reach the heart.
The men cast out in party-matches,
Then sowther a' in deep debauches;
Ae night they're mad wi' drink an' whoring,
Niest day their life is past enduring.

They find little joy in their sports and balls, or at the race meetings, just making sure that they are seen in all the right places. The men get drunk and throw their money away on prostitutes and gambling, and wake up next day with massive hangovers.

party-matches = groups; *sowther* = make up; *deep debauches* = heavy drinking; *niest* = next

The ladies arm-in-arm in clusters.
As great an' gracious a' as sisters;
But hear their absent thoughts o' ither,
They're a' run-deils an' jads thegither.
Whyles, owre the wee bit cup an' platie,
They sip the scandal-potion pretty;
Or lee-lang nights, wi' crabbit leuks
Pore owre the devil's pictur'd beuks;
Stake on a chance a farmer's stackyard,
An' cheat like onie unhang'd blackguard

The women act so sisterly and gracious while they sip their tea and seek the latest scandal about their friends. Or they sit, scowling, while they play cards, gambling with their tenant's livelihood, and cheating shamelessly.

jad = ill-tempered woman; *platie* – plate; *crabbit leuks* = sour-faced; *devil's pictur'd beuks* = playing cards; *stackyard* = stockyard

There's some exceptions, man an' woman;
But this is Gentry's life in common.

There are a few exceptions, but not many.

By this time the sun was out o' sight,
An' darker gloamin brought the night;
The bum-clock humm'd wi' lazy drone;
The kye stood rowtin i' the loan;
When up they gat an' shook their lugs,
Rejoic'd that they were na *men* but *dogs*,
An' each took aff his several way,
Resolv'd to meet some ither day.

By now darkness was falling. Beetles were droning in the twilight, and the cattle were lowing in the fields. The two dogs arose, shook themselves, and considered how fortunate they were to be dogs and not men. They each went his own way vowing to meet again.

gloamin' = twilight; *bum-clock* = drone beetle; *kye* = cattle; *lugs* = ears

The Cotter's Saturday Night

INSCRIBED TO R. AIKEN, ESQ.

Let not ambition mock their useful toil,
Their homely joys, and destiny obscure;
Nor grandeur hear; with a disdainful smile,
The short and simple annals of the poor,
—————-Gray

Cotters, or cottagers were the labouring classes of the farming community, the people who dug the ditches and cleared the stones from the fields. People to whom life was an ongoing struggle against poverty and starvation, and the people for whom Burns had a burning respect and admiration. Proud, proud people who were both God-fearing and law-abiding citizens, and whose aspirations were seldom greater than to be allowed to feed and house their families. Once again the Bard presents himself as a true champion of the working-classes, again displaying his contempt for the paraphernalia of Church and State. Burns wrote this wonderful poem when he was 26 years old, and dedicated it to Robert Aiken, one of the targets of Holy Willie's venomous tirades, and to whom the poem is addressed in the opening lines.

My lov'd, my honour'd, much respected friend!
No mercenary bard his homage pays;
With honest pride, I scorn each selfish end,
My dearest meed, a friend's esteem and praise;
To you I sing, in simple Scottish lays,
The lowly train in life's sequester'd scene;
The native feelings strong, the guileless ways;
What Aiken in a cottage would have been;
Ah! tho' his worth unkown, far
   happier there I ween.

The poem starts with Burns paying his respects to Robert Aiken, explaining to him that had he been born a cottager, then this is how life would have been, and telling him that he may have been a happier man for it.

meed = reward; *lay* = song; *ween* = expect

November chill blaws loud wi' angry sough;
The short'ning winter-day is near a close;
The miry beasts retreating frae the pleugh;
The black'ning trains o' craws to their repose;
The toil-worn Cotter frae his labor goes,
This night his weekly moil is at an end,
Collects his spades, his mattocks and his hoes;
Hoping the morn in ease and rest to spend,
And weary o'er the moor, his course does
hameward bend.

The scene changes to the cotter wearily returning homewards on a Saturday evening, hoping to spend the following morning resting his tired body. The returning horses, covered in mud from the ploughing, and the masses of crows flying to their nests paints a very vivid picture.

blaws = blows; *sough* = sigh; *miry* = muddy; *frae the pleugh* = from the plough; *trains o' craws* = masses of crows; *moil* = labour *mattock* = pickaxe; *hameward* = homeward

At length his lonely cot appears in view,
Beneath the shelter of an aged tree;
Th' expectant wee-things, toddling,
        stacher through
To meet their dad,with flichterin' noise
        and glee,
His wee-bit ingle, blinkin' bonilie,
His clean hearth-stane, his thrifty wifie's smile,
The lisping infant prattling on his knee,
Does a' his weary kiaugh and care beguile,
An' makes him quite forget his labor an' his toil.

As he approaches his cottage, he is met by his toddlers who are happy to see their father, and as he sits by his fireside, his toils and tribulations are forgotten in the comfort of his home and his loving wife.

cot = cottage; *wee-things* = small children; *stacher* = walk unsteadily; *flichterin'* = fluttering; *ingle* = fireside, *hearth-stane* = hearth-stone; *wifie* = wife; *kiaugh* = trouble

Belyve, the elder bairns come drappin' in,
At service out, amang the farmers roun';
Some ca' the pleugh, some herd, some tentie rin
A cannie errand to a neebor town;
Their eldest hope, their Jenny, woman grown,
In youthfu' bloom, love sparkling in her e'e,
Comes hame; perhaps to show a braw
        new gown,
Or deposit her sair-won penny-fee,
To help her parents dear, if they in hardship be.

Eventually the older children start arriving home. They have been working for local farmers, or running errands to a nearby town. The eldest daughter, Jenny, is almost a grown woman but she understands the need to help out with the family budget.

belyve = eventually; *bairns* = children; *drappin'* = dropping; *ca' the pleugh* = drive the plough; *tentie rin a cannie errand* = carefully run a small errand; *neebor* = neighbour; *e'e* = eye; *braw* = fine; *sair won penny-fee* = hard earned small wage

With joy unfeign'd, brothers and sisters meet,

And each for other's weelfare kindly spiers;
The social hours, swift-wing'd, unnotic'd fleet;
Each tells the uncos that he sees or hears.
The parents, partial, eye their hopeful years;
Anticipation forward points the view,
The mother, wi' her needle an' her sheers,
Gars auld claes look amaist as weel's the new;
The father mixes a', wi' admonition due.

This is a family of true brotherly and sisterly love and affection, and time flies as each recounts the events of the week, while the parents listen and wonder what life has ahead for their offspring. The mother keeps busy with her sewing and repairing, while the father offers words of wisdom.

weelfare = welfare; *spiers* = asks; *fleet* = fly by; *unco* = unusual; *sheers* = scissors; *gars auld claes look amaist as weel's the new* = makes old clothes seem like new; *a' wi'* = all with

Their master's and their mistress's commands,
The younkers a' are warned to obey;
And mind their labors wi' an eydent hand,
And ne'er, tho' out o' sight, to jauk or play;
An' O! be sure to fear the Lord alway!
And mind your duty, duly, morn and night;
Lest in temptation's path ye gang astray,
Implore His counsel an' assisting might;
'They never sought in vain that sought the
        Lord aright.'

Right and wrong are deeply defined in this family, and the young people are taught not only to obey their employers, but more importantly, also to follow the word of God at all times and never be afraid to ask for His advice.

younkers = youngsters; *eydent* = diligent; *jauk* = fool about; *gang* = go; *aright* = in the right way

But, hark! a rap comes gently to the door;
Jenny, wha kens the meaning o' the same,
Tells how a neebor lad came o'er the moor,
To do some errands, and convoy her hame.
The wily mother sees the conscious flame
Sparkle in Jenny's e'e, and flush her cheek;
Wi' heart-struck anxious care, enquires
        his name,
While Jenny, hafflins is afraid to speak;
Weel-pleas'd the mother hears it's nae wild,
        worthless rake

A young suitor arrives to court Jenny, the eldest daughter. Jenny's embarrassment, and the mother's relief that he is not a ne'er–do-well illustrate a situation familiar in many families.

rap = knock; *wha kens* = who knows; *cam o'er* = came over; *hafflins* = half; *weel pleas'd* = well pleased; *nae* = no; *rake* = waster

Wi' kindly welcome, Jenny brings him ben;
A strappin' youth, he taks the mother's eye;
Blythe Jenny sees the visit's no ill-ta'en;
The father cracks o' horses, pleughs, an' kye.
The youngster's artless heart o'erflows wi' joy,
But blate an' laithfu', scarce can weel behave;
The mother, wi' a woman's wiles can spy,
What makes the youth sae bashfu' an' sae grave;
Weel pleas'd to think her bairn's respected
    like the lave.

Jenny is relieved to see no disapproval of the visit. Her mother obviously likes the lad and father is happy to discuss farming matters with him. The lad is bashful and serious, which pleases the mother who recognises that he respects her daughter.
ben = through; *strappin'* = well-built; *taks* = takes; *no ill- taen* = not ill-taken; *cracks* = talks; *kye* = cattle; *blate an' laithfu'* = sheepish and bashful; *the lave* = the others

O happy love! where love like this is found;
O heart-felt raptures! bliss beyond compare!
I've paced much this weary, mortal round,
And sage experience bids me this declare—
'If Heaven a draught of heavenly
        pleasure spare,
One cordial in this melancholy vale,
'Tis when a youthful, loving, modest pair
In other's arms, breathe out the tender tale,
Beneath the milk-white thorn that scents
        the ev'ning gale.'

At this point, Burns recounts the many times that he himself has experienced the joys of love, and waxes lyrical accordingly.

Is there, in human form, that bears a heart—
A wretch! a villain! lost to love and truth!
That can, wi' studied, sly, ensaring art,
Betray sweet Jenny's unsuspecting youth?
Curse on his perjur'd arts!
        dissembling, smooth!
Are honour, virtue, conscience, all exil'd?
Is there no pity, no relenting ruth,
Points to the parent fondling o'er their child?
Then paints the ruin'd maid, and their
        distraction wild?

He goes to ask how anyone could take advantage of an innocent like Jenny, and curses the wrongdoers for the shame they bring to entire families. One wonders if the Bard is wearing a hairshirt at this point, and if these lines are directed at his far from blameless life.
perjur'd arts = lies; *dissembling* = masking; *ruth* = remorse

But now the supper crowns their simple board,
The whalesome parritch, chief o' Scotia's food;
The soupe their only hawkie does afford,
That, 'yont the hallan snugly chows her cood;
The dame brings forth in complimental mood,
To grace the lad, her weel-hain'd kebbuck fell,
An' aft he's prest, an' aft he ca's it guid;
The frugal wife, garrulous, will tell,
How 'twas a towmond auld, sin' lint was i'
    the bell.

Supper consists of porridge served with milk from their only cow, happily settled behind the partition that seperates her from the living quarters, and just to impress a little, the mother produces a cheese that has lain for a year, wrapped in flax.

halesome parritch = wholesome porridge; *yont* = beyond; *hallan* = partition; *chows her cood* = chews the cud; *weel hain'd kebbuck* = cheese she has saved; *aft* = often; *ca's it guid* = calls it good; *towmond auld* = twelve-month old; *sin' lint was i' the bell* = since flax was in flower

The cheerfu' supper done, wi' serious face,
They, round the ingle, form a circle wide;
The sire turns o'er, wi' partriachal grace,
Th big ha'-Bible, ance his father's pride.
His bonnet rev'rently is laid aside,
His lyart haffets wearing thin and bare;
Those strains that once did sweet in Zion glide,
He wales a portion with judicious care;
'And let us worship God!' he says with
    solemn air.

With supper finished, the family sit around the fireplace. The father removes his hat, revealing thin, greying hair, then brings out the cherished family Bible. He selects a chapter and solemnly tells the family to prepare to worship God.

round the ingle = round the fireplace; *ha'-Bible* = family-Bible; *ance* = once; *bonnet* = a working man's cap; *lyart haffets* = grey temples; *wales* = selects

They chant their artless notes in simple guise,
They tune their hearts, by far the noblest aim;
Perhaps *Dundee's* wild-warbling measures rise,
Or plaintive *Martyrs*, worthy o' the name;
Or noble *Elgin* beets the heavenward flame,
The sweetest far of Scotia's holy lays;
Compar'd with these, Italian trills are tame;
The tickl'd ear no heart-felt raptures raise;
Nae unison hae they, with our Creator's praise.

The family join together in singing a well-known psalm, possibly to one of the traditional Scottish airs rather than to one of the joyless Italian tunes which many people favoured.

holy-lays = religious music

The priest-like father reads the sacred page,
How Abram was the friend of God on high;
Or, Moses bade eternal warfare wage
With Amalek's ungracious progeny;
Or, how the royal Bard did groaning lie
Beneath the stroke of Heaven's avenging ire;
Or Job's pathetic plaint, and wailing cry;
Or rapt Isaiah's wild, seraphic fire;
Or other holy Seers that tune the sacred lyre.

Now the father reads the Scriptures in a truly reverent and ministerial fashion, telling the ancient stories from the Bible to his hushed family.

plaint = lamentation; *lyre* = harp

Perhaps the Christian volume is the theme,
How guiltless blood for guilty men was shed;
How He, who bore in Heav'n the
    second name,
Had not on earth whereon to lay his head;
How His first followers and servants sped;
The precepts sage they wrote to many a land;
How He, who lone in Patmos banished,
Saw in the sun a mighty angel stand,
And heard great Bab'lons doom
pronounc'd by Heaven's command.

Burns now appears to be contemplating the wisdom of the Bible as he writes of the life of Jesus Christ. His knowledge of the Holy Book is impressive as he tells of St John's exile in Patmos, and how he saw the Angel Michael, and heard the order to destroy Babylon, considered by some to be a name describing all heretical religions.

Then kneeling down to Heaven's
    Eternal King,
The saint, the father, and the husband prays;
Hope 'springs exulting on triumphant wing,'
That thus they shall all meet in future days:
There, ever bask in uncreated rays,
No more to sigh, or shed the bitter tear,
Together hymning their Creator's praise,
In such society, yet still more dear;
While circling Time moves round in an
    eternal sphere.

The father exults the praises of the Lord and prays for the day when the family meet in Heaven, where all cares will be forgotten, and their days will be spent in praise of the Lord.

Compar'd with this, how poor Religion's pride,
In all the pomp of method, and of art;
When men display to congregations wide
Devotion's ev'ry grace, except the heart!
The Power, incens'd, the pageant will desert,
The pompous strain, the sacredotal stole;
But, hap'ly, in some cottage far apart,
May hear, well-pleas'd, the language of the soul;
And in His Book of Life the inmates
        poor enrol.

Here again the poet declares his contempt for the pomp and ceremony of the Church, and the lack of heartfelt devotion of many of those who profess to be devout. Their beliefs are hollow when stood against those of the cottagers.

sacredotal = priestly; *haply* = perhaps

Then homeward all take off their sev'ral way,
The youngling cottagers retire to rest:
The parent-pair their secret homage pay,
And proffer up to Heaven the warm request,
That He who stills the raven's clam'rous nest,
And decks the lily fair in flow'ry pride,
Would, in the way His wisdom sees the best,
For them and for their little ones provide;
But, chiefly, in their hearts with Grace
        Divine preside.

As the family gathering breaks up and they set of to their various destinations, the parents pray to God that He will provide for all of them, but more importantly, that they will be blessed with His Holy Grace.

youngling = young

From scenes like this, old Scotia's
        grandeur springs,
That makes her lov'd at home, rever'd abroad:
Princes and lords are but the breath of kings,
'An honest man's the noblest work of God;'
And certes, in fair Virtue's heavenly road,
The cottager leaves the palace far behind;
What is a lordling's pomp? a cumbrous load,
Disguising oft the wretch of human kind,
Studied in arts of Hell, in wickedness refin'd!

This simplicity of belief is what appears to make Scotland so beloved around the world. Burns does not hesitate to use Alexander Pope's words about there being nothing more noble than an honest man, at the same time pointing out that Lord and Prince are but titles given out by kings. In terms of love and devotion, a cottage is a much worthier place than a palace.

certes = certainly; *cumbrous* = cumbersome

O Scotia! my dear, my native soil!
For whom thy warmest wish to Heav'n is sent!
Long may thy hardy sons of rustic toil
Be blest with health, and peace, and
  sweet content!
And O! may Heaven their simple
  lives prevent
From Luxury's contagion, weak and vile!
Then however crowns and coronets be rent,
A virtuous populace may rise the while,
And stand a wall of fire, around their
  much- lov'd isle.

Expressing his love for Scotland, the land of his birth, Burns prays that the peace and contentment of its working class will never be ruined by exposure to the luxururies which promote avarice, and that no matter who wears the crown, the population will stand united to protect their beloved country.

O Thou! who pour'd the patriotic tide,
That stream'd thro' Wallace's
  undaunted heart,
Who dar'd to, nobly, stem tyrannic pride,
Or nobly die, the second glorious part;
(The patriot's God, peculiarly Thou art,
His friend, inspirer, guardian, and reward!)
O never, never Scotia's realm desert;
But still the patriot, and the patriot-bard
In bright succession raise, her ornament
  and guard!

Finally, he pleads with God, who filled the veins of great Scots such as William Wallace with patriotic blood which helped fight against the tyrants, that He should never desert the Scots as he is the true God of the patriotic Scottish Nation.
dar'd = dared

Halloween

Yes! Let the rich deride, the proud disdain
The simple pleasures of the lowly train:
To me more dear, more congenial to my heart
One native charm, than all the gloss of art ——GOLDSMITH

Another of the Bard's lengthy works, this time describing some of the ancient customs and beliefs associated with Halloween. These customs had ceased many years before Rab wrote this piece, and he is relying largely upon the stories told to him as a child . In my opinion, this is one of the more difficult of Burns' works to understand as it is completely written in the Auld Scots.

Upon that night, when fairies light
On Cassilis Downans dance,
Or owre the lays, in splendid blaze,
On sprightly coursers prance;
Or for Colean, the rout is taen,
Beneath the moon's pale beams;
There up the Cove, to stray an' rove,
Amang the rocks an' streams
To sport that night:

The fairies are about on Halloween, dancing in the light of the moonlight on the hillocks and heading out towards Culzean Castle and Culzean Bay.
Cassilis Downans = a house on the banks of the river Doon

Amang the bonie, winding banks,
Where Doon rins, wimplin clear:
Where Bruce ance ruled his martial ranks,
An' shook his Carrick spear;
Some merry, friendly, countra-folks,
Together did convene,
To burn their nits, an' pou their stocks,
An' haud their Halloween
Fu' blythe that night.

Close to the Banks of the Doon, where Robert the Bruce once ruled, a crowd of country people are gathered for a Halloween party, where they will observe some old traditions.
nits = nuts; *pou their stocks* = counting the grain on a stalk of corn in pairs. To have an odd grain left meant little chance of marriage; *haud* = hold; *fu blythe* = merry

The lasses feat, an' cleanly neat,
Mair braw than when they're fine;
Their faces blithe, fu' sweetly kythe,
Hearts leal, an' warm, an' kin':
The lads sae trig, wi' wooer-babs
Weel knotted on their garten;
Some unco blate, an' some wi' gabs
Gar lasses' hearts gang startin
Whyles fast that night.

The girls were dressed for the occasion and the lads wore love knots on their garters.
feat = spruce; kythe = display; leal = loyal; trig = smart; wooer-babs = love-knots; garten = garters; unco blate = very shy; wi' gabs = talk freely; gar = make

Then, first an' foremost, thro' the kail,
Their stocks maun a' be sought ance;
They steek their een, an' grape an' wale
For muckle anes, an' straught anes.
Poor hav'rel Will fell aff the drift,
An' wandered thro' the bow-kail,
An' pow't, for want o' better shift,
A runt was like a sow-tail
Sae bow't that night.

Into the field with eyes covered to try and find a stalk of corn. The stalk of corn can only be used once so it is important to get a strong one. Silly Will wanders into the cabbage patch, and pulls a stalk so bent it's like a sow's tail. maun = must; steek their een = close their eyes; grape an' wale = grope and choose; muckle anes = big ones; straught = straight; hav'rel = silly; fell aff the drift = got left behind; bow-kail = cabbage; pow't = pulled; bow't = bent

Then, straught or crooked, yird or nane,
They roar an' cry a' throw'ther;
The vera wee-things, toddling, rin,
Wi' stocks out-owre their shouther:
An' gif the custock's sweet or sour,
Wi' joctelegs they taste them;
Syne cozilie, aboon the door,
Wi' cannie care, they've plac'd them
To lie that night.

They all return through the yard with their stalks, the little children with long ones they carry over their shoulders. They cut the pith to see if it is sweet or sour then place them carefully around the door. throw'ther = in disorder; gif = if; custock = pith; joctelegs = clasp-knife; yird or nane = dirty or not; vera = very; rin = run; aboon = around; cannie = careful

The lasses staw frae 'mang them a',
To pou their stalks o' corn;
But Rab slips out, and jinks about,
Behint the muckle thorn:
He grippet Nelly, hard an' fast;
Loud skirl'd a' the lasses;
But her tap-pickle maist was lost,
Whan kiutlin in the fause-house
Wi' him that night.

The girls sneak out to pull their stalks of corn, but Rab grabs Nelly and as all the girls scream he pulls her into the frame of the haystack.

skirl'd = screamed; *tap-pickle maist* = uppermost grain in stalk of oats; *her tap-pickle maist was lost* = euphemism for losing virginity; *kiutlin* = cuddling; *fause-house* = frame of haystack

The auld guid-wife's weel-hoorded nits
Are round an' round divided,
An' monie a lads an' lasses' fates
Are there that night decided:
Some kindle, couthie, side by side,
An' burn thegither trimly;
Some start awa wi' saucy pride,
An' jump out-owre the chimlie
Fu' high that night.

An old lady dishes out nuts in another Halloween ritual. If two people's nuts roast well together, then all is well, but some explode and fly up the chimney indicating bad omens.

weel-hoorded = well-hoarded; *kindle couthie* = burn comfortably; *chimlie* = chimney

Jean slips in twa, wi' tentie e'e;
Wha 'twas, she wadna tell;
But this is *Jock*, and this is *me*,
She says in to hersel:
He bleez'd owre her, an' she owre him,
As they wad never mair part;
Till fuff! he started up the lum,
And Jean had e'en a sair heart
To see 't that night.

Jean put two nuts on the fire without disclosing who her chosen man was. They seemed an ideal couple, but she was distressed when her intended's nut exploded and shot up the chimney.

tentie e'e = attentive eye; *bleez'd* = blazed; *lum* = chimney

Poor Willie, wi' his bow-kail runt,
Was burnt wi' primsie Mallie;
An' Mary, nae doubt, took the drunt,
To be compar'd to Willie:
Mall's nit lap out, wi' pridefu' fling,
An' her ain fit, it brunt it;
While Willie lap, an' swoor by jing,
'Twas just the way he wanted
To be that night.

Willie, with his misshapen stalk was paired off with a demure young lady who took the huff at being compared with him. Her nut flew out of the fire and burnt her foot while Willie swore that he didn't care anyway.

primsie = demure; *drunt* = huff; *lap* = leapt; *ain fit* = own foot; *swoor* = swore; *brunt* = burnt

Nell had the fause-house in her min',
She pits hersel an' Rob in;
In loving bleeze they sweetly join
Till white in ase they're sobbin;
Nell's heart was dancin at the view;
She whisper'd Rob to leuk for 't:
Rob, stownlins, pri'ed her bonie mou,
Fu cozie in the neuk for 't,
Unseen that night.

Nell had memories of her earlier encounter with Rob as she puts their nuts in together. She was thrilled to see them burn happily until they became ash and Rob and her kissed tenderly in a corner unseen by the others.

ase = ash; *leuk* = look; *stownlins* = stealthily; *mou* = mouth; *neuk* = nook

But Merran sat behint their backs,
Her thoughts on Andrew Bell;
She lea's them gashing at their cracks,
An' slips out by hersel:
She thro' the yard the nearest taks,
An' for the kiln she goes then,
An' darklins grapit for the bauks,
And in the blue-clue throws then,
Right fear't that night.

Merran has Andrew Bell on her mind and leaves the others gossiping as she tries another method of seeing into the future. By throwing blue yarn into the kiln would reveal ones' lover. She was very brave as a demon was believed to inhabit the kiln.

gashing at their cracks = gossiping; *darklins* = darkness; *grapit* = grabbed; *blue-clue* = blue yarn

An' ay she win't, an' ay she swat—
I wat she made nae jaukin;
Till something held within the pat,
Guid Lord! but she was quakin!
But whether 'twas the Deil himsel,
Or whether 'twas a bauk-en,
Or whether it was Andrew Bell,
She did na wait on talkin
To spier that night.

She wound the yarn until something caught it, then she ran off shaking with terror without waiting to see if it was Andrew Bell, the beam or the Devil himself.

win't = wound; *swat* = sweat; *spier* = ask; *wat* = assure; *nae jaukin* = didn't idle; *pat* = pot; *bauk-en* = beam end;

Wee Jenny to her graunie says,
'Will you go wi' me, graunie?
I'll eat the apple at the glass,
I gat frae uncle Johnie;'
She fluff't her pipe wi' sic a lunt,
In wrath she was sae vap'rin,
She notic't na, an aizle brunt
Her braw, new, worstet apron
Out thro' that night.

When Jenny asked her Granny to come with her whilst she ate an apple at the mirror (another Halloween custom that would show your future husband), the older woman flew into a rage and puffed hard upon her pipe, not even noticing the burn mark on her new apron.

fluff't = puffed; *lunt* = puff of smoke; *aizle* = ember

'Ye little skelpie-limmer's-face!
I daur you try sic sportin,
As seek the Foul Thief onie place,
For him to spae your fortune:
Nae doubt but ye may get a sight!
Great cause ye hae to fear it;
For monie a ane has gotten a fright,
An' liv'd an' died deleeret,
On sic a night.

Hurling abuse at the youngster, she dared her to try this as it would tempt the devil to appear, and others have been left in a state of madness because of seeing him.

skelpie-limmer's face = young hussy; *daur* = dare; *Foul Thief* = Devil; *spae* = tell; *deleeret* = delirious; *sic* = such

'Ae hairst afore the Sherra-moor,
I mind as weel's yestreen,
I was a gilpey then, I'm sure
I was na past fyfteen:
The simmer had been cauld an' wat,
An' stuff was unco green;
An' ay a rantin kirn we gat,
An' just on Halloween
It fell that night.

'Our stibble-rig was Rab M'Graen,
A clever, sturdy fallow
His sin gat Eppie Sim wi' wean,
That liv'd in Achmacalla:
He gat hemp-seed, I mind it weel,
An' he made unco light o't;
But monie a day was by himsel,
He was sae sairly frighted
That vera night.'

Then up gat fechtin Jamie Fleck,
An' he swoor by his conscience,
That he could saw hemp-seed a peck;
For it was a' but nonsense:
The auld guidman raught down the pock,
An' out a handfu' gied him;
Syne bad him slip frae 'mang the folk,
Sometime when nae ane see'd him
An' try't that night.

She has a clear memory of a Halloween party just before the Battle of Sherriffmuir when she was only fifteen. It had been a cold and wet summer and everything was uncommonly green.

hairst = harvest; *gilpey* = young girl; *simmer* = summer; *cauld an' wat* = cold and wet; *rantin kirn* = wild party

One fellow had spread out hemp-seed which was supposed to reveal the Devil, and although he made a joke of it, he was really scared afterwards.

stibble-rig = chief-harvester; *wean* = child

This tempted one of the lads to declare that it was all nonsense and that he would spread out the seed to prove it. An old man gave him a handful of seed but he waited until nobody was watching before he set out to try it.

fechtin = fighting; *raught* = reached; *pock* = bag; *syne bad him* = soon bade him

He marches thro' amang the stacks,
Tho' he was something sturtin;
The graip he for a harrow taks,
An' haurls at his curpin:
And ev'ry now and then he says,
'Hemp-seed I saw thee,
An' her that is to be my lass
Come after me, an' draw thee
As fast this night.'

Slightly frightened, he marches through the hay-stacks, hurling the pitchfork behind him, and repeating the rhyme.
sturtin = troubled; *graip* = pitchfork; *haurls at his curpin* = hurls it behind him

He whistl'd up *Lord Lennox' March*,
To keep his courage cheery;
Altho' his hair began to arch,
He was sae fley'd an' eerie;
Till presently he hears a squeak,
An' then a grane an' gruntle;
He by his shouther gae a keek,
An' tumbled wi' a wintle
Out-owre that night.

His hair was standing on end with fear, when he heard some srange noises, and glancing over his shoulder tumbled over in terror.
fley'd an' eerie = terror stricken; *grane* = groan; *shouther* = shoulder; *keek* = glance; *wintle* = somersault

He roar'd a horrid murder-shout,
In dreadfu' desperation!
An' young an' auld come rinnin out,
An' hear the sad narration:
He swoor 'twas hilchin Jean M'Craw,
Or crouchie Merran Humphie,
Till stop! she trotted thro' them a';
An' wha was it but Grumphie
Asteer that night?

His screams of terror brought the others running to help. He swore that he was followed by two of the most undesirable females in the area, but they discovered that he had been terrified by a pig on the loose.
hilchin = crippled; *crouchie* = hunchback; *Grumphie* = the pig; *asteer* = astir

Meg fain wad to the barn gaen,
To winn three wechts o' naething,
But for to meet the Deil her lane,
She pat but little faith in:
She gies the herd a pickle nits,
An' twa red-cheekit apples,
To watch, while for the barn she sets,
In hopes to see Tam Kipples
That vera night.

Meg would have gone to the barn to sieve out some corn, and she wasn't too concerned about meeting the Devil. She handed over her apples and nuts to the shepherd to look after for her while she went in search of Tam Kipples.

fain = gladly; *wad* = would; *winn* = separate corn from chaff; *wecht* = sieve; *herd* = shepherd

She turns the key, wi' cannie thraw,
An' owre the threshold ventures;
But first on Sawnie gies a ca',
Syne bauldly in she enters:
A ratton rattl'd up the wa',
An' she cry'd, Lord preserve her!
An' ran thro' midden-hole an' a',
An' pray'd wi' zeal and fervour,
Fu' fast that night.

She opened the barn door carefully, calling first for Sandy, then as she entered, a rat scurried up the wall scaring her so much that she ran straight through the muck-heap.

cannie thraw = careful turn; *Sawnie* = Sandy; *bauldly* = boldly; *ratton* = rat; *midden- hole* = dung-heap

Then hoy't out Will, wi' sair advice;
They hecht him some fine braw ane;
It chanc'd the stack he faddom't thrice,
Was timmer-propt for thrawin;
He taks a swirlie, auld moss-oak
For some black, gruesome carlin;
An' loot a winze, an' drew a stroke,
Till skin in blypes cam haurlin
Aff's nieves that night.

They coaxed Will out with a promise of something good. He thought he was putting his arms three times round a stack, but it was a timber prop he had hold of. He then mistook an old tree for a witch and punched it until his knuckles were bleeding.

hecht = urged; *faddom't* = fathomed; *timmer-propt* = propped up; *swirlie* = gnarled; *loot a winze* = cursed; *drew a stroke* = struck; *blypes* = shreds; *haurlin* = hurling; *nieves* = fists

A wanton widow Leezie was,
As cantie as a kittlin;
But och! that night, amang the shaws,
She gat a fearful settlin!
She thro' the whins, an' by the cairn,
An' owre the hill gaed scrievin;
Whare three laird's lands met at a burn,
To dip her left sark-sleeve in,
Was bent that night.

Lizzie the widow was set on trying yet
another method of finding a partner. If a lass
were to immerse the left sleeve of her
nightdress in the waters of a stream, the face
of her intended would be revealed to her.
cantie as a kittling = lively as a kitten; *scrievin*
= ran swiftly; *whin* = gorse

Whyles owre a linn the burnie plays,
As thro' the glen it wimpl't;
Whyles round a rocky scaur it strays,
Whyles in a wiel it dimpl't;
Whyles glitter'd to the nightly rays,
Wi' bickerin, dancin dazzle;
Whyles cookit underneath the braes,
Below the spreading hazlel
Unseen that night.

The burn ran over a waterfall and round
the rocks until it reached a pool under the
hazel tree where it was hidden from the
moonlight.
linn = waterfall; *wimpl't* = wimpled; *scaur*
= cliff; *cookit* = hidden; *wiel* = eddy

Amang the brachens, on the brae,
Between her an' the moon,
The Deil, or else an outler quey,
Gat up an' gae a croon:
Poor Leezie's heart maist lap the hool;
Near lav'rock-height she jumpit,
But mist a fit, an' in the pool
Out-owre the lugs she plumpit,
Wi' a plunge that night.

Poor Lizzie was leaning over the pool
when she was suddenly scared by a strange
noise which could have been the devil, or
more likely a heifer lowing. She jumped
up in terror and landed over her ears in
the pool.
outler quey =heifer in a field; *croon* = low
(cattle); *maist lap the hool* = nearly jumped
out of her body; *lav'rock* = skylark; *mist a fit*
= missed her footing; *owre the lugs* = over
the ears

In order, on the clean hearth-stane,
The luggies three are ranged;
An' ev'ry time great care is taen
To see them duly changed;
Auld uncle John, wha wedlock's joys
Sin' Mar's years did desire,
Because he gat the toom dish thrice,
He heav'd them on the fire,
In wrath that night.

Three wooden dishes are arranged on the hearth, but frustrated old uncle John, who has picked the wrong one three times, was so mad that he threw them on the fire. *luggies* = wooden dishes; *Mar's year* = 1715, the Jacobite Rebellion; *toom* = empty

Wi' merry sangs, an' friendly cracks,
I wat they did na weary;
And unco tales, an' funnie jokes,
Their sports were cheap an' cheery:
Till butter'd sow'ns, wi' fragrant lunt,
Set a' their gabs a-steerin;
Syne, wi' a social glass o' strunt,
They parted aff careerin
Fu' blythe that night.

The evening carried on with stories and jokes as the folks enjoyed their simple party, until it was time for a final drink and a stagger home. *cracks* = chat; *butter'd sow'ns* = sour puddings; *lunt* = steam; *gabs a-steerin* = tongues wagging; *strunt* = alchohol; *wat* = assure

The Auld Farmer's New-Years Morning Salutation to his Auld Mare, Maggie

ON GIVING HER THE ACCUSTOMED RIPP OF CORN TO HANSEL IN THE NEW YEAR.

A lovely poem in which the farmer relives the many years that he has spent with his beloved old mare.

A Guid New-Year I wish thee, Maggie!
Hae, there's a ripp to thy auld baggie:
Tho' thou's howe-backit now, an' knaggie,
I've seen the day,
Thou could hae gane like ony staggie
Out-owre the lay.

The farmer reminds his old mare that although she is showing her age, he can remember her running like a colt. *hae* = here; *ripp* = handful of unthreshed corn; *auld baggie* = old stomach; *thou's howe-backit* = you're hollow-backed; *an' knaggie* = and knobbly; *hae gaen* = have gone; *onie staggie* = any stag; *out-owre the lay* = over the meadow

Tho' now thou's dowie, stiff an' crazy,
An' thy auld hide as white's a daisie,
I've seen thee dappl't, sleek an' glaizie,
A bonie gray:
He should been tight that daur't to raize thee,
Ance in a day.

Although the mare is now stiff and drooping, in her youth she had been a beautiful grey with a shiny coat, full of spirit. *thou's dowie* = you're sad; *hide* = coat; *dappl't* = dappled; *glaizie* = shiny; *bonie* = beautiful; *tight* = prepared; *daur't* = dared; *raize* = excite; *ance* = once

Thou ance was i' the foremost rank,
A filly buirdly, steeve, an' swank;
An' set weel down a shapely shank,
As e'er tread yird;
An' could hae flown out-owre a stank,
Like ony bird.

The mare had been as elegant and trim as any that walked on earth, and she could fly over pools like a bird. *buirdly, steeve an' swank* = strong, firm and elegant; *e'er tread yird* = ever walked on earth; *out-owre a stank* = over a pool

It's now some nine-an'-twenty year,
Sin' thou was my guid-father's mear;
He gied me thee, o' tocher clear,
An' fifty mark;
Tho' it was sma', 'twas weel-won gear,
An' thou was stark.

Twenty-nine years have now passed since he was given the mare as part of his wife's dowry, along with some money, and although it was not much, it did not matter as the horse was strong. *guid-father's meere* = father-in-law's mare; *gied* = gave; *tocher* = dowry; *stark* = strong

When first I gaed to woo my Jenny,
Ye then was trottin wi' your Minnie:
Tho' ye was trickie, slee an' funnie,
Ye ne'er was donsie;
But hamely, tawie, quiet an' cannie,
An unco sonsie.

When the farmer was courting, the mare was still a young foal running beside her mother, and although lively, she was well behaved.
gaed to woo = went to court; minnie = mother; slee = shy; donsie = mischievous; hamely = homely; tawie = docile; unco sonsie = very well-mannered

That day, ye pranc'd wi' muckle pride,
When ye bure hame my bonie bride:
An' sweet an' gracefu', she did ride.
Wi' maiden air!
Kyle-Stewart I could bragged wide,
For sic a pair.

When the bride arrived on the mare's back, the farmer was the proudest man in the county to have two such beautiful ladies.
wi' muckle = with great; bure hame = carried home; Kyle-Stewart = Ayrshire

Tho' now ye dow but hoyte and hobble,
An' wintle like a saumont-coble,
That day, ye was a jinker noble,
For heels an' win'!
An' ran them till they a' did wauble,
Far, far behin'!

The old horse struggles to walk properly, but he remembers when she could outrun all the others.
dow = can; hoyte = stagger; saumont-coble = salmon-boat; wintle = swing fom side to side; jinker = goer; wauble = wobble

When thou an' I were young an' skiegh,
An' stable meals at fairs were driegh,
How thou would prance, an' snore an' scriegh,
An' tak the road !
Towns-bodies ran, an' stood abiegh,
An' ca't thee mad.

Neither farmer nor mare enjoyed the tedium of the fairs, and the horse would prance and snort until they were on the road, shocking the townies with their speed.
skiegh = skittish; driegh = dreary; wad = would; snore = snort; scriegh = whinny; abiegh = at a distance; ca't = called

When thou was corn't, an' I was mellow,
We took the road ay like a swallow:
At brooses thou had ne'er a fellow,
For pith an' speed;
But ev'ry tail thou pay't them hollow,
Whare'er thou gaed.

When the mare was fed and the farmer was happy, they would ride like the wind. Nothing could catch them at the traditional wedding races.
corn't = fed; brooses = wedding race from the church to the home of the bridegroom; pith = vigour; pay't = paid

The sma', droop-rumpl't, hunter cattle
Might aiblins waur't thee for a brattle;
But sax Scotch mile, thou try't their mettle,
An gar't them whaizle:
Nae whip nor spur, but just a wattle
O' saugh or hazel.

Small hunters might win in a sprint, but over a distance she'd leave them behind without the need of whip or spurs.
sma' = small; *droop-rumpl't* = short-rumped; *aiblins waur't thee for a brattle* = perhaps beat you in a short sprint; *sax* = six; *gar't them whaizle* = made them wheeze; *a wattle o' saugh* = a wand of willow

Thou was a noble fittie-lan',
As e'er in tug or trow was drawn!
Aft thee an' I, in aught hours gaun,
On guid March-weather,
Hae turn'd sax roods beside our han',
For days thegither.

The farmer tells her what a wonderful plough-horse she had been, and how much land they had turned over in a working day.
fittie-lan' = rear left-hand plough-horse; *aft* = often; *aught* = eight; *gaun* = gone; *sax rood* = acre and a half; *beside our han'* = by ourselves; *thegither* = together

Thou never braing't, an' fetch't an' fliskit,
But thy auld tail thou wad hae whiskit,
An' spread abreed thy weel-fill'd brisket,
Wi' pith an' pow'r,
Till sprittie knowes wad rair't an' riskit,
An' slypet owre.

She never did anything unexpected while ploughing, pulling willingly over the roughest ground, and ignoring the danger.
Braing't = lunged; *fetch't* = stopped suddenly; *fliskit* = fretted; *spread abreed thy weel-fill'd brisket* = thrust out your chest; *sprittie knowes* = tufted hillocks; *wad rair't an' riskit an' slypet owre* = would roar and rack until they broke up

When frosts lay lang, an' snaws were deep,
An' threaten'd labor back to keep,
I gied thy cog a wee-bit heap
Aboon the timmer;
I ken'd my Maggie wad na sleep
For that, or simmer.

During the difficulties of a severe winter, she would be given more feed, as the farmer knew she would not stop to rest until summer.
lang = long; *snaws* = snows; *cog* = dish; *timmer* = edge; *ken'd* = knew

In cart or or car thou never reestit;
The steyest brae thou wad hae fac'd it;
Thou never lap, an' sten't, an' breastit,
Then stood to blaw;
But just thy step a wee thing hastit,
Thou snoov't awa.

The mare never stopped to rest when working, and she would go at a steep hill with no visible effort.

reestit = become restless; *steyest brae* = steepest slope; *lap, an sten't, an' breestit* = leapt, or sprang or lunged; *blaw* = blow; *hastit* = faster; *snoov't awa* = went smoothly on

My pleugh is now thy bairntime a',
Four gallant brutes, as e'er did draw;
Forbye sax mae, I've sell't awa,
That thou has nurst:
They drew me thretteen pund an' twa,
The vera warst.

The ploughing team now consists of four of the mare's offspring, with another six having been sold to give the farmer a good profit.

pleugh = plough; *bairntime* = offspring; *forbye* = besides; *sax mae* six more; *sell't awa* = sold; *nurst* = nursed; *thretteen pund* = thirteen pounds; *vera warst* = very worst

Mony a sair darg we twae hae wrought,
An' wi' the weary warl' fought!
An' mony an anxious day, I thought
We wad be beat!
Yet here to crazy age we're brought,
Wi' something yet.

The farmer reminds the mare of the many hard days they have shared together and how, in spite of everything, they are still here to enjoy their old-age.

sair darg = hard day's work; *twae* = two; *warl'* = world

An' think na, my auld, trusty servan',
That now perhaps thou's less deservin',
An' thy auld days may end in starvin';
For my last fow,
A heapit stimper, I'll reserve ane
Laid by for you.

He reassures the mare that although her working days are over, she need never worry about being fed as he would starve himself before Maggie went hungry.

fow = bushel; *heapit stimper* = heaped quarter peck; *ane laid by* = one set aside

We've worn to crazy years thegither;
We'll toyte about wi' ane anither;
Wi' tentie care I'll flit thy tether
To some hain'd rig,
Whare ye may nobly rax your leather,
Wi' sma' fatigue.

The pair have aged together and will totter around in their old age. Maggie will have her own space to graze in peace for the rest of her life.

toyte = totter; *tentie* = prudent; *flit* = remove; *hain'd rig* = reserved space; *rax your leather* = fill your stomach; *sma' fatigue* = little exertion

Scotch Drink

Gie him strong drink until he wink,
That's sinking in despair;
An' liquor guid, to fire his bluid,
That's prest wi' grief and care;
There let bowse, an' deep carouse,
Wi' bumpers flowing o'er,
Till he forgets his loves or debts,
An' minds his griefs no more.
Solomon's proverbs, xxxi, 6,7.

Here we have fairly lengthy poem dedicated to the virtues of Scotch Whisky, and at the same time taking the opportunity to slam the imposition of tax upon such a popular drink.

It would appear that illegal stills were not uncommon in those distant days, and the excisemen also come under attack for their constant pursuit of such stills.

Let other poets raise a fracas,
'Bout vines and wines, and drucken Bacchus,
An' crabbit names an' stories wrack us,
An' grate our lug;
I sing the juice Scotch bear can make us,
In glass or jug.

Burns has no interest in the praise of wines, nor in listening to others tell tales of Bacchus. For him, the only true drink comes from the barley of Scotland – whisky! *drucken* = drunken; *crabbit* = ill- natured; *wrack* = punish; *grate our lug* = irritate our ear; *bear* = barley

O Thou, my Muse! guid auld Scotch drink!
Whether thro' wimplin worms thou jink,
Or richly brown, ream owre the brink,
In glorious faem.
Inspire me, till I lisp an' wink,
To sing thy name!

As the whisky winds its way through the coils of the distilling apparatus, he is inspired by the rich, brown liquid foaming in the still. *wimplin'* = waving; *jink* = dodge; *ream* = froth; *faem* = foam

Let husky wheat the haughs adorn
An' aits set up their awnie horn,
An' pease and beans at e'en or morn,
Perfume the plain:
Leeze me on thee, John Barleycorn,
Thou king o' grain!

The Bard has no objection to the sight of fields of wheat, oats, peas and beans, but nevertheless his blessings are given to barley, the king of grain. *haughs* = meadows; *aits* = oats; *awnie* = bearded; *pease* = peas, *leeze on thee* = blessings on you; *John Barleycorn* = whisky

On thee aft Scotland chows her cood,
In souple scones, the wale o' food!
Or tumbling in the boiling flood
Wi' kail an' beef;
But when thou pours thy strong
heart's blood,
There thou shines chief.

Food fills the wame an' keeps us livin';
Tho' life's a gift no' worth receivin',
When heavy dragg'd wi' pine an' grievin';
But oil'd by thee,
The wheels o' life gae down-hill, scrievin',
Wi' rattlin' glee.

Thou clears the head o' doited Lear,
Thou cheers the heart o' drooping Care;
Thou strings the nerves o' Labour sair,
At's weary toil;
Thou ev'n brightens dark Despair
Wi' gloomy smile.

Aft, clad in massy, siller weed,
Wi' gentles thou erects thy head;
Yet, humbly kind in time o' need,
The poor man's wine;
His wee drap parritch, or his bread,
Thou kitchens fine.

Although Scotland depends on barley for the making of favourite scones, or to thicken up the soup, it is only when in liquid form that its true value is revealed
aft = often; *chows her cood* = eats her food; *souple scones* = soft barley cakes; *wale* = choice; *kail* = cabbage

Food fills our bellies and keeps us alive, but life can seem to be nothing more than burdensome, weary toil, and whisky can help that life much more cheerful.
wame = belly; *leivin'* = living; *heavy dragg'd* = worn out; *wi' pine an' grievin'* = with suffering and grieving; *scrievin'* = gliding easily; *rattlin'* = lively

Whisky can clear muddled heads as well as help dispel care and pain. Even the deepest despair can be lightened with a glass of whisky.
doited Lear = stupid customs

The gentry may serve their whisky in fancy silver cups, but it can always be relied on to be the poor man's wine and to supplement his meagre meal.
clad in massy siller weed = dressed in heavy silver; *gentles* = gentry; *wee drap parritch* = small drop of porridge; *kitchens* = makes palatable

Thou art the life o' public haunts,
But thee, what were our fairs and rants?
Ev'n godly meetings o' the saunts,
By thee inspir'd,
When gaping, they besiege the tents,
Are doubly fir'd.

How dull life would be without whisky. Festivals and Fairs are much livelier when it is present, and the tents where it is sold are always thronged with thirsty people. *public haunts* = taverns; *what were our fairs and rants* = that was our pleasure and joy; *saunts* = saints; *fir'd* = affected

That merry night we get the corn in,
O sweetly, then, thou reams the horn in!
Or reekin' on a New-Year mornin'
In cog or bicker,
An' just a wee drap sp'ritual burn in,
An' gusty sucker!

Harvest time is always cause for celebration, but on New Year's morning, whisky is especially enjoyed steaming hot, with a drop of water from the burn and a touch of sugar.
reams the horn in = froths in the cup; *reekin'* = smoking; *cog or bicker* = wooden dishes; *gusty sucker* = sugar

When Vulcan gies his bellows breath,
An' ploughmen gather wi' their graith.
O rare! to see thee fizz an' freath
I' th' lugget caup!
Then Burnewin come on like death
At ev'ry chaup.

When ploughmen gather at the smithy, the whisky froths in the cup, and the blacksmith hammers more heartily after a drop.
when Vulcan gies his bellows braith = in the heat of the smithy; *graith* = harness; *fizz an' freath* = hiss and froth; *lugget caup* = a two-handled cup; *Burnewin* = blacksmith; *chaup* = blow

Nae mercy then, for airn or steel;
The brawnie, bainie, ploughman chiel,
Brings hard owrehip, wi' sturdy wheel,
The strong forehammer,
Till block an' studdie ring an' reel.
Wi' dinsome clamour.

With no mercy for the iron or steel on which he is working, the blacksmith's muscular forearm causes his hammer to make the anvil ring out aloud.
airn = iron; *bainie* = muscular; *chiel* = young man; *owrehip* = a method of hammering; *block an' studdie* = anvil and smithy; *dinsome* = noisy

When skirlin weanies see the light,
Thou maks the gossips clatter bright,
How fumblin' cuifs their dearies slight,
Wae worth the name!
Nae howdie gets a social night,
Or plack frae them.

While celebrating a new baby with a drop of whisky, the women gossip about their husbands and forget to reward the midwife. *skirlin' weanies* = shrieking babies; *clatter bright* = chatter noisil;, *fumblin' cuifs* = awkward fools; *dearies slight* = insult their loved ones; *wae worth* = woe befall; *howdie* = midwife; *plack* = a small coin

When neebors anger at a plea,
An' just as wud as wud can be,
How easy can the barley-brie
Cement the quarrel!
It's aye the cheapest lawyer's fee,
To taste the barrel,

Here the Bard speaks words of wisdom as he points out that it is far cheaper to have a drink with a neighbour to resolve a quarrel than to pay the fees of a lawyer. *neebor* = neighbour; *wud* = mad; *barley-brie* = whisky; *aye* = always

Alake! that e'er my Muse has reason,
To wyte her countrymen wi' treason!
But monie daily weet their weason
Wi' liquors nice.
An' hardly, in a winter season,
E'er spier her price.

Sad to say, but we have reason to accuse some of our countrymen of treason because they consume drinks other than whisky, and they do not even ask the price. *alake* = alas; *wyte* = blame; *weet their weason* = wet their throats; *spier* = ask

Wae worth that brandy, burnin' trash!
Fell source o' monie a pain an' brash!
Twins monie a poor, doylt, drucken hash
O' half his days;
An' sends, beside, auld Scotland's cash
To her warst faes.

Brandy is trash which causes painful hangovers and is the reason for so many lost working-days. What's more, the revenue from brandy goes to support the country's enemies. *fell* = biting; *brash* = sickness; *twins* = deprives; *doylt drucken hash* = stupid drunken fellow; *warst faes* = worst foes

Ye Scots, wha wish auld Scotland well!
Ye chief, to you my tale I tell,
Poor, plackless devils like mysel'!
It sets you ill,
Wi' bitter dearthfu' wines to mell,
Or foreign gill.

If you wish Scotland well, then do not bother with fancy, foreign wines. They will do you no good at all. *chief* = mainly; *plackless* = penniless; *dearthfu'* = expensive; *mell* = to meddle; *gill* = a measure of whisky

May gravels round his blather wrench,
 An' gouts torment him, inch by inch,
Wha twists his gruntle wi' a glunch
O' sour disdain, Out owre a glass o'
whisky-punch Wi' honest men!

May anyone who sneers at a man who enjoys a glass of whisky with his friends have a bladder that feels like gravel, and suffer from gout. *may gravels round his bladder wrench* = may kidney-stones give him pains in his bladder; *twists his gruntle wi' a grunch* = screws his face up in a frown

O Whisky! soul o' plays an' pranks!
Accept a Bardie's gratefu' thanks!
When wanting thee, what tuneless cranks
Are my poor verses!
Thou comes - they rattle i' their ranks,
At ither's arses!

Burns acknowledges that his verses are often tuneless noises until he has had a glass of whisky, then the words come pouring out. *plays and pranks* = games and jokes; *cranks* = creakings; *ither's arses* = others backsides

Thee, Ferintosh! O sadly lost!
Scotland lament frae coast to coast!
Now colic-grips, an' barkin' hoast
May kill us a',
For loyal Forbes' chartered boast
Is ta'en awa!

In reparation for damage done during the Jacobite Rebellion, Ferintosh Distillery (owned by the Forbes family) had been freed from paying excise duty. This privilege was withdrawn in 1785, and the price of whisky escalated, depriving men of their favourite tipple. *colic grips* = illness takes hold; *barkin'hoast* = barking cough; *ta'en awa* = taken away

Thae curst horse-leeches o' the Excise,
Wha mak the whisky stells their prize!
Haud up thy han', Deil, ance, twice, thrice!
There, seize the blinkers
An' bake them up in brunstane pies
For poor damn'd drinkers.

Closing illicit stills was one of the main activities of the despised exciseman, and the devil is called upon to deal with them harshly. *horse-leeches* = blood-suckers; *stells* = stills; *haud up thy han'* = hold up your hand; *blinkers* = a form of contempt; *brunstane* = brimstone

Fortune! if thou'll but gie me still
Hale breeks, a scone, an' whisky gill,
An' rowth o' rhyme to rave at will,
Tak a' the rest,
An' deal 't about as thy blind skill
Directs the best.

All the Bard wants from life are whole trousers, some food to eat along with his whisky, and some rhyme to produce at will. With these, he can accept whatever life has in store for him.

hale breeks = whole trousers; *rowth o'* = abundance of; *rave* = utter

To a Louse

Here we have one of the Bard's masterpieces, illustrating in memorable lines just how easy it is to have the totally incorrect impression of how we see and are seen by our fellow mortals. The opening lines of the final verse are renowned throughout the world.

Ha! whare ye gaun, ye crowlin' ferlie?
Your impudence protects you sairly:
I canna say but ye strunt rarely,
Owre gauze and lace;
Tho', faith! I fair, ye dine but sparely,
On sic a place.

When he first notices the louse, he marvels at its nerve to roam over this fine lady. *whare ye gaun* = where are you going; *crowlin' ferlie* = crawling marvel; *sairly* = sorely; *ow're* = over; *sic* = such

Ye ugly, creepin, blastit wonner.
Detested, shunn'd, by saunt an' sinner
How daur ye set your fit upon her,
Sae fine a lady !.
Gae somewhere else and seek your dinner
On some poor body.

Now he suggests that it is quite wrong for it to be on such a fine lady, and it should find some poor person on which to seek its meal. *blastit wonner* = worthless wonder; *saunt* = saint; *fit* = foot; *sae* = so

Swith! in some beggar's hauffet squattle,
There ye may creep, and sprawl,
and sprattle,
Wi' ither kindred, jumping cattle;
In shoals and nations;
Whaur horn nor bane ne'er daur unsettle
Your thick plantations.

He tells the louse that it would be much more at home with a beggar, sharing that space with its peers in the parasite world where there would be little chance of being routed out by a comb. *swith* = quick; *hauffet* = sideburns; *squattle* = squat; *sprattle* = scramble; *ither* = other; *horn nor bane* = a comb made from horn or bone; *daur* = dare

Now haud you there! ye're out o' sight,
Below the fatt'rils, snug and tight,
Na faith ye yet ! ye'll no' be right
Till ye've got on it,
The vera tapmost, tow'rin height
O' Miss's bonnet.

Now hold on! The creature has disappeared and it is not going to be content until it is right on top of the lady's hat. *haud ye there* = wait; *fatt'rils* = ribbon ends; *vera* = very; *tow'rin* = towering

My sooth! right bauld ye set your nose out,
As plump an' grey as onie grozet;
O for some rank, mercurial rozet,
Or fell, red smeddum,
I'd gie you sic a hearty dose o't
Wad dress your droddum!

Here he sees that the louse is quite plump, and is as grey as a gooseberry. He wishes he had some insect repellent to use on it. *bauld* = bold; *grozet* = gooseberry; *rozet* = rosin; *fell red smeddum* = biting red powder; *o't* = of it; *wad* = would; *dress your droddum* = hurt you in the trousers

I wad na been surpris'd to spy
You on an auld wife's flannen toy;
Or aiblins some bit duddie boy,
On's wylecoat;
But Miss's fine Lunardi! fye!
How daur ye do 't?

He would expect the creature to be on an old lady's flannel cap, or on a lad's ragged vest, but not on a fine Lunardi bonnet. *wad na been* = would not have been; *auld wife's flannen toy* = old woman's flannel cap with side flaps; *aiblins* = perhaps; *duddie* = ragged; *wyliecoat* = a flannel vest; *daur* = dare

Oh Jenny, dinna toss your head
An' set your beauties a' abread!
Ye little ken what cursed speed
The blastie's makin!
Thae winks an' finger-ends, I dread
Are notice takin'!

He now makes a silent plea that the lady does not shake her head and spread out her hair as she is totally unaware of what Burns is watching with such fascination. *dinna* = do not; *yer* = your; *set your beauties a' abread* = toss your curls; *ken* = know; *blastie* = ugly little creature

O wad some Pow'r the giftie gie us
To see oursels as ithers see us!
It wad frae monie a blunder free us,
An' foolish notion,
What airs in dress an' gait wad lea'e us,
An' ev'n devotion!

Finally, the poet asks us to consider ourselves – are we really all that we think we are. Would we stop making foolish comments about others if we understood just how they saw us? *monie* = many; *lea'e* = leave; *wad* = would

Love and Liberty – a Cantata

Burns was drinking in Poosie Nansie's tavern in Mauchline, watching the antics of a group of beggars, when he decided to embark upon this work. It was his only attempt to write something that could be staged and appears to have been influenced by 'The Beggar's Opera.' This is another wonderfully descriptive piece, full of life and vitality.

RECITATIVO

When lyart leaves bestrew the yird,
Or wavering like the bauckie-bird,
Bedim cauld Boreas' blast;
When hailstanes drive wi' bitter skyte,
And infant frosts begin to bite,
In hoary cranreuch drest;
Ae night at e'en a merry core
O' randie, gangrel bodies,
In Poosie Nansie's held the splore,
To drink their orra duddies;
Wi' quaffing and laughing,
They ranted an' they sang,
Wi' jumping an' thumping,
The vera girdle rang.

It was the start of winter and a group of beggars were drinking noisily in the inn.
lyart = withered; yird = ground; bauckie-bird = bat; Borea's blast = north-wind; skyte = lash; hoary cranreuch = hoar frost; core o' randie, gangrel bodies = gang of unruly ruffians; held the splore = a dinking bout was held; orra duddies = spare rags; ranred = roistered; the vera girdle = the very griddle

First, niest the fire, in auld red rags,
Ane sat, weel brac'd wi' mealy bags,
And knapsack a' in order;
His doxy lay within his arm;
Wi' usquebae an' blankets warm—
She blinket on her sodger:
An' ay he gied the tozie drab
The tither skelpin' kiss,
While she held up her greedy gab
Just like an aumous dish.
Ilk smack still, did crack still,
Line onie cadger's whup;
Then staggering an' swaggering,
He roar'd this ditty up:—

Next to the fire sat an old soldier, his uniform in rags, and with his female companion in his arms, warm with whisky and covered in blankets. Kissing her loudly, he suddenly stood up and began to sing.
niest = next; brac'd wi' mealy bags = fed with oatmeal, the common alms at that time; doxy = sweetheart; usquebae = whisky; sodger = soldier; tozie = tipsy; drab = slut; gab = mouth; aumous = alms; cadger's whup = hawker's whip

AIR

TUNE: *Soldier's Joy*

I am a son of Mars, who have been in
    many wars,
And show my cuts and scars wherever I come;
This here was for a wench, and that other in
    a trench,
When welcoming the French at the sound
    of the drum.
Lal de daudle, etc..

The old soldier had fought in many wars and was always pleased to show off his battle scars – some for women, others for trenches.

My prenticeship I past, where my leader
    breath'd his last,
When the bloody die was cast on the
    heights of Abram;
And I served out my trade when the gallant
    game was play'd,
And the Moro low was laid at the sound of
    the drum.

He goes on to describe the many bloody encounters in which he has been involved. *heights of Abram* = General Wolfe's routing of the French at Quebec in 1759; *the Moro* = the fortress defending Santiago in Cuba, stormed by the British in 1762

I lastly was with Curtis among the
    floating batt'ries,
And there I left for witness an arm and a limb;
Yet let my country need me, with Elliot to
    head me
I'd clatter on my stumps at the sound of the
    drum.

His sevice career had ended at the siege of Gibraltar where he had lost an arm and a leg, but he would still fight if called upon. *Curtis* = Admiral Sir Roger Curtis; *Elliot* = General George Elliot

And now tho' I must beg, with a wooden
    arm and leg,
And many a tatter'd rag hanging over
    my bum,
I'm as happy with my wallet, my bottle
    and my callet,
As when I us'd in scarlet to follow a drum.

Although reduced to begging, he is just as happy with his lot as he was as a soldier. *callet* = prostitute

What tho', with hoary locks, I must stand
    the winter shocks,
Beneath the woods and rocks oftentimes
    for a home,
When the tother bag I sell and the tother
    bottle tell,
I could meet a troop of hell, at the sound
of a drum.

He is now forced to sleep outdoors in all weathers, but as long as he can sell something and buy a bottle he will face up to the Devil's army.

RECITATIVO

He ended; and the kebars sheuk
Aboon the chorus roar;
While frightened rattons backward leuk,
An' seek the benmost bore;
A fairy fiddler frae the neuk,
He skirl'd out, *Encore!*
But up arose the martial chuck,
An' laid the loud uproar.

The rafters shook with the applause as he finished, but before he could take an encore, the camp whore rose to her feet and all was quiet.

kebars sheuk = rafters shook; *aboon* = above; *rattons* = rats; *benmost bore* = innermost hole; *martial chuck* = camp whore

AIR
TUNE: *Sodger Laddie*

I once was a maid, tho' I cannot tell when,
And still my delight is in proper young men;
Some one of a troop of dragoons was
    my daddie,
No wonder I'm fond of a sodger laddie.
Sing, lal de lal, etc.,

She had no idea of her age but knew that her father had been a dragoon, so she loved all the young soldiers.

The first of my loves was a swaggering blade,
To rattle the thundering drum was his trade;
His leg was so tight, and his cheek was
    so ruddy,
Transported was I with my sodger laddie.

Her first love had been a drummer and she had been besotted by him.

But the godly old chaplain left him in
    the lurch,
The sword I forsook for the sake of
    the church;
He ventur'd the soul, and I risket the body,
'Twas then I prov'd false to my sodger laddie.
One and all, cry out, Amen!

However, an affair with the camp chaplain
soon put an end to her relationship with
the drummer.

Full soon I grew sick of my sanctified sot,
The regiment at large for a husband I got;
From the gilded spontoon to the fife I
    was ready,
I asked no more but a sodger laddie.

She rapidly grew sick of the chaplain and
made herself available to anyone in the
regiment, irrespective of rank.

But the Peace it reduc'd me to beg in despair,
Till I met my old boy in a Cunningham Fair,
His rags regimental they flutter'd so gaudy,
My heart it rejoic'd at a sodger laddie.

Peacetime reduced her to poverty and
despair until she met up with her soldier,
his ragged uniform attracting her to him.

And now I have liv'd – I know not how long!
And still I can join in a cup and a song,
But whilst with both hands I can hold the
    glass steady,
Here's to thee, my hero, my sodger laddie.

And now she's lived, she doesn't know for
how long and she can still join in with
the drinking and singing – while she can
hold her glass, she'll toast her soldier.

RECITATIVO

Poor Merry-Andrew in the neuk
Sat guzzling wi' a tinkler hizzie;
They mind't na wha the the chorus teuk,
Between themselves they were sae busy:
At length, wi' drink an' courting dizzy,
He stoiter'd up an' made a face;
Then turn'd, an' laid a smack on Grizzie,
Syne tun'd his pipes wi' grave grimace:

Merry-Andrew was busily engaged in
drinking with his tinker girl friend, paying
no attention to what was going on, until
he rose drunkenly, kissed the girl, and
with a serious face, tuned up his pipes.
tinkler-hizzie = tinker hussy; *teuk* = took,
stoiter'd = staggered; *syne* = then

133

AIR

TUNE: *Auld Sir Symon*

Sir Wisdom's a fool when he's fou;
Sir Knave is a fool in a session;
He's there but a prentice I trow,
But I am a fool by profession.

The wise man and the knave may be fools when they're drunk, but he is a fool at all times.
fou = drunk; *trow* = trust

My grannie she bought me a beuk,
And I held awa to the school:
I fear I my talent misteuk,
But what will ye hae of a fool?

His grandmother bought him a book, and he went to school, but just wasted his time. *held awa* = went off; *beuk* = book; *misteuk* = mistook

For a drink I would venture my neck;
A hizzie's the half o' my craft;
But what could ye other expect,
Of ane that's avowedly daft.

He would do anything for a drink, and girls were half of his downfall, but what else could one expect from one so stupid?

I ance was tied up like a stirk,
For civilly swearing and quaffing!
I, ance was abused i' the kirk,
For towsing a lass i' my daffin'.

He has been humiliated by the courts and the church for his misdeeds. *tyed up like a stirk* = put in an iron collar and chained to a post; *towsing a lass i' my daffin'* = oblique reference to having sex out of marriage

Poor Andrew that tumbles for sport
Let naebody name wi' a jeer;
There's even, I'm tauld, i' the Court
A tumbler ca'd the Premier.

Let nobody miscall him because he is a clown. He has been told that the prime-minister is also a clown.
tauld = told

Observ'd ye yon reverend lad
Mak faces to tickle the mob?
He rails at our mountebank squad–
Its rivalship just i' the job.

Watch how the preacher puts on funny expressions while sermonising. It's just what Andrew does to amuse the crowds.

And now my conclusion I'll tell,
For faith! I'm confoundedly dry;
The chiel that's a fool for himsel',
Guid Lord! he's far dafter than I.

He may have been born stupid, but a man who's a fool to himself is even more so.

RECITATIVO

Then neist outspak a raucle carlin,
Wha kent fu' weel to cleek the sterlin',
For monie a pursie she had hookit,
An' had in mony a well been doukit;
Her love had been a Highland laddie,
But weary fa' the waefu woodie!
Wi' sighs an' sobs she thus began
To wail her braw John Highlandman:

The next on her feet was a fat old hag, well
experienced in stealing and picking pockets,
and who had been ducked in many wells for
her misdemeanours. She told of her love for
a highlander amid sobs and tears.

raucle carlin = fat hag; *cleek the sterlin'* = steal
money; *douked* = ducked; *woodie* = dimwit

AIR

TUNE: *O, an ye were dead, Guidman*

CHORUS

Sing hey my braw John Highlandman!
Sing ho my braw John Highlandman!
There's not a lad in a' the lan'
Was match for my John Highlandman!

A Highland lad my love was born,
The Lalland laws he held in scorn;
But he still was faithfu' to his clan,
My gallant, braw John Highlandman.

She was in love with a Highlander.
lalland = lowland

With his phillibeg, an' tartan plaid,
An' guid claymore down by his side,
The ladies' hearts he did trepan,
My gallant, braw John Highlandman.

The ladies all loved him in his kilt and with
his claymore.
phillibeg = short kilt; *claymore* = broadsword;
trepan = ensnare

We ranged a' from Tweed to Spey,
An' liv'd like lords an' ladies gay,
For a Lalland face he fearèd nane,
My gallant, braw John Highlandman.

They travelled the lenght and breadth of
Scotland living well off their spoils.

They banishid him beyond the sea,
But ere the bud was on the tree,
Adown my cheeks the pearls ran,
Embracing my John Highlandman.

He was to be deported and tears ran down
her cheeks as she embraced him.

But och! they catch'd him at the last,
And bound him in a dungeon fast:
My curse upon them every one,
They've hang'd my braw John Highlandman!

However, when he was eventually caught,
the punishment was changed to hanging.

And now a widow, I must mourn
The pleasures that will ne'er return;
No comfort but a hearty can,
When I think on John Highlandman.

She now mourns for her past life and has
no comfort apart from the drink.

RECITATIVO

A pigmy scraper wi' his fiddle,
Wha' used at trystes an' fairs to driddle,
Her strappin' limb an' gawsie middle
(He reach'd nae higher)
Had hol'd his heartie like a riddle,
An' blawn't on fire.

A midget fiddler stood up to tell how he had
lost his heart to the much larger lady.
trystes = cattle round-ups; *driddle* = work very
slowly; *gawsie* = buxom; *blawn't* = blown it

Wi' hand on hainch, an' upward e'e,
He croon'd his gamut, one, two, three,
Then in an *arioso* key,
The wee Apollo
Set off wi' *allegretto* glee
His *giga* solo.

Gazing skywards and with hand on hip,
the little fellow sang chirpilly.
hainch = haunch

AIR

TUNE: *Whistle owre the lave o't*   *lave o't* = rest of it.

CHORUS

I am a fiddler to my trade,
An' a' the tunes that e'er I play'd
The sweetest still to wife or maid,
Was 'Whistle owre the lave o't.'

Let me ryke up to dight that tear,   He will wipe any tears and take good care
An' go wi' me an' be my dear,   of her.
An' then your ev'ry care an' fear   *ryke* = reach; *dight* = wipe.
May whistle owre the lave o't.

At kirns an' weddings we'se be there,   They will play at all sorts of functions and
An' O', sae nicely's we will fare;   they'll do well, drinking without a care in
We'll bouse about till Daddie Care   the world.
Sings *Whistle owre the lave o't.*   *kirns* = merrymaking at end of harvest

Sae merrily's the banes we'll pyke,   They will enjoy a life of eating and of
An' sun oursels about the dyke;   relaxation with no worries to weigh them
An' at our leisure, when ye like,   down.
We'll whistle owre the lave o't!   *banes* = bones; *pyke* = pick; *dyke* = wall

But bless me wi' your heav'n o' charms,   If she gives in to him he will play his fiddle
An' while I kittle hair on thairms,   and ensure her wellbeing.
Hunger, cauld, an' a' sick harms,   *kittle hair on thairms* = tickle the fiddle
May whistle owre the lave o't.   strings

RECITATIVO

Her charms had struck a sturdy caird,
As weel as poor gut-scraper;
He tak's the fiddler by the beard,
An' draws a roosty rapier–
He swore by a' was swearing worth,
To speet him like a pliver,
Unless he would from that time forth
Relinqish her for ever.

Unfortunately for the midget, the lady's charms had also attracted the attention of another tinker who threatened to murder the midget if he carried on with his amorous pursuit.

caird = tinker; *roosty rapier* = rusty sword; *speet* = skewer; *pliver* = plover

Wi' ghastly e'e, poor Tweedle-Dee
Upon his hunkers bended,
And pray'd for grace wi' ruefu' face,
An' sae the quarrel ended.
But tho' his little heart did grieve
When round the tinkler prest her,
He feign'd to snirtle in his sleeve,
When thus the caird address'd her:

The midget had no choice but to concede, although he managed a quiet snigger when he heard the tinker address the lady.

hunkers = haunches; *snirtle* = snigger

AIR
TUNE: *Clout the Cauldron*

My bonny lass, I work in brass,
A tinkler is my station;
I've travell'd round all Christian ground
In this my occupation.
I've ta'en the gold, an' been enroll'd
In many a noble squadron;
But vain they search'd when off I march'd
To go an' clout the cauldron.

He was a tinker who worked with brass, and although he had often taken the King's bounty to join the army, he had no qualms about deserting when the brass cauldron needed a patch.

Despise that shrimp, that wither'd imp,
Wi' a' his noise an' caperin';
An' take a share wi' those that bear
The budget and the apron.
An' by that stoup, my faith an' houp!
And by that dear Kilbaigie!
If e'er ye want, or meet wi' scant,
May I ne'er weet my craigie.

He pleads with her to ignore the midget
and join him in his brass business. Not
another drop of liquor will he drink if he
should let her down.

stowp = cup; *Kilbaigie* = a nearby whisky
distillery; *weet my craigie* = wet my throat

RECITATIVO

The caird prevail'd – th' unblushing fair
In his embraces sunk,
Partly wi' love, o'ercome sae sair,
An' partly she was drunk.
Sir Violino, with an air
That show'd a man o' spunk,
Wish'd unison between the pair,
And made the bottle clunk
To their health that night.

The tinker won the affections of the lady,
but only because she was too drunk to
resist. The fiddler appeared to take his
defeat with good grace and drunk the
health of the tinker and the woman.

But urchin Cupid shot a shaft,
That play'd a dame a shavie,
The fiddler rak'd her fore and aft,
Behint the chicken cavie.
Her lord, a wight o' Homer's craft,
Tho' limping wi' the spavie,
He hirpl'd up, an' lap like daft,
An' shor'd them *Dainty Davie*
O' boot that night.

However, he eventually persuaded her to
join him in lovemaking behind the
chicken sheds, and when the tinker
discovered them he appears to have
offered the midget his lady friend free for
the rest of the night.

hurchin = urchin; *shavie* = trick; *chicken
cavie* = hen-coop; *spavie* = bone-disease;
shor'd = offered; *boot* = free

He was a care-defying blade
As ever Bacchus listed,
Tho' fortune sair upon him laid,
His heart, she ever miss'd it.
He had no wish but — to be glad,
Nor want but — when he thirsted;
He hated nought but — to be sad,
An thus the Muse suggested
His sang that night.

The tinker was not someone to be burdened with care, he was happy when his thirst was quenched so he stood up to give a song when requested.

AIR
TUNE; *For a' that, an' a' that*

CHORUS

For a' that, an' a' that,
An' twice as muckle's a' that,
I've lost but ane, I've twa bebin'.
I've wife eneugh for a' that.

I am a Bard of no regard,
Wi' gentle folks an' a' that,
But Homer-like the glowran byke,
Frae town to town I draw that.

He may be a nobody to the educated people, but crowds of ordinary people enjoy listening to him.
glow'rin' byke = staring crowds

I never drank the Muses' stank,
Castalia's burn, an' a' that;
But there it streams an' richly reams,
My Helicon I ca' that.

Without the benefit of a formal education, he is still able to find inspiration for his work.
stank = pool; *reams* = froth

Great love I bear to a' the fair,
Their humble slave, an' a' that;
But lordly will, I hold it still
A mortal sin to thraw that.

thraw = thwart

In raptures sweet, this hour we meet,
Wi' mutual love an' a' that;
But for how lang the flee may stang,
Let inclination law that!

He understands that love can come and go
as quickly as an insect bite.
flie = fly; *stang* = sting

Their tricks an' crafts hae put me daft,
They've ta'en me in, an' a' that;
But clear your decks, an' here's the Sex!
I like the jads for a' that.

He may have been taken in by the wiles of
young women on many occasions, but he
still loves them all.
jads = young women

CHORUS

For a' that, an' a' that,
An' twice as muckle's a' that,
My dearest bluid, to do them guid,
They're welcome till't for a' that.

RECITATIVO

So sang the Bard – and Nansie's wa's
Shook wi' a thunder of applause,
Re-echo'd from each mouth;
They toom'd their pocks, an' pawn'd their duds,
They scarcely left to co'er their fuds,
To quench their lowan drouth.
Then owre again, the jovial thrang

Thunderous applause greeted the poet as
the crowd frantically emptied their pockets
and sold their belongings to pay for another
drink as they beseeched him to sing again.
room'd their pocks = emptied their pockets;
co'er their fuds = cover their backsides; *lowan*
drouth = burning thirst; *lowse* = untie

The poet did request
To lowse his pack, an' wale a sang
A ballad o' the best;
He rising, rejoicing,
Between his twa Deborahs,
Looks round him, an' found them
Impatient for the chorus.

wale = choose

his twa Deborahs =see Judges v. 12

AIR

TUNE: *Jolly Mortals, fill your Glasses*

CHORUS

A fig for those by law protected!
Liberty's a glorious feast!
Courts for cowards were erected,
Churches built to please the priest.

See! the smoking bowl before us,
Mark our jovial, ragged ring!
Round and round take up the chorus,
And in raptures let us sing.

The final verses of the Cantata are dedicated to praising the lifestyle of the beggars and asking which is more important, pleasure or treasure?

What is title? what is treasure?
What is reputation's care?
If we lead a life of pleasure,
'Tis no matter how or where!

With the ready trick and fable,
Round we wander all the day;
And at night, in barn or stable,
Hug our doxies on the hay.

Does the train-attended carriage
Thro' the country lighter rove?
Does the sober bed of marriage
Witness brighter scenes of love?

Life is all a variorium,
We regard not how it goes;
Let them cant about decorum,
Who have characters to lose.

Here's to budgets, bags and wallets!
Here's to all the wandering train!
Here's our ragged brats and callets!
One and all, cry out–Amen!

callets = wenches.

The Lass O' Ballochmyle

Burns set eyes upon a young lady while out for an evening stroll, and being the great romantic, was so excited by her beauty that he composed the following verses in her honour. In an attempt to ingratiate himself with the lass, Wilhelmina Alexander, he wrote to her, enclosing the poem in the obvious hope that they might form some sort of relationship. However, Wilhelmina was not prepared to play the poet's game. Possibly she was aware of his reputation, and she chose to ignore Burns' advances. She never married, but kept the poet's tribute throughout her life.

'Twas even, the dewy field were green,
On every blade the pearls hang;
The zephyrs wanton'd round the bean,
And bore its fragrant sweets alang;
In every glen the mavis sang,
All Nature listening seem'd the while,
Except where greenwood echoes rang,
Among the braes o' Ballochmyle.

With careless step I onward stray'd,
My heart rejoic'd in Nature's joy,
When musing in a lonely glade,
A maiden fair I chanc'd to spy:
Her look was like the morning's eye,
Her air like Nature's vernal smile;
The lilies' hue and roses die
Bespoke the Lass o' Ballochmyle.

Fair is the morn in flow'ry May
And sweet is night in autumn mild;
When roving thro' the garden gay,
Or wand'ring in the lonely wild;
But Woman, Nature's darling child!
There all her charms she does compile,
Even there her other works are foil'd,
By th' bonie Lass o' Ballochmyle.

O! had she been a country maid,
And I the happy country swain,
Tho' shelter'd in the lowest shed
That ever rose on Scotland's plain!
Thro' weary winter's wind and rain,
With joy, with rapture, I would toil;
And nightly to my bosom strain
The bonie Lass o' Ballochmyle!

Then Pride might climb the slipp'ry steep,
Where fame and honours lofty shine;
And thirst of gold might tempt the deep,
Or downward seek the Indian mine;
Give me the cot below the pine,
To tend the flocks or till the soil;
And every day have joys divine
With the bonie Lass o' Ballochmyle.

Adam Armour's Prayer

It must be said that not everything written by Burns was beautiful and romantic. Indeed, some of his works are unsavoury in the extreme. This is a sordid tale of how a gang of local youths, which included Jean Armour's brother, took the law into their own hands and inflicted painful punishment upon a lass who had a reputation as a prostitute. The girl had certainly been before the Kirk Session to answer for her conduct, but so had many others, as Burns was all too aware.

Gude pity me, because I'm little,
For though I am an elf o' mettle
And can, like ony wabster's shuttle
Jink there or here;
Yet scarce as lang's a guid kail whittle,
I'm unco queer.

Adam may be little but he can move quickly and he thinks he's got worth.
Gude = God; *wabster* = weaver; *kail-whittle* = *cabbage knife*

An' now thou kens our woefu' case;
For Geordie's Jurr we're in disgrace,
Because we stang'd her through the place,
An' hurt her spleuchan',
For which we daurna show our face
Within the clachan.

They've run the girl through the village tied to a pole, causing her serious injury, and now they're on the run.
kens = knows; *jurr* = maidservant; *stang'd* = rode her on a pole; *spleuchan* = genitalia; *daurna* = dare not; *clachan* = village

And now we're dern'd in glens and hollows,
And hunted, as was William Wallace,
Wi' constables, thae blackguard fallows,
An' sodgers baith;
But Gude preserve us frae the gallows,
That shamefu' death!

They're now in hiding from the forces of law.
dern'd = concealed; *sodgers* = soldiers

Auld, grim, black-bearded Geordie's sel';
O, shake him owre the mouth o' Hell!
There let him hing, and roar, an' yell
Wi' hideous din,
And if he offers to rebel,
Then heave him in!

Geordie = George Gibson, the girl's employer and landlord of Poosie Nansies.

When Death comes in wi' glimmerin blink,
An' tips auld drucken Nanse the wink,
May Sautan gie her doup a clink
Within his yett,
An' fill her up wi' brimstone drink,
Red-reekin het.

When Nansie dies, he hopes that Satan will be extremely cruel to her.
drucken = drunken; *gie her doup a clink* = smack her backside; *yett* = gate; *het* = hot

There's Jockie an' the hav'rel Jenny,
Some devil seize them in a hurry,
And waft them in th' infernal wherry
Straught through the lake,
An' gie their hides a noble curry
Wi' oil of aik!

Their family are also in the request for cruel treatment.

straught = straight
aik = oak

As for the jurr, puir worthless body!
She's got mischief enough already;
Wi' stranget hips and buttocks bluidy
She suffer'd sair!
But may she wintle in a woody,
If she whore mair!

The girl has suffered enough, but should she go back to her old ways then he hopes she will hang.
stanget hips = bruised by the pole; *wintle in a woody* = hang from a noose

The Inventory

Following in the aftermath of the war in America, William Pitt introduced a whole range of taxes to bolster the country's sagging finances. These included tax on carriage horses, carriages and servants. Burns responded to his demand in a very amusing, tongue in cheek rhyme.

Sir, as your mandate did request,
I send you here a faithfu' list
O' guids an' gear, an' a' my graith   *guids an' gear* = wordly goods
To which I'm clear to gi'e my aith.   *aith* = oath

Imprimis, then, for carriage cattle: *carriage cattle* = cart-horses
I hae four beasts o' gallant mettle,
As ever drew afore a pettle: *pettle* = plough-scraper
My *Lan'-afore's* a guid auld 'has been' *Lan'-afore's* = front, left hand horse of the
An' wight an' wilfu' a' his days been: four; *wight an' wilfu'* =strong-willed
My *Lan'-ahins* a weel gaun fillie,   *Lan'-ahins* = rear, left hand horse
That aft has borne me hame frae Killie,   *Killie* = Kilmarnock
An' your auld borough monie a time,   *auld borough* = (old town) the town of Ayr
In days when riding was nae crime.
But ance, when in my wooing pride
I, like a blockhead, boost to ride,   *boost* = had to
The wilfu' crearure sae I pat to,—
(Lord pardon a' my sins, an' that too!)
I play'd my fillie sic a shavie,   *shavie* = trick
She's a' bedevil'd wi' the spavie.   *spavie* = swelling on her shanks
My *Fur-ahin's* a wordy beast   *Fur-ahin's* = rear, right-hand horse
As e'er in tug or tow was trac'd.   *tug or trow* = harness
The fourth's a Highland Donald hastie,
A damn'd red-wud Kilburnie blastie!   *blastie* = mad pest
Foreby, a cowte o' cowtes the wale,   *cowte o' cowtes* = pick of the colts
As ever ran afore a tail:
If he be spar'd to be a beast,
He'll draw me fifteen pund at least.   *pund* = pound

Wheel-carriages I hae but few,
Three carts, an' twa are feckly new;
An auld wheelbarrow, mair for token,
Ae leg an' baith the trams are broken;
I made a poker o' the spin'le,
An' my auld mither brunt the trin'le.

feckly = partly

trams = shafts

brunt the trin'le = burnt the wheel

For men, I've three mischievous boys,
Run-deils for fechtin an' for noise:
A gaudsman ane, a thresher t'other,
Wee Davoc hauds the nowte in fother.
I rule them as I ought, discreetly,
An' aften labour them compleatly;
An' ay on Sundays duly nightly,
I on the *Questions* targe them tightly,
Till, faith! wee Davoc's grown sae gleg,
Tho scarcely langer than your leg,
He'll screed you aff 'Effectual Calling',
As fast as onie in the dwalling.
I've nane in female servan' station,
(Lord keep me ay frae my tempation!):
I hae nae wife; and that my bliss is,
An' ye hae laid nae tax on misses;
An' then, if kirk folk dinna clutch me,
I ken the deevils darena touch me.
Wi' weans I'm mair than than weel
    contented;
Heav'n sent mae ane mair than I wanted!
My sonsie, smirking, dear-bought Bess,
She stares the daddie in her face,
Enough of ought, ye like but grace:
But her, my bonie, sweet wee lady,
I've paid enough for her already;
An' gin ye tax her or her mither,
By the Lord, ye'se get them a' thegither!

deils for fechtin = devils for fighting
gaudsman = cattle-drover
hauds the nowte in fother = feeds the cattle

Questions = Catechisms, discipline
gleg = clever

screed = recite
dwalling = house

misses = mistresses

weans = children

She stares her daddie in her face = she's like her father

gin ye = should you

And now, remember, Mr Aiken,
Nae kind o' licence out I'm takin:
Frae this time forth, I do declare
I'se ne'er ride horse nor hizzie mair;   *hizzie* = hussie
Thro dirt and dub for life I'll paidle,   *dub* = puddles
Ere I sae dear pay for a saddle;
I've sturdy bearers, Gude be thankit!
And a' my gates on foot I'll shank it   *I'll shank it* = will walk
The Kirk and you may tak you that,
It puts but little in your pat;   *pat* = pot
Sae dinna put me in your beuk,   *beuk* = book
Nor for my ten white shillings leuk.

This list wi' my ain han' I've wrote it,
The day an' date as under notit;
Then know all ye whom it concerns,

Ssubscripsi huic,
ROBERT BURNS

Mossgiel, February 22nd, 1786.

To a Mountain Daisy

The Bard was going through a very unhappy period in his life when he wrote this poem and his deep unhappiness is clearly illustrated in the melancholy tone.

It would seem that the boredom of ploughing allowed him time for deep meditation, for it was on such an occasion that the sight of a daisy caught his eye and inspired the following words.

Wee, modest, crimson-tipped flow'r
Thou's met me in an evil hour;
For I maun crush amang the stoure
Thy slender stem:.
To spare thee now is past my pow'r
Thou bonie gem

The ploughman is speaking to the daisy and apologising for its accidental uprooting, but unfortunately, at this stage there is nothing he can do about it.

maun = must; *amang the stoure* = among the dust

Alas, it's no thy neebor sweet,
The bonie lark, companion meet,
Bending thee 'mang the dewy weet,
Wi' spreckl'd breast!
When upward-springing, blythe, to greet
The purpling east.

He explains that sadly it was not a friendly lark which was bending the flower stalks as it sprang upward to meet the sun rising in the east. *no'* = not; *neebor* = neighbour; *'mang the dewy weet* = among the dewy wet; *spreckled* = speckled; *the purpling east* = the sunrise

Cauld blew the bitter-biting north
Upon thy early, humble birth;
Yet cheerfully thou glinted forth
Amid the storm,
Scarce rear'd above the parent-earth
Thy tender form.

Although the bitter north wind was blowing when it came through the surface, the daisy had still appeared bright and cheerful throughout the storm, although it was so small that its head barely rose above the earth. *Cauld* = cold; *north* = north wind

The flaunting flow'rs our gardens yield,
High shelt'ring woods and wa's maun shield;
But thou, beneath the random bield
O' clod or stane,
Adorns the histie stibble field.
Unseen, alane.

Gardens may have beautiful flowers but they are sheltered by woods and walls. The daisy has to survive alone, surrounded by mud and earth and stone, seldom seen by anyone.

wa's = walls; *maun* = must; *bield o' clod or stane* = shelter of earth or stone; *histie stibble field* = field of dry stubble; *alane* = alone

There, in thy scanty mantle clad,
Thy snawie bosom sun-ward spread,
Thou lifts thy unassuming head
In humble guise;
But now the share uptears thy bed,
And low thou lies!

There was the daisy with only a few petals to protect it as it rose humbly towards the sun, and now the plough has torn it from its bed and laid it low.
scanty mantle clad = barely covered; *snawie* = snowy; *share uptears* = plough uproots

Such is the fate of artless maid,
Sweet flow'ret of the rural shade!
By love's simplicity betray'd
And guileless trust,
Till she, like thee, all soil'd, is laid
Low i' the dust.

Such is the fate of the innocent young maiden who has been betrayed by love and trust. She has nothing to look forward to until, like the daisy, she shares its fate and death returns her to the dust.
flow'ret = little flower; *guileless* = simple

Such is the fate of simple Bard,
On life's rough ocean luckless starr'd
Unskilful he to note the card
Of prudent lore,
Till billows rage, and gales blow hard,
And whelm him o'er

The Bard has had little luck throughout his lifetime, and has been neither sufficiently wordly nor prudent to avoid the storms of life which now threaten to overcome him.

Such fate to suffering worth is giv'n
Who long with wants and woes has striv'n,
By human pride or cunning driv'n
To mis'rys brink;
Till wrench'd of ev'ry stay but Heav'n
He, ruin'd, sink!

He is resigned to whatever fate has in store for him as his problems have driven him to the point of total despair. Everything in his life is bleak and there is little chance of salvation. Only ruination seems certain. *wants and woes* = poverty and grief; *striv'n* = struggled; *ev'ry stay but Heav'n* = nothing left but death

Ev'n thou who mourn'st the Daisy's fate,
That fate is thine – no distant date;
Stern Ruin's plough-share drives, elate,
Full on thy bloom;
Till, crush'd beneath the furrow's weight
Shall be thy doom!

Finally, he compares the fate of the daisy to what is in store for himself as he believes that his own death is imminent. He sees no escape from the harshness of his own life!
elate = proudly; *furrow's weight* = the earth turned over by the plough

Second Epistle to Davie

A BROTHER POET

Although Robert Burns was a prolific writer of letters, most of which were composed in the very formal manner so popular at the time, he delighted in corresponding with his fellow poets in rhyme as this one to David Sillar demonstrates.

Auld Neebor,
I'm three times doubly o'er your debtor,
For your auld-farrant, frien'ly letter;
Tho' I maun say 't, I doubt ye flatter;
Ye speak sae fair;
For my puir, silly, rhyming clatter
Some less maun sair.

He starts by thanking his friend for the flattering letter which he had received.
auld-farrant = old- fashioned; *puir* = poor; *clatter* = chatter; *maun sair* = must serve

Hale be your heart, hale be your fiddle!
Lang may your elbuck jink an' diddle,
To cheer you thro' the weary widdle
O' war'ly cares,
Till bairns' bairns kindly cuddle
Your auld, grey hairs!

He hopes that Davie will remain fit and healthy and live to have grandchildren.
elbuck = elbow; *jink and diddle* = dance up and down; *widdle* = strife; *war'ly* = wordly; *bairns' bairns* =grandchildren

But Davie, lad, I'm red ye're glaikit;
I'm tauld the Muse ye hae negleckit;
An' gif it's sae, ye sud be lickit
Until ye fyke;
Sic han's as you sud ne'er be faikit,
Be hain't wha like.

He's dismayed to find that Davie is not composing rhymes at the moment, as a gift such as his should be used. In fact he should be whipped into action again.
red ye're glaikit = regret you're foolish; *gif* = if; *lickit* = whipped; *fyke* = fidget; *sud* = should; *faikit* = excused; *hain't* = except

For me, I'm on Parnassus' brink,
Rivin the words to gar them clink;
Whyles daez't wi' love, whyles daez't wi' drink,
Wi' jads or Masons;
An' whyles, but ay owre late, I think;
Braw sober lessons.

Burns feel he is on the edge of a mountain trying to make his words rhyme, and he is distracted by girls or drinking with his Masonic friends.
rivin = tearing up; *gar them clink* = make them rhyme; *jads* = hussies

Of a' the thoughtless sons o' man,
Commen' me to the Bardie clan;
Except it be some idle plan
O' rhyming clink,
The devil-haet that I sud ban,
They never think.

He prefers his fellow poets to any other group of men. They have a casual attitude to life that he enjoys.

devil-haet = Heaven-forbid

Nae thought, nae view, nae scheme o' livin',
Nae care to gie us joy or grievin',
But just the pouchie put the nieve in,
An' while ought's there,
Then, hiltie-skiltie, we gae scrievin',
An' fash nae mair.

They live for the moment with little concern for the future, and get by on very little.
pouchie = pocket; *nieve* = fist; *hiltie-skiltie* = helter-skelter; *scrievin* = careering; *fash* = worry

Leeze me on rhyme! it's ay a treasure,
My chief, amaist my only pleasure;
At hame, a-fiel', at wark or leisure,
The Muse, poor hizzie!
Tho' rough an' raploch be her measure,
She's seldom lazy.

Bless his poetry. It's his greatest pleasure in life and he can enjoy it anywhere.
amaist = almost; *rough an' raploch* = rough and ready

Haud to the Muse, my dainty Davie;
The warl' may play you monie a shavie,
But for the Muse, she'll never leave ye,
Tho' e'er sae puir;
Na, even tho' limpin wi the spavie
Frae door to door.

Stick to your talent, Davie, and no matter what life has in store for you, you will always have that ability.
monie a shavie = many a trick; *spavie* = bone disease affecting the leg

Epistle to a Young Friend

Burns wrote the following words in 1786 to a young man named Andrew Hunter Aitken who was about to make his way in the world. The advice he offers is a pleasure to read as it shows the wonderful insight that he had into his fellow beings. However, it appears that the Bard was not always able to follow the guidelines which he gave so readily to young Andrew.

I lang hae thought, my youthfu' friend,
A something to have sent you,
Tho' it should serve nae ither end
Than just a kind memento;
But how the subject-scheme may gang,
Let time and chance determine;
Perhaps it may turn out a sang;
Perhaps, turn out a sermon.

Rab has been thinking of writing to Andrew for some time, but has no idea if his words will turn out to be a song or a sermon. Perhaps just something to keep as a reminder of their friendship.
lang hae = long have; *nae ither* = no other; *gang* = go; *sang* = song

Ye'll try the world soon, my lad;
And Andrew dear, believe me,
You'll find mankind an unco squad,
And muckle may they grieve ye:
For care and trouble set your thought,
Ev'n when your end's attained;
And a' your views may come to nought,
Where ev'ry nerve is strained.

Andrew will discover that mankind is made up of people of varied assortment, many of whom will cause him grief. He should be prepared to face adversity at all times and accept that his plans may come to nothing.
unco = strange; *muckle* = much

I'll no say, men are villains a':
The real, harden'd wicked,
Wha hae nae check but human law,
Are to a few restricked;
But, och! mankind are unco weak,
An' little to be trusted;
If *Self* the wavering balance shake,
It's rarely right adjusted!

Not all men are out and out villains, but few can be totally trusted, and should he cross the line between right and wrong, he will find it difficult to come back.
wha hae nae = who have nothing

Yet they wha fa' in Fotune's strife,
Their fate we should na censure;
For still, th' important end of life,
They equally may answer:
A man may hae an honest heart,
Tho' poorith hourly stare him;
A man may take a neebor's part,
Yet hae nae cash to spare him.

He must not criticise his fellow men as everyone will have to answer for their sins on the Day of Judgement, nor should he should judge anyone according to their wealth as the man facing poverty can still be kind and caring.

wha fa' = who fall; *poortith* = poverty; *neebor's* = neighbour's

Ay free, aff han', your story tll,
When wi' a bosom cronie;
But still, th' important end of life,
Ye scarcely tell to onie:
Conceal yourself as weel's ye can
Frae critical dissection;
But keek thro' ev'ry other man,
Wi' sharpen'd, sly inspection.

Talk freely to your friends, but never reveal your innermost secrets. Always maintain your reserve to prevent criticism and keep a wary eye on others.

aff han' = off hand; *bosom cronie* = best friend; *keek* = glance

The sacred lowe o' weel-plac'd love,
Luxuriantly indulge it;
But never tempt th' illicit rove,
Tho' naething should divulge it:
I waive the quantum o' th sin,
The hazard of concealing;
But, och! it hardens a' within,
And petrifies the feeling!

When you find true love, you have found real joy. Although others may tempt you and there is no danger of being caught out, you must resist, for it will remain on your conscience and be blight on your life.

lowe = flame; *weel - plac'd* = well placed; *illicit rove* = infidelity; *waive the quantum* = reject the amount

To catch Dame Fortune's golden smile,
Assidious wait upon her;
And gather gear by ev'ry wile
That's justify'd by honour;
Not for to hide it in a headge,
Nor for a train attendant;
But for a glorious priviledge
Of being independent.

You must pursue your fortune through hard work, and take pride in your belongings, safe in the knowledge that you have acquired them by honest endeavour.

gear = wealth

The fear o' Hell's a hangman's whip
To haud the wretch in order;
But where ye feel your honour grip,
Let that ay be your border:
Its slightest touches, instant pause –
Debar a' side-pretences;
And resolutely keep its laws,
Uncaring consequences.

Although the fear of Hell may keep others in check, all that is required of him is an honest mind and a strong conscience. With these, he can look forward to a blameless life.

haud = hold

The great creator to revere,
Must sure become the creature;
But still the peaching cant forbear,
And ev'n the rigid feature;
Yet ne'er with wits profane to range
Be complaisance extended;
An athiest's laugh's a poor exchange
For Deity offended!

He must always have faith in God and learn to tolerate the stony-faced preachers. Never blaspheme nor use profanity.

When ranting round in Pleasure's ring,
Religion may be blinded;
Or if she gie a random sting,
It may be little minded;
But when on Life we're tempest-driv'n,
A conscience but a canker –
A correspondence fix'd wi' Heaven,
Is sure a noble anchor!

It's very easy to forget religion when enjoying oneself, but even when temptation is at its greatest and his conscience is being strained to its utmost, then the strenght of his beliefs will carry him through.

ranting = frolicking; *canker* = corruption

Adieu, dear, amiable youth!
Your heart can ne'er be wanting!
May prudence, fortitude and truth,
Erect your brow undaunting.
In ploughman phrase,
'God send you speed,'
Still daily to grow wiser;
And may you better reck the rede,
Than ever did th' adviser!

Now, self-deprecation on the part of Burns as he finishes the epistle by hoping that Andrew will take more heed of his advice than he did himself.

reck the rede = heed the advice

Lines Written on a Bank Note

The following lines were actually written upon a one-guinea note in 1786. At the time, Burns was giving a good deal of thought to the idea of emigrating to Jamaica believing that this might be a means of escaping from his ever present problems.

Few of us will have difficulty relating to the heart-felt words of this poem.

Wae worth thy pow'r, thou cursed leaf!   *wae worth* = woe befall
Fell source of all my woe and grief,   *fell source* = cause
For lack o' thee I've lost my lass,
For lack o' thee I scrimp my glass!   *scrimp my glass* = limit my drinking
I see the children of affliction
Unaided, thro' thy curs'd restriction.
I've seen the oppressor's cruel smile
Amid his hapless victim's spoil;
And for thy potence vainly wish'd   *potence* = power
To crush the villain in the dust.
For lack o' thee, I leave this much-lov'd shore,
Never, perhaps, to greet old Scotland more!

R.B.

The Farewell

Robert Burns was in no doubt that his future lay in the West Indies. His many skirmishes with the Kirk and the problems which he was having to face because of his relationship with his wife's family were taking their toll. He wrote several pieces dwelling on this, and expressing his sorrow at being forced to leave his beloved Scotland. This is a fairly sentimental poem, written in the summer of 1786, in which he tells of his sorrow at his impending separation from his wife, his family and friends.

> *The valiant, in himself, what can he suffer?*
> *Or what does he regard his single woes?*
> *But when, alas! he multiplies himself,*
> *To dearer selves, to the lov'd tender fair*
> *To those whose bliss, whose beings hang upon him,*
> *To helpless children – then, Oh then he feels*
> *The point of misery, festering in his heart,*
> *And weakly weeps his fortunes like a coward:*
> *Such, such am I!— undone! –* THOMSON'S *Edward and Eleanor*

Farewell, old Scotia's bleak domains,
Far dearer than the torrid plains,
Where rich ananas blow!   *Ananas* = pineapples
Farewell, a mother's blessing dear!
A brother's sigh, a sister's tear!
My Jean's heart-rending throe!
Farewell, my Bess! tho' thou'rt bereft   *Bess* = his illegimate daughter, Elizabeth
Of my paternal care,
A faithful brother I have left,   *faithful brother* = Gilbert Burns
My part in him thou'lt share!
Adieu too, to you too,
My Smith, my bosom frien';   *My Smith* = James Smith
When kindly you mind me,
O, then befriend my Jean!

What bursting anguish tears my heart;
From thee, my Jeany, must I part!
Thou, weeping, answ'rest –'No!'
Alas! misfortune stares my face,
And points to ruin and disgrace,
I for thy sake must go!
Thee, Hamilton, and Aiken dear,   Gavin Hamilton. Robert Aiken
A grateful, warm adieu:
I with much-indebted tear
Shall still remember you!
All-hail then, the gale then
Wafts me from thee, dear shore!
It rustles, and whistles
I'll never see thee more!

Reply to a Trimming Epistle Received from a Tailor

Robert Burns was not a man to take insults lying down. A tailor by the name of Thomas Walker had sent Burns twenty-six dreary stanzas in the hope that Burns would reply to him in verse. Burns ignored them completely, but when the Kilmarnock Edition was published, Walker wrote complaining of the poet's morals, prompting Burns to respond with this jocular and deeply sarcastic poem.

What ails ye now, ye lousy bitch
To thrash my back at such a pitch?
Losh, man, hae mercy wi' your natch,
Your bodkin's bauld.
I didna suffer half as much
Frae Daddie Auld.

Burns hurls abuse at the tailor and points out that the local minister was not as harsh on him as Walker.
thresh = thrash; *Losh* = Lord; *natch* = notching-blade; *bodkin* = large needle

What tho' at times when I grew crouse,
I gie their wames a random pouse,
Is that enough for you to souse
Your servant sae?
Gae mind your seam, ye prick-the-louse,
And jag-the-flea!

If I get in the mood for making love to the girls, what's it to do with you? Mind your own business.
crouse = bold; *wames* = bellies; *pouse* = thrust; *souse* = hit; *prick-the-louse* = nit-picker; *jag-the-flea* = flea

King David o' poetic brief
Wrocht 'mang the lasses sic mischief
As filled his after-life wi' grief,
An' bluidy rants;
An' yet he's rank'd amang the chief
O' lang-syne saunts.

King David was one for the girls, but he still became one of the leading saints.
wrocht = wrought; *rants* = rows; *lang-syne* = long ago; *saunts* = saints

And maybe Tam, for a' my cants,
My wicked rhymes, an' drucken rants,
I'll gie auld Clove Clootie's haunts
An unco slip yet,
An' snugly sit amang the saunts,
At Davie's hip yet!

Burns feels that he might yet escape the Devil and take his place among the saints.
cants = songs. *Cloven Clootie* = the Devil

But, fegs, the Session says I maun
Gae fa' upo' anither plan
Than garrin lasses coup the cran,
Clean heels owre body,
An' sairly thole their mother's ban
Afore the howdy.

But before that, the Session want him to appear once more to answer for his misdeeds with the girls.

fegs = faith; *maun* = must; *garrin'* = making; *coup the cran* = upset the cart

This leads me on to tell for sport
How I did with the Session sort:
Auld Clinkum at the inner port
Cried three times 'Robin!
Come hither lad, and answer for't,
Ye're blamed for jobbin'!'

He goes on to relate his experience with the Session when the bell-ringer summoned him.

Clinkum = bell-ringer; *jobbin'* = fornication

Wi' pinch I put a Sunday face on,
An' snoov'd awa before the Session
I made an open, fair confession —
I scorned to lie –
An' syne Mess John, beyond expression,
Fell foul o' me.

Putting on a pious expresson, he admitted to the Session that they were correct. Their leader fell upon him in rage.

snoov'd = walked purposefully; *Mess* = master

A fornicater-loun he call'd me,
An' said my faut frae bliss expell'd me.
I own'd the tale was true he tell'd me,
But what the matter?
(Quo' I) 'I fear unless ye geld me,
I'll ne'er be better!'

He told Burns that his sins would bar him from Heaven. Rab replied that the only way to stop him chasing the girls was for him to be gelded.

loun = rogue; *gelded* = castrated

'Geld you!' (quo he) 'an' what for no?
If that your right hand, leg or toe
Should ever prove your sp'ritual foe,
You should remember
To cut it aff – an' what for no
Your dearest member!'

Rab was a bit taken aback when the leader agreed with him. After all, if one's arm or leg was causing problems, then cut it off, so why not Rab's offending parts?

'Na, na, (quo I) 'I'm no for that,
Gelding's nae better than 'tis ca't;
I'd rather suffer for my my faut,
A hearty flewit,
As sair owre hips as ye can draw't,
Tho' I should rue it.

Rab thought this was was not a good idea
and suggested that a flogging might be
more in order.

flewit = flogging

'Or gin ye like to end the bother,
To please us a' – I've just ae ither;
When next wi' yon lass I forgather,
Whate'er betide it,
I' ll frankly gie her 't a' thegither,
An' let her guide it.'

He wondered if it might be an idea to let
the next girl who he seduces to do the
flogging.

But, Sir, this pleas'd them warst of a',
An' therefore, Tam, when that I saw,
I said 'Guid night' an' came awa,
An' left the Session:
I saw they were resolv'd a'
On my oppression.

This did not go down too well and as he
set off homeward he could see that they
were bent on his downfall.

My Highland Lassie O

Burns turned to Mary Campbell shortly after his affair with Jean Armour was brought to an end by Jean's father. Burns' opinion of Mary Campbell is at odds with those of others in his family who considered her to be no more than a slut, and it certainly appears that Campbell was no upholder of morals. However, Rab must have been stricken as he had decided that the two of them would travel to the West Indies to start a new life together.

This plan was not to be fulfilled as Mary died shortly before they were due to depart, and it remains unclear to this day whether she died from fever or childbirth.

CHORUS
Within the glen sae bushy, O,
Aboon the plain sae rashy, O,
I set me down wi right guid will,
To sing my Highland lassie, O!

Nae gentle dames, tho' ne'er sae fair,
Shall ever by my Muse's care:
Their titles a' are empty show;
Gie me my Highland lassie, O!

O, were yon hills and vallies mine,
Yon palace and yon gardens fine,
The world then the love should know
I bear my Highland lassie, O!

But fickle fortune frowns on me,
And I maun cross the raging sea;
But while my crimson currents flow,
I'll love my Highland lassie, O!

Although thro' foreign climes I range,
I know her heart will never change;
For her bosom burns with honour's glow,
My faithful Highland lassie, O!

For her I'll dare the billows roar,
For her I'll trace a distant shore,
That Indian wealth may lustre throw
Around my Highland lassie, O!

She has my heart, she has my hand,
By secret troth and honor's band!
'Till the mortal stroke shall lay me low,
I'm thine, my Highland lassie, O!

Farewell the glen sae bushy, O!
Farewell the plain sae rashy, O!
To other land I now must go
To sing my Highland lassie, O!

Epigram on Rough Roads

Burns was so disgusted with the condition of the roads on one of his journeys that he wrote the following lines about them. Another poem which is as meaningful today as when he wrote it.

I'm now arrived – thanks to the gods!
Thro' pathways rough and muddy,
A certain sign that makin' roads
Is no' this people's study:

Altho' I'm not wi' Scriptur cram'd,
I'm sure the Bible says,
That heedless sinners shall be damn'd,
Unless they mend their *ways*.

To an Old Sweetheart

Burns wrote these lines to Miss Peggy Thomson of Kirkoswald, a one time sweetheart, but since married. This is one of several poems written during the time that he was seriously contemplating a new life in the West Indies, so this short poem is a note of goodbye.

Once fondly lov'd, and still remember'd dear,
Sweet early object of my youthful vows,
Accept this mark of friendship, warm, sincere,
(Friendship! 'tis all cold duty now allows.)

And while you read the simple, artless rhymes,
One friendly sigh for him – he asks no more,
Who, distant, burns in flamin' torrid climes,
Or haply lies beneath th' Atlantic roar.

The Gloomy Night is Gath'ring Fast

The following lines were composed as Burns walked home from a visit to his friend Dr.
Lawrie. Again, it was during the time that he considered emigration to the West Indies
was inevitable, and the prospect of such a move filled him with a sense of foreboding.

The gloomy night is gath'ring fast,
Loud roars the wild, inconstant blast;
Yon murky cloud is filled with rain,
I see it driving o'er the plain;
The hunter now has left the moor,
The scatt'red coveys meet secure;
While I here wander, prest with care,
Along the lonely banks of Ayr.

The Autumn mourns her rip'ning corn
By early Winter's ravage torn;
Across her placid, azure sky,
She sees the scowling tempest fly;
Chill runs my blood to hear it rave;
I think upon the stormy wave,
Where many a danger I must dare,
Far from the bonie banks of Ayr.

'Tis not the surging billows roar,
'Tis not that fatal, deadly shore;
Tho' death in ev'ry shape appear,
The wretched have no more to fear:
But round my heart the ties are bound;
The heart transpierc'd with many a wound;
These bleed afresh, those ties I tear,
To leave the bonie banks of Ayr.

Farewell, old Coila's hills and dales,
Her heathy moors and winding vales;
The scenes where wretched Fancy roves;
Pursuing past unhappy loves!
Farewell my friends! farewell my foes!
My peace with these, my love with those-
The bursting tears my heart declare,
Farewell, my bonie banks of Ayr!

On Meeting with Lord Daer

Lord Daer was the first aristocrat Burns was to encounter socially and he was obviously very excited at the prospect. They met at the home of an Ayrshire professor who was entertaining the peer at his country house. Lord Daer was at that time a student at Edinburgh University, and must have been considered a radical by his fellow peers as he was in favour of both parliamentary reform and the French revolution. He died in France at an early age and thus never inherited the title of the Earl of Selkirk.

This wot ye all whom it concerns;
I, Rhymer Rab, alias Burns
October twenty-third,
A ne'er-to-be-forgotten day,
Sae far I sprachl'd up the brae,
I dinner'd wi' a Lord.

Burns wants the world to know that he has dined with a Lord.
wot = know; *sprachl'd up the brae* = clambered up the hill

I've been at drucken Writers' feasts,
Nay, been bitch-fou 'mang Godly Priests;
(Wi' rev'rence be it spoken!)
I've even join'd the honor'd jorum,
When mighty Squireships o' the Quorum
Their hydra drouth did sloken.

He recalls many occasions when he has dined with lawyers and priests, frequently inebriated.
drucken Writers = drunken lawyers; *bitch-fou* = completely drunk; *jorum* = drinking vessel; *hydra drouth did sloken* = many people drank

But wi' a Lord – stand out my shin!
A Lord, a Peer, an Earl's son!—
Up higher yet, my bonnet!
An sic a Lord! — lang Scotch ell twa,
Our Peerage he looks o'er them a',
As I look o'er my sonnet.

But he has never dined with nobility, and this particular nobleman is over six feet tall, quite a height at that time in history.
shin = climb; *lang Scotch ell twa* = over six feet

But O, for Hogarth's magic pow'r,
To shew Sir Bardie's willyart glow'r,
An' how he star'd an' stammer'd!
When goavin's he'd been led wi' branks,
An' stumpin' on his ploughman shanks,
He in the parlour hammer'd.

He wished that William Hogarth, the painter, had been on hand to record his expression as he was led into the parlour to meet the Lord.
Sir Bardie's willyart glow'r = Burns' timid look; *goavin's* = dazed; *branks* = bridles; *stumpin'* = walking stiffly; *shanks* = legs

To meet good Stewart little pain is,
Or Scotia's sacred Demosthenes;
Thinks I: 'They are but men!'
But 'Burns'!- 'My Lord'-Good God! I doited!
My knees on ane anither knoited,
As faultering I gaed ben.

Mere mortals are one thing, but meeting a Lord made him nervous and tongue-tied.
doited = blundered; *knoited* = knotted; *gaed ben* = went through

I sidling shelter'd in a neuk,
An' at his Lordship staw a leuk,
Like some portentous omen;
Except good sense and social glee,
An' (what surpris'd me) modesty,
I marked naught uncommon.

Still overcome by the occasion, Burns stood in a corner stealing glances at the Lord, and was surprised at how modest and normal the young man was.
sidling shelter'd in a neuk = edged into a corner; *staw a leuk* = stole a glance

I watch'd the symptons o' the Great,
The gentle pride, the lordly state,
The arrogant assuming;
The fient a pride, nae pride had he,
Nor sauce, nor state, that I could see,
Mair than an honest ploughman!

Burns had witnessed the arrogance of aristocrats before, but Lord Daer displayed none of their traits. In fact he felt that the young Lord's attitude to life was little different to his own.
fient = friend; *mair* = more

Then from his Lordship I shall learn,
Henceforth to meet with unconcern
One rank as weel's another;
Nae honest, worthy man need care,
To meet wi' noble, youthfu' Daer,
For he but meets a Brother.

This meeting has shown the poet that all men are equal, irrespective of rank or title, and that an honest man can hold his head high in any company.

Address to Edinburgh

Burns wrote this tribute to the city shortly after his arrival in Edinburgh. Its style is a bit stiff, slightly pompous, and almost Anglicised – rather how the citizens of Edinburgh are perceived by their counterparts in the west.

Edina! Scotia's darling seat!
All hail thy palaces and tow'rs,
Where once, beneath a Monarch's feet
Sat Legislation's sov'reign pow'rs!
From marking wildly-scatt'red flow'rs,
As on the banks of Ayr I stray'd,
And singing, lone, the ling'ring hours,
I shelter in thy honor'd shade.

Here Wealth still swells the golden tide,
As busy trade his labours plies;
There Architecture's noble pride
Bids elegance and splendour rise:
Here Justice, from her native skies,
High wields her balance and her rod;
There Learning, with his eagle eyes,
Seeks Science in her coy abode.

Thy sons, Edina, social, kind,
With open arms the stranger hail;
Their views enlarg'd, their lib'ral mind,
Above the narrow, rural vale;
Attentive still to Sorrow's wail,
Or modest Merit's silent claim:
And never may their sources fail!
And never envy blot their name!

Thy daughters bright thy walks adorn,
Gay as the gilded summer sky,
Sweet as the dewy, milk-white thorn,
Dear as the raptur'd thrill of joy!
Fair Burnett strikes th' adoring eye,   Eliza Burnett
Heav'ns beauties on my fancy shine:
I see the Sire of Love on high,
And own his work indeed divine!

There, watching high the least alarms,
Thy rough, rude fortress gleams afar;
Like some bold vet'ran, grey in arms,
And marked with many a seamy scar:
The pond'rous wall and massy bar,
Grim-rising o'er the rugged rock,
Have oft withstood assailing war,
And oft repell'd th' invader's shock.

With awe-struck thought and pitying tears,
I view that noble, stately dome,
Where Scotia's kings of other years,
Fam'd heroes! had their royal home:
Alas, how chang'd the times to come!
Their royal name low in the dust!
Their hapless race wild-wand'ring roam!
Tho' rigid Law cries out ' 'Twas just!'

Wild beats my heart to trace your steps,
Whose ancestors, in days of yore,
Thro' hostile ranks and ruin'd gaps
Old Scotia's bloody lion bore;
Ev'n I, who sing in rustic lore,
Haply my sires have left their shed,
And fac'd grim Danger's loudest roar,
Bold-following where your fathers led!

Edina, Scotia's darling seat!
All hail thy palaces and tow'rs;
Where once beneath a Monarch's feet,
Sat Legislation's sov'reign pow'rs!
From marking wildly cat'red flow'rs,
As on the banks of Ayr I stray'd,
And singing, lone, the ling'ring hours,
I shelter in thy honor'd shade.

Address to a Haggis

No Burns Supper could ever take place without the wonderful ritual of the Address to the Haggis. This recital is usually performed in a very theatrical and flamboyant manner and can be totally incomprehensible to the non-Scot (and truth be told, even to some Scots). It is a truly wonderful poem, full of humour, although some find the language daunting.

There is one school of thought that thinks Burns wrote 'To a Haggis' as a piece of fun and never intended it to be taken seriously. Others believe it to be a tribute to the strength of the working-classes. No matter! It has become part of the Scottish tradition and will never, ever be forgotten.

Fair fa' your honest, sonsie face,
Great chieftain o' the puddin'-race!
Aboon them a' ye tak your place,
Painch, tripe or thairm;
Weel are ye wordy o' a grace
As lang's my arm.

This begins with a simple statement. The haggis is the greatest of all puddings, greater than stomach, tripe or guts, and well worth this long grace.
sonsie = jolly; *puddin-race* = meat puddings or sausages; *aboon* = above ; *painch, tripe or therm* = animal entrails; *weel* = well; *wordy* = worthy; *lang* = long; *airm* = arm

The groaning trencher there ye fill,
Your hurdies like a distant hill,
Your pin wad help to mend a mill,
In time o' need,
While thro' your pores the dews distil,
Like amber bead.

It fills the platter and its buttocks look like a distant hill. Its skewer is large enough to repair a mill, and the moisture oozing from it is as beautiful as amber beads.
groaning trencher = laden platter; *hurdies* = hips or buttocks; *pin* = skewer; *wad* = would

His knife see rustic labour dight,
An' cut you up wi' ready slight,
Trenching your gushing entrails bright,
Like onie ditch;
And then, O what a glorious sight,
Warm-reekin, rich!

With a skilled hand, the server cuts through the skin which flows open like a ditch as the insides gush forth. But what a glorious sight with its warm, steaming richness.
dight = to clean; *trenching* = cutting open; *ony* = any; *warm-reekin* = warm smelling

Then, horn for horn, they stretch an' strive,
Deil tak the hindmost, on they drive,
Till a' their weel-swall'd kytes belyve
Are bent like drums;
Then auld Guidman, maist like to rive,
'Bethankit' hums

Spoonful by spoonful, everyone digs in
and the devil take the slowest eater until
all are replete. Then the bulging elder of
the family leans back and gives his thanks.
horn = a spoon; *weel-swall'd kytes* = full
bellies; *bent like drums* = tight as drums;
auld = old; *maist* = most; *rive* = burst;
bethankit = God be thanked

Is there that owre his French ragout,
Or olio that wad staw a sow,
Or fricassee wad make her spew
Wi' perfect sconner,
Looks down wi' sneerin, scornfu' view
On sic a dinner?

Can anyone who has eaten that fancy
French rubbish, so disgusting as to make a
pig throw up, dare to look down his nose
and sneer at such a dinner.
owre = over; *ragout/olio* = savoury dishes of
meat and vegetables; *staw a sow* = stop a pig;
fricasse = dish of fowl or rabbit; *spew* =
vomit; *sconner* = disgust; *sic* = such

Poor devil! see him owre his trash,
As feckless as a wither'd rash,
His spindle shank a guid whiplash,
His nieve a nit;
Thro' bluidy flood or field to dash,
O how unfit!

Look at that poor devil bent over the
rubbish he is eating. He's as weak as a
withered rush. His legs are skinny and his
fist is no bigger than a nut. No venturing
into the battle-field for him, he's too unfit.
feckless = helpless; *spindle-shank* = thin leg;
guid = good; *nieve* = fist; *nit* = nut

But mark the Rustic, haggis-fed,
The trembling earth resounds his tread,
Clap in his walie nieve a blade,
He'll mak it whisslle.
An' legs, an' arms, an' heads will sned,
Like taps o' thrissle.

But see that labourer fed on haggis. The
earth trembles under his feet and in his great
fist a sword would whistle through the air,
lopping off legs, arms and heads as though
they were no more than the tops of thistles.
walie nieve = large fist; *blade* = sword; *whissle*
= whistle; *sned* = lop off; *taps o' thrissle* = tops
of thistle

Ye Pow'rs, wha mak mankind your care,
And dish them out their bill o' fare,
Auld Scotland wants nae skinking ware
That jaups in luggies;
But, if ye wish her gratefu' prayer
Gie her a Haggis!

You Powers who look after mankind and provide us with our food. Scotland does not want watery rubbish splashing about in dishes. If you want her grateful thanks. give her a haggis.

bill-o'-fare = menu; *skinking ware* = watery rubbish; *jaups* = splashes; *luggie* = wooden dish with handles; *gie* = give

Elegy on the Death of Robert Ruisseux

Robert Burns appears to have had no fear of death. In fact on reading some of his work, it would seem that there were times in his life when he might have regarded it as a welcome relief from the tribulations which he suffered. This is a mock elegy written about himself, the name Ruisseaux being French for stream, or burn.

Now Robin lies in his last lair,
He'll gabble rhyme, nor sing nae mair;
Cauld poverty, wi' hungry stare,
Nae mair shall fear him;
Nor anxious fear, nor cankert care,
E'er mair come near him.

He is now in his grave and secure from the tribulations that have dogged him during his lifetime.

cankert = crabbed

To tell the truth, they seldom fash'd him,
Except the moment that they crush'd him;
For sune as chance or fate had hush'd, 'em
Tho' e'er sae short,
Then wi' a rhyme or sang he lash'd 'em,
And thought it sport.

His enemies seldom succeeded in suppressing him for he was usually able to extract revenge by lampooning them in verse.

fash'd = worried; *sune* = soon

Tho' he was bred to kintra–wark,
And counted was baith wight and stark,
Yet that was never Robin's mark
To mak a man;
But tell him he was learn'd and clark,
Ye roos'd him then!

Although born into the life of a farm worker, he never judged a man by his physical strength, only by his knowledge, and was always pleased to be recognised as an educated man.

kintra-wark = country work; *baith wight and stark* = both stout and strong; *clark* = scholarly; *roos'd* = flattered

The Guidwife of Wauchope House, to Robert Burns, the Airshire Bard
Feb 1787

This is a wonderful, witty poem, not written by Burns, but sent to him by Mrs Elizabeth Scott, a very talented lady who lived in Wauchope House, close to Jedburgh. She had read the Kilmarnock Edition and was obviously very impressed by it. Mrs Scott tells the Bard that she doubts he really is a ploughman as she knows of no ploughman who could quote from the Greek Classics, or who would be able to make jokes about the country's political leaders. In fact, she feels that such knowledge could only be gleaned by close association with such people. She would much prefer to spend an evening listening to the Bard than entertaining dull aristocrats.

My canty, witty, rhyming ploughman,   *canty* = lively
I hafflins doubt, it is na' true, man,   *hafflins* = partly
That ye between the stilts was bred,
Wi' ploughman school'd, wi' ploughman fed.
I doubt it sair, ye've drawn your knowledge   *doubt it sair* = really doubt it
Either frae grammar school, or colledge.
Guid troth, your saul and body baith   *saul* = soul; *baith* = both
War' better fed, I'd gie my aith,   *war* = were; *aith* = oath
Than theirs, who sup sour milk and parritch,   *sup* = drink
An' bummil thro' the single caritch.   *bummil* = mumble; *caritch* = catechism
Whaever heard the ploughman speak,
Could tell if Homer was a Greek?
He'd flee as soon upon a cudgel,
As get a single line of Virgil.
An' then sae slee ye crack your jokes   *slee* = sly
O' Willie Pitt and Charlie Fox.
Our great men a' sae weel descrive,   *descrive* = describe
An' how to gar the nation thrive,   *gar* = make
Ane maist wad swear ye dwelt amang them,
An' as ye saw them, sae ye sung them.
But be ye ploughman, be ye peer,
Ye are a funny blade, I swear.
An' tho' the cauld I ill can bide,

Yet twenty miles, an' mair, I'd ride,
O'er moss an' muir , an' never grumble,   *muir* = moor
If my auld yad shou'd gae a stumble,   *yad* = mare
To crack a winter-night wi' thee,
An' hear thy sangs, an' sonnets slee.
A guid saut herring, an' a cake   *saut* = salt
Wi' sic a chiel a feast wad make.
I'd rather scour your rumming yill,   *rumming yill* – beer glass
Or eat o' cheese and bread my fill,
Than wi' dull lairds on turtle dine,
An' ferlie at their wit and wine.   *ferlie* = marvel
O, gif I kend but whare ye baide,
I'd send to you a marled plaid;
'Twad haud your shoulders warm and braw,
An' douse at kirk, or market shaw.
Far south, as weel as north, my lad,
A' honest Scotsmen lo'e the maud.
Right wae that we're sae far frae ither;
Yet proud I am to ca' ye brither.

Your most obed. E.S.

To the Guid Wife of Wauchope House

MRS SCOTT

This is Burns' reply to Mrs Elizabeth Scott's wonderful poem.

I mind it weel, in early date,
When I was beardless, young, and blate,
An' first cou'd thresh the barn,
Or haud a yokin at the pleugh,
An' tho' fu' foughten sair eneugh,
Yet unco proud to learn;
When first amang the yellow corn
A man I reckon'd was,
An' wi' the lave ilk merry morn
Could rank my rig an' lass:
Still shearing, and clearing
The tither stooked raw,
Wi' clavers an' havers,
Wearing the time awa'.

Burns harks back to his early years when he was learning the business of farming. He and the girl he worked with could do a full days work although it was exhausting. He gathered the corn and she put it into sheaves or stooks.

mind it weel = remember it well; *blate* = shy; *haud a yokin* = do a day's work; *foughten* = tired; *lave* = others; *ilk* = each; *tither* = other; *clavers an' havers* = nonsense and chatter; *An' tho' fu' foughten sair eneugh* = and though tired and sore

E'n then, a wish (I mind its pow'r),
A wish that to my latest hour
Shall strongly heave my breast,
That I for poor auld Scotland's sake
Some useful plan, or book could make,
Or sing a sang at least.
The rough burr-thistle spreading wide
Amang the bearded bear,
I turn'd the weeding heuk aside,
An' spar'd the symbol dear.
No nation, no station,
My envy e'er could raise:
A Scot still, but blot still,
I knew nae higher praise.

Even when he was so young he wished that he could write a book or compose a song for the glory of Scotland. He was so proud of his country that he would not cut down thistles, (the emblem of Scotland) when weeding. He can think of no higher station in life than being born a Scot.

beardy bear = barley; *weeding heuk* = hook

But still the elements o' sang
In formless jumble, right an' wrang,
Wild floated in my brain;
'Till on the that hairst I said before,
My partner in the merry core,
She rous'd the forming strain.
I see her yet, the sonsie quean
That lighted up my jingle,
Her pauky smile, her kittle een,
That gart my heart-strings tingle!
So tiched, bewitched,
I rav'd ay to myself;
But bashing and dashing,
I kend na how to tell.

Hale to the sex, ilk guid chiel says,
Wi' merry dance on winter-days,
An' we to share in common!
The gust o' joy, the balm of woe,
The saul o' life, the heav'n below
Is rapture-giving Woman.
Ye surly sumphs, who hate the name,
Be mindfu' o' your mither;
She, honest woman, may think shame
That ye're connect'd with her!
Ye're wae men, ye're nae men,
That slight the lovely dears;
To shame ye, disclain ye,
Ilk honest birkie swears.

The words tumbled around in his head until one harvest when he was inspired to write a poem about his partner.(Nelly Kilpatrick of Handsome Nell fame). Her smile and her eyes were his inspiration but he was too shy to tell her how he felt about her.

hairst = harvest; core = crowd; sonsie quean = good-natured girl; kittle een = shrewd eyes; gart = made

He wishes good health to all women, who he feels give joy to life, but mocks any man who thinks ill of women as their own mothers might disown them for being so churlish.

saul = soul; sumphs = boorish people; birkie = fellow

For you, na bred to barn an' byre,
Wha sweetly tune the Scottish lyre,
Thanks to you for your line.
The marl'd plaid ye kindly spare,
By me should gratefully be ware;
'Twad please me to the Nine.
I'd be mair vauntie o' my hap,
Douce hingin owre my curple,
Than onie ermine ever lap,
Or proud imperial purple.
Farewell then, lang hale then,
An' plenty be your fa'
May losses and crosses
Ne'er at your hallan ca'.

He thanks Mrs Scott for her epistle and appreciates that she was not bred for country work. She has given him a partly coloured plaid which he will wear more proudly than if it were an ermine robe, and he hopes her life will be free from tragedy.

marl'd = partly coloured; *ware* = worn; *vauntie* = proud; *hap* = covering; *douce* = soberly; *curple* = leather strap which holds saddle on horse; *lang hale* = long health; *fa'* = lot; *hallan* = hallway, porch

March, 1787, R. Burns

To Mr McAdam of Craigengillan

IN ANSWER TO AN OBLIGING LETTER HE SENT IN THE COMMENCEMENT OF MY
POETIC CAREER

McAdam had acquired wealth and status through his work in improving methods of agriculture, and had written to Burns, apparently to congratulate him upon his poetry. There is a certain amount of hypocrisy contained in poems such as this, that show that although Burns scorned the rich and famous in his verses, he was nevertheless flattered to receive their accolades.

Sir, o'er a gill I gat your card,
I trow it made me proud;
'See wha tak's notice o' the Bard!'
I lap, and cry'd fu loud.

Burns thanks McAdam for his card, he's delighted that he's been noticed.
o'er a gill = over a drink; *trow* = promise; *lap* = jumped

Now deil-ma-care about their jaw,
The senseless, gawky million;
I'll cock my nose aboon them a',
I'm roos'd by Craigengillan!

He doesn't care what the masses think of him for he has been praised by the gentry.
jaw = gossip; *gawky* = clumsy; *roos'd* = praised

'Twas noble, Sir; 'twas like yoursel,
To grant your high protection:
A great man's smile, ye ken fu' well,
Is ay a blest infection.

Burns flatters McAdam by saying that MacAdam smiling upon Burns' work has truly blessed it.

Tho', by his banes wha in a tub
Match'd Macedonian Sandy!
On my ain legs thro dirt and dub,
I independent stand ay.

Although McAdam is a match for Alexander the Great, Burns can always stand independent.
banes = bones; *Macedonian Sandy* = Alexander the Great; *dub* = puddle

And when those legs to guid, warm kail,
Wi' welcome canna bear me,
A lee dyke-side, a sybow-tail,
An' barley-scone shall cheer me.

When he gets old and infirm, Burns will be content with a simple life and diet.
kail = broth; *lee dyke-side* = sheltered wall; *sybow-tail* = spring onion

Heaven spare you lang to kiss the breath
O' monie flow'ry simmers,
An' bless your bonie lasses baith,
I'm tauld they're loosome kimmers!

An' God bless young Dunaskin's laird,
The blossom of our gentry!
An' may he wear an auld man's beard,
A credit to his country!

He hopes McAdam will enjoy long life, and
blesses his beautiful daughters.

simmers = summers; *loosome* = lovable;
kimmers = young girls

Burns then blesses him again, wishing
that he lives to be an old man.

Lament For the Absence of William Creech

William Creech was a prominent figure within the literati in Edinburgh. His bookshop in the High Street was the central meeting point for writers, lawyers, and men of letters. He was also responsible for publishing much of Burns' works and the two had an amicable relationship until Creech became reticent about paying Burns his due fees. This led to a distinct cooling down of the relationship, but the following poem was written before that occurrence when the two were still friendly.

Auld chuckie Reekie's sair distrest
Down droops her ance weel-burnish'd crest,
Nae joy her bonie buskit nest
Can yield ava:
Her darling bird that she lo'es best,
Willie's awa.

Edinburgh is distressed as the darling of her society, Willie, has gone away.
Auld Reekie = Edinburgh; *chuckie* = mother-hen; *buskit* = well-trimmed; *ava* = at all; *droops* = drops

O, Willie was a witty wight,
And had o' things an unco sleight!
Auld Reekie' ay he keepit tight,
An' trig an' braw;
But now they'll busk her like a fright,
Willie's awa!

Willie was a man of wit who kept things running smoothly, but now he's away, there's trouble
wight = chap; *sleight* = skill; *trig and braw* = neat and handsome; *busk* = dress; *fright* = freak; *unco sleight* = uncommon skill

The stiffest o' them a' he bow'd;
The bauldest o' them a' he cow'd;
They durst nae mair than he allow'd,
That was a law:
We've lost a birkie well worth gowd—
Willie's awa!

He was a leader in society and his word was considered to be law.
bauldest = boldest; *durst* = dared; *birkie* = fellow; *gowd* = gold

Now gawkies, tawpies, gowks, and fools,
Frae colleges and boarding-schools
May sprout like simmer puddock-stools
In glen or shaw:
He wha could brush them down to mools,
Willies awa!

Now all those pretentious people will be unrestrained.
gawkies = silly people; *tawpies* = silly girls; *gowks* = fools; *simmer* = summer; *puddock-stools* = tadpoles; *mools* = dust

The brethren o' the Commerce Chaumer
May mourn their loss wi' doolful clamour:
He was a dictionar and grammar
Among them a':
I fear they'll now mak monie a stammer:
Willie's awa!

The business community relied on him
to correct their spelling and grammar,
but mistakes will now be made.
Chaumer = Chamber; *doolful* = doleful

Nae mair we see his levee door
Philosophers and Poets pour,
And toothy Critics by the score,
In bloody raw:
The adjutant o' a' the core,
Willie's awa!

No more morning receptions will take
place while he's away.
levee = early morning reception by a
person of distinction

Now worthy Greg'rys Latin face,
Tyler's and Greenfield's modest grace,
McKenzie, Stewart, such a brace
As Rome ne'er saw,
They a' maun meet some ither place—-
Willie's awa!

Edinburgh's men of letters must find
another meeting place.

Poor Burns ev'n 'Scotch Drink' canna
quicken,
He cheeps like some bewilder'd chicken
Scar'd frae its minnie and the cleckin,
By hoodie-craw.
Grief's gien his heart an unco kickin,
Willie's awa!

Even a drop of Scotch cannot inspire
Burns. He feels quite lost without Creech.
minnie = mother; *cleckin* = brood;
hoodie-craw = carrion crow

Now ev'ry sour-mou'd, girnin blellum,
And Calvin's folk, are fit to tell him;
Ilk self-conceited critic-skellum
His quill may draw:
He wha could brawlie ward their blellum,
Willie's awa!

All of his critics can now write
about him without trepidation
girnin = crying; whining; *blellum* =
babbler; *skellum* = scoundrel

Up wimpling, stately Tweed I've sped,
And Eden scenes on crystal Jed,
And Ettrick banks, now roaring red
While tempests blaw;
But every joy and pleasure's fled,
Willie's awa!

Although he's witnessed the beauty of the border counties, it seems meaningless without Creech.

May I be Slander's common speech,
A text for Infamy to preach,
And lastly, streekit out to bleach
In winter snaw,
When I forget thee, Willie Creech,
Tho' far awa!

May Burns be slandered and infamous and stretched out in the snow to bleach should he forget Creech.
streekit = stretched

May never wicked Fortune touzle him,
May never wicked men bamboozle him,
Until a pow as auld's Methusalem
He canty claw!
Then to the blessed new Jerusalem,
Fleet-wing awa!

May Creech never have bad luck or be cheated and grow old in peace.
pow = head; *canty claw* = cheerfully scratch

Sonnet on William Creech

In sharp contrast to the previous poem, Burns composed this sonnet about Creech some time afterwards. His feelings towards the publisher had been soured over a dispute about money, and the adulation in which he held Creech has long since evaporated.

A little upright, pert, tart, tripping wight,   *wight* = fellow
And still his precious self his dear delight;
Who loves his own smart shadow in the streets
Better than e'er the fairest She he meets.
Much spacious lore, but little understood.
(Veneering oft outshines the solid wood),
His solid sense by inches you must tell,
But mete his subtle cunning by the ell!
A man of fashion, too, he made his tour,
Learn'd 'Vive la bagatelle et vive l'amour':
So travell'd monkies their grimaces improve,
Polish their grin – nay, sigh for ladies love!
His meddling vanity, a busy fiend,
Still making work his selfish craft must mend.

Bonie Dundee

An old ballad revised by the Bard. The central theme is of a young maiden left pregnant by a passing soldier. The opening line which refers to a 'hauver-meal bannock' is an early version of the modern 'having a bun in the oven.'

'O whar gat ye that hauver-meal bannock?'
'O silly blind body, O dinna ye see?
I gat it frae a young brisk sodger laddie
Between Saint Johnston and bonie Dundee.

The girl is asked who got her pregnant and she replies that the father is a soldier.

'O gin I saw the laddie that gae me 't!
Aft has he doudl'd me upon his knee;
May Heaven protect my bonie Scots laddie,
And send him safe hame to his babie and me!

She wishes that he'll be protected and return home safe.

O, gin = Oh that; doudl'd = dandled

'My blessin's upon thy sweet, wee lippie!
My blessin's upon thy bonie e'e-brie!
Thy smiles are sae like my blyth sodger laddie,
Thou's ay the dearer and dearer to me!

The mother blesses her child who reminds her of the father.

'But I'll big a bow'r on yon bonie banks,
Whare Tay rins wimplin by sae clear;
An' I'll cleed thee in the tartan sae fine,
And mak thee a man like thy daddie dear.'

She will build a shelter for them and clothe the boy in tartan just as his father was.

big = build; cleed = clothe

To Symon Gray

Robert Burns may have been inclined to offer advice to Andrew Aiken, but when pestered by a retired London businessman, Symon Gray, who had taken up residence in the Borders and who fancied himself to be a fellow poet, his response was very different. Gray must have been a very thick-skinned individual for he sent three samples of his poems to Burns for approval, and the replies simply became coarser and ruder.

Symon Gray,
You're dull today.
Dullness, with redoubted sway,
Has seized the wits of Symon Gray.

Dear Cimon Gray,
The other day,
When you sent me some rhyme,
I could not then just ascertain
Its worth, for want of time.

But now today, good Mr. Gray,
I've read it o'er and o'er.
Tried all my skill, but find I'm still
Just where I was before.

We auld wives' minions gie our opinions,   *auld wives minions* = old women's darlings
Solicited or no';
Then of its fau'ts my honest thoughts   *fau'ts* = faults
I'll give – and here they go.

Such damn'd bombast no time that past
Will show, or time to come,
So, Cimon dear, your song I'll tear,
And with it wipe my bum.

On Scaring Some Water-fowl in Loch Turit

Robert Burns detested hunting and had nothing but contempt for those who enjoyed killing any form of wildlife in the supposed pursuit of pleasure. This poem demonstrates his sympathies towards the water-fowl that fell under the hunter's gun, and although he appreciates the need of wild creatures to hunt in order to survive, he cannot excuse his fellow man for the atrocities which they commit upon nature's innocents.

Why, ye tenants of the lake,
For me your wat'ry haunts forsake?
Tell me, fellow creatures, why
At my presence thus you fly?
Why disturb your social joys,
Parent, filial, kindred ties?

Burns asks why the waterfowl fly away when he is present.

Common friend to you and me,
Nature's gifts to all are free:
Peaceful keep your dimpling wave,
Busy feed, or wanton lave;
Or, beneath the sheltering rock,
Bide the surging billows shock.

wanton lave = idly rest

bide = endure

Conscious, blushing for our race,
Soon, too soon, your fears I trace.
Man, your proud, usurping foe,
Would be lord of all below:
Plumes himself in freedom's pride,
Tyrant stern to all beside.

He talks of man's tyrany and is embarrassed.

The eagle, from the cliffy brow,
Marking you his prey below,
In his breast no pity dwells,
Strong necessity compels.
But Man, to whom alone is giv'n
A ray direct from pitying Heav'n,
Glories in his heart humane –
And creatures for his pleasure slain.

The eagle also preys on the waterfowl, yet this is necessary. Man slays for pleasure.

191

In these savage, liquid plains,
Only known to wand'ring swains,
Where the mossy riv'let strays,
Far from human haunts and ways;
All on Nature you depend,
And life's poor season peaceful spend.

The waterfowl hides where no-one goes.
wand'ring swains = wandering lovers
riv'let = rivulet or stream

Or, if Man's superior might
Dare invade your native right,
On the lofty ether borne,
Man with all his powers you scorn;
Swiftly seek, on clanging wings,
Other lakes, and other springs;
And the foe you cannot brave,
Scorn at least to be his slave.

What if man invades the birds right of flight?
lofty ether borne = carried high in the air

Epitaph For William Michie

Burns wrote many epitaphs in his day, some sad, some amusing, some cutting. This one however was a spoof, for following a night of hard drinking, William, or Ebenezer Michie, as was his correct name, keeled over in drunken stupor prompting Burns to write the following few lines.

Here lie Willie Michie's banes:
O Satan, when you tak him,
Gie him the schulin o your weans,
For clever deils he'll mak them!

banes = bones; *schulin* =schooling; *weans* = children; *deils* = devils

Where, Braving Angry Winter's Storms

Margaret, or Peggy, Chalmers was yet another young lady whose beauty had bewitched Robert Burns, and who joined the ranks of those who had turned down his proposal of marriage. He was certainly distressed to discover that she was to be married to a banker and wrote to her outlining his feelings.

Where braving angry winter's storms,
The lofty Ochils rise,
Far in their shade my Peggy's charms
First blest my wondering eyes:

As one who by some savage stream
A lonely gem surveys,
Astonish'd doubly marks its beam
With art's most polish'd blaze.

Blest be the wild, sequester'd glade,
And blest the day and hour,
Where Peggy's charms I first survey'd,
When first I felt their pow'r!

The tyrant Death, with grim controul
May seize my fleeting breath,
But tearing Peggy from my soul
Must be a stronger death.

Ca' the Yowes to the Knowes

This particularly beautiful ballad has a melody that is always a joy to hear. It is the Bard's second version of the song. The Clouden refers to a tributary of the River Nith, and the silent towers are the remains of Lincluden Abbey.

Chorus
Ca' the yowes to the knowes,
Ca' them where the heather grows,
Ca' them where the burnie rowes,
My bonie dearie.

ca' the yowes to the knowes = call the sheep to the hills; *yowes =* ewes; *knowes =* knolls; *where the burnie rowes =* where the stream is running

Hark the mavis e'ening sang
Sounding Clouden's woods amang,
Then a-faulding let us gang,
My bonie dearie.

Once the sheep are safely settled, they will set off.
mavis = thrush; *a-faulding =* through the gates of the sheep-fold

We'll gae down by Clouden side,
Thro' the hazels spreading wide,
O'er the waves that gently glide,
To the moon sae clearly.

They will walk by the riverside and watch the moonbeams reflect from the water.

Yonder Clouden's silent towers,
Where, at moonshine's midnight hours,
O'er the dewy bending flowers
Fairies dance sae cheery.

The ruined abbey is where one can see fairies dance at midnight.

Ghaist nor bogle shalt thou fear,
Thou'rt to Love and Heav'n sae dear
Nocht of ill may come thee near,
My bonie dearie.

The lass is too precious for any harm to befall her.
ghaist nor bogle = ghost or demon, *nocht =* nought

I'm O'er Young to Marry Yet

This is another old song revitalised by Burns and which is a particular favourite at any Burns Supper. A young girl is apparently not overjoyed at the prospect of marriage and is using her tender years as an excuse.

CHORUS
I'm o'er young, I'm o'er young,
I'm o'er young to marry yet!
I'm o'er young, 'twad be a sin
To tak me frae my mammie yet.

I'm far too young to marry, it would be a sin to take me from home.

I am my mammie's ae bairn,
 Wi' unco folk I weary, Sir;
And lying in a man's bed,
I fley'd it make me eerie,Sir.

She's an only child and finds strangers boring. She's frightened of going to bed with a man.
ae bairn = only child; *fley'd* = afraid;
eerie = frightened

Hallowmass is come and gane,
The nights are lang in winter, Sir,
And you an' I in ae bed,
In trowth, I dare na venture,Sir!

It's deep winter and she dares not go to bed with him.
Hallowmass = first week of November;
trowth = truth

Fu' loud an' shrill the frosty wind
Blaws thro' the leafless timmer, Sir;
But if ye come this gate again,
I'll aulder be gin simmer, Sir.

timmer = trees; *gin simmer* = by summer

O, That I Were Where Helen Lies

Anyone who holds a preconceived idea that the Scots are rather dour and unromantic will surely have a different view after reading this poem. It is an old ballad, rewritten by the Bard, and is the true, tragic tale of a lass who was just too popular.

Helen Irvine lived in the village of Kirkconnel in the sixteenth century and had a lover named Adam Fleming. A rival suitor, besotted with jealousy, fired a shot at Fleming, but Helen tried to come between the two men and was fatally wounded by the bullet. Fleming drew his sword and immediately slew the assailant, but rather than face trial, he fled to Spain where he joined the army. Years later, he returned to Kirkconnel where he died and was buried in a grave beside his beloved Helen.

O that I were where Helen lies,
Night and day on me she cries;
O that I were where Helen lies
In fair Kirkconnel lee.   *lee* = lea; *evermair* = evermore
O Helen fair beyond compare,
A ringlet of thy flowing hair,
I'll wear it still for ever mair
Until the day I die.

Curs'd be the hand that shot the shot,
And curs'd be the gun that gave the crack!
Into my arms bird Helen lap,   *lap* = leapt; *na ye* = not you; *sair* = sore; *spake*
And died for sake o' me!   *nae mair* = spoke no more; *meikle* = much
O think na ye but my heart was sair;
My Love fell down and spake nae mair;
There did she swoon wi' meikle care
On fair Kirkconnel lee.

I lighted down, my sword did draw,   *lighted down* = dismounted; *sma'* = small
I cutted him in pieces sma';
I cutted him in pieces sma'
On fair Kirkconnel lee.
O Helen chaste, thou wert modest,
If I were with thee I were blest,
Where thou lies low and takes thy rest
On fair Kirkconnel lee.

I wish my grave was growing green,
A winding sheet put o'er my e'en,
And I in Helen's arms lying
In fair Kirkconnel lee!
I wish I were where Helen lies!
Night and day on me she cries:
O, that I were where Helen lies
On fair Kirkconnel lee.

winding sheet = shroud
o'er my e'en = over my eyes

The Birks of Aberfeldie

The Bard was inspired to write these verses as he stood admiring the falls of Aberfeldy. This is a simple and beautiful song, written in 1787, which remains a favourite at Burns Suppers and ceillidhs to this day. This song has a particularly haunting melody which will stay with you forever once you hear it played.

CHORUS
Bonie lassie, will ye go,
Will ye go, will ye go;
Bonie lassie, will ye go
To the birks of Aberfeldie.   birks = birches

Now simmer blinks on flow'ry braes,
And o'er the crystal streamlets plays,
Come, let us spend the lightsome days
In the birks of Aberfeldie!

The little birdies blythely sing,
While o'er their heads the hazels hing,   hing = hang
Or lighty flit on wanton wing
In the birks of Aberfeldie.

The braes ascend like lofty wa's,
The foamy stream, deep-roaring, fa's   fa's = falls
O'erhung wi' fragrant-spreading shaws,
The birks of Aberfeldie.

The hoary cliffs are crown'd wi' flowers,
White o'er the linns the burnie pours,   linns = waterfalls
And rising weets wi' misty showers
The birks of Aberfeldie.

Let Fortune's gifts at random flee,
They ne'er shall draw a wish frae me;
Supremely blest wi' love and thee
In the birks of Aberfeldie.

A Rose-bud by My Early Walk

The young lady to whom this tribute was penned was a mere twelve-year old at the time of writing. Jean Cruikshank was the daughter of an Edinburgh school-master and was already an accomplished musician when the Bard wrote the following verses in her honour.

A rose-bud by my early walk
Adown a corn-inclosed bawk,   *bawk* = footpath
Sae gently bent its thorny stalk,
All on a dewy morning.

Ere twice the shades o' dawn are fled,
In a' its crimson glory spread,
And drooping rich the dewy head,
It scents the early morning.

Within the bush her covert nest
A little linnet fondly prest,
The dew sat chilly on her breast,
Sae early in the morning.

She soon shall see her tender brood,
 The pride, the pleasure o' the wood,
Amang the fresh green leaves bedew'd,
Awake the early morning.

So thou dear bird, young Jeany fair,
On trembling string or vocal air,
Shall sweetly pay the tender care
That tents thy early morning!   *tents* = guards

So thou, sweet rose-bud, young and gay,
Shalt beauteous blaze upon the day,
And bless the parent's evening ray
That watch'd thy early morning!

Clarinda, Mistress of My Soul

Robert Burns' affair with Agnes McLehose, or Nancy, as she was known to her friends, stretched out over some five years. Nancy was a married woman, estranged from her husband, so in order to avoid scandal they devised a code whereby she would become Clarinda, and he Sylvander. Nancy eventually sailed off to Jamaica to attempt a reconciliation with her husband, a departure which prompted the writing of one of the Bard's most beautiful and famous songs, *Ae Fond Kiss*. The affair was the source of many other romantic letters and verses that are are still enthralling to read today. Sadly, Nancy's voyage to Jamaica was a lost cause. Her husband had taken a mistress, and Nancy had no option but to return home, only to find that her beloved Sylvander had also moved to pastures new and had lost interest in her.

Clarinda, mistress of my soul,
The measur'd time is run!
The wretch beneath the dreary pole
So marks his latest sun.

To what dark cave of frozen night
Shall poor Sylvander hie,   *hie* = hasten
Depriv'd of thee, his life and light,
The sun of all his joy?

We part – but by these precious drops
That fill thy lovely eyes,
No other light shall guide my steps
Till thy bright beams arise !

She, the fair sun of all her sex,
Has blest my glorious day;
And shall a glimmering planet fix
My worship to its ray.

Verses to Clarinda

Sent with a pair of wine glasses.

Fair Empress of the Poet's soul
And Queen of poetesses,
Clarinda, take this little boon,   *boon* = gift
This humble pair of glasses;

And fill them high with generous juice,
As generous as your mind;
And pledge me in the generous toast:
'The whole of human kind!'

'To those who love us!' second fill;
But not to those whom *we* love,
Lest we love those who love not us!
A third— 'To thee and me, love!'

'Long may we live! Long may we love!
And long may we be happy!
And may we never want a glass
Well charg'd with generous nappy!'   *nappy* = ale or liquor

Rattlin', Roarin' Willie

William Dunbar was one the Bard's drinking cronies in Edinburgh. He was a Writer to the Signet and was also a very active member of a drinking club known as the Crochallan Fencibles in which he was given the rank of colonel. It seems likely that this club was the source of many of Burns' bawdy ballads and tales.

O, rattlin, roarin Willie,
O, he held to the fair,
An' for to sell his fiddle
And buy some other ware;
But parting wi' his fiddle,
The saut tear blin't his e'e——
And rattlin, roarin Willie,
Ye're welcome hame to me.

Willie went to the fair to sell his fiddle, but on parting with it he began to cry.

rattlin = roistering; *saut* = salt; *blin't* = blinded

O Willie, come sell your fiddle,
O, sell your fiddle sae fine!
O Willie, come sell your fiddle,
And buy a pint o wine!
If I should sell my fiddle,
The warld would think I was mad;
For monie a rantin day
My fiddle and I hae had.

He's encouraged to sell it and buy drink, but he and the fiddle have had some great times together.

rantin = rollicking

As I came by Crochallan,
I cannily keekit ben,
Rattlin, roarin Willie,
Was sitting at yon boord-en';
And amang guid companie;
Rattlin, roarin Willie,
Ye're welcome hame to me.

cannily keeked = looked cautiously

boord-en' = table-end

Of A' the Airts The Wind Can Blaw

In this eloquent tribute to his new bride, Jean Armour, the Bard expresses his joy and delight at being with her, and explains how the beauties of nature constantly bring her to mind.

Of a' the airts the wind can blaw
I dearly like the west,
For there the bonie lassie lives,
The lassie I lo'e best;

There's wild-woods grow, and rivers row
And monie a hill between;
But day and night my fancy's flight
Is ever wi' my Jean.

I see her in the dewy flowers,
I see her sweet and fair;
I hear her in the tunefu' birds,
I hear her charm the air;

There's not a bonie flower that springs
By fountain, shaw or green;
There's not a bonie bird that sings
But minds me o' my Jean.

airts = directions; *blaw* = blow;
rowe = roll

shaw = wooded dell

The Banks of Nith

Burns was extremely fond of the River Nith and was inspired to write the following verses in compliment as he ran by the banks of the river one morning.

The Thames flows proudly to the sea,
Where royal cities stately stand;
But sweeter flows the Nith to me,
Where Cummins ance had high command.   *Cummins* = probably a reference to the
When shall I see my honor'd land,   Comyn family
That winding stream I love so dear?
Must wayward Fortune's adverse hand
For ever, ever keep me here?

How lovely, Nith, thy fruitful vales,
Where bounding hawthorns gaily bloom;
How sweetly wind thy sloping dales,
Where lambkins wanton thro' the broom!   *lambkins wanton thro' the broom* =
Tho' wandering, now, must be my doom,   lambs wander through the broom
Far from thy bonie banks and braes,
May there my latest hours consume,
Amang the friends of early days!

Tam Glen

The Bard had a total aversion to the custom of marrying daughters off to rich suitors and was always in favour of loving relationships. This song relates to an old St. Valentine's Day tradition of drawing lots for sweethearts.

My heart is a-breaking, dear tittie,
Some counsel unto me come len',
To anger them a' is a pity,
But what will I do wi' Tam Glen?

The lass pleads with her sister to advise her on how to prevent a quarrel with her parents over her choice of suitors.
tittie = sister

I'm thinking, wi' sic a poor fellow,
In poortith I might mak a fen';
What care I in riches to wallow,
If I maunna marry Tam Glen?

Poverty may be her destiny, but that would be preferable to losing her sweetheart.
wi' sic = with such; *poortith* = poverty; *fen'* = shift; *maunna* = must not

There's Lowrie the laird o' Dumeller ;
'Guid day to you' – brute! he comes ben,
He brags and he blaws o' his siller,
But when will he dance like Tam Glen?

The local laird may be rich, but he'll never be able to dance like the man she loves.
comes ben = comes in; *blaws o' his siller* = boasts of his riches

My minnie does constantly deave me,
And bids me beware o' young men,
They flatter, she says, to deceive me –
But wha can think sae o' Tam Glen?

Her mother has warned her to beware of flattery from young men, but Tam would not deceive her.
minnie = mother; *deave* = deafen

My daddie says, gin I'll forsake him,
He'd gie me guid hunder marks ten,
But if it's ordain'd I maun take him,
O, wha will I get but Tam Glen?

Her father has offered her a cash bribe to take the laird, but her heart still says no.
gin = if; *guid hunder* = good hundred; *maun* = must

Yestreen at the Valentines' dealing,
My heart to my mou gied a sten,
For thrice I drew ane without failing,
And thrice it was written 'Tam Glen!'

At the Valentine's draw she was startled to pick Tam's name out three times in a row.
yestreen = last night; *my heart to my mou gied a sten* = my heart jumped to my mouth

The last Hallowe'en I was waukin
My droukit sark-sleeve, as ye ken—
His likeness came up the house staukin,
And the very grey breeks o' Tam Glen!

An old Halloween tradition where a lass puts her arm in a stream to reveal her true love.
wauken = awake; *droukit sark-sleeve* = drenched shirt sleeve; *staukin* = stalking; *breeks* = breeches

Come, counsel, dear tittie, don't tarry!
I'll gie you my bonie black hen,
Gif you will advise me to marry,
The lad I lo'e dearly, Tam Glen.

Finally, she offers her sister her hen if she will back her up in her choice of sweetheart.
gif = if

Elegy on Captain Matthew Henderson

A GENTLEMAN WHO HELD THE PATENT FOR HIS
HONOURS IMMEDIATELY FROM ALMIGHTY GOD.

Burns and Captain Henderson became acquainted during the poet's stay in Edinburgh where they were fellow lodgers in a house in St. James Square. Henderson had been a man of considerable wealth, but had blown his fortune on the high life and gambling. He certainly made a great impression upon Burns.

This poem is also a wonderful indication of the amount of wildlife to be found in Ayrshire in the eighteenth century, particularly interesting to hear Burns referring to bitterns —- long gone from Scotland.

But now his radiant course is run,
For Matthew's course was bright:
His soul was like the glorious sun,
A matchless, Heavenly light.

O Death, thou tyrant fell and bloody!
The meikle Devil wi' a woodie
Haurl thee hame to his black smiddie,
O'er hurcheon hides,
And like stock-fish come o'er his studdie
Wi' thy auld sides.

Death is compared to the Devil carrying a noose, and is told to drag itself over hedge-hog hides and be soundly beaten. *meikle* = large; *woodie* = noose; *haurl* = drag; *smiddie* = smithy; *hurcheon hide* = hedgehog skin; *studdie* = anvil; *stock-fish* = unsalted fish

He's gane, he's gane! he's frae us torn,
The ae best fellow e'er was born!
Thee, Matthew, Nature's sel' shall mourn,
By wood and wild,
Where, haply, Pity strays forlorn,
Frae man exil'd.

Matthew has gone from us forever, and all of nature will mourn his passing. *gane* = gone; *ae* = one

Ye hills, near neebors o' the starns,
That proudly cock your cresting cairns!
Ye cliffs, the haunts of sailing yearns,
Where Echo slumbers!
Come join ye, Nature's sturdiest bairns,
My wailing numbers.

The hills, the nearest neighbours of the stars, and the cliffs where eagles fly are called upon to join together in mourning. *neebors* = neighbours; *starns* = stars; *cresting cairns* = peaks; *yearns* = eagles; *bairns* = children

Mourn, ilka grove the cushat kens!
Ye hazly shaws and briery dens!
Ye burnies wimplin' down your glens,
Wi' toddlin' din,
Or foaming, strang, wi' hasty stens,
Frae lin to lin!

Now, every grove, hollow and wood, as well as the meandering stream, must mourn.
ilka = every; cushat = wood-pigeon; kens = knows; hazly shaws = wooded dells; burnies = streams; wimplin' = meandering; toddlin' din = tinkling sound; strang = strong; hasty stens = short bursts; frae = from; lin = waterfall

Mourn, little harebells o'er the lea;
Ye stately foxgloves, fair to see;
Ye woodbines, hanging bonilie,
In scented bowers;
Ye roses on your thorny tree,
The first o' flowers.

It is now the turn of the flora to be called to mourn.
bonilie =beautifully

At dawn, when every glassy blade
Droops with a diamond at his head;
At ev'n, when beans their fragrance shed,
I' the rustling gale;
Ye maukins, whiddin' thro' the glade,
Come join my wail!

At dawn, every dew-tipped blade of grass will bow its head, and in the evening the violet-white flowers will lose their fragrance in the wind. Even the hares are called to mourn.
maukins = hares; whiddin' = scudding

Mourn, ye wee songsters o' the wood;
Ye grouse that crap the heather bud;
Ye curlews, calling thro' a clud;
Ye whistling plover;
And mourn, ye whirring paitrick brood;
He's gane forever!

Now it is the turn of all songbirds and game-birds to mourn as he is gone forever.
crap = crop; clud = cloud; paitrick = partridge; gane = gone

Mourn, sooty coots and speckled teals;
Ye fisher herons, watching eels;
Ye duck and drake, wi' airy wheels
Circling the lake;
Ye bitterns, till the quagmire reels,
Rair for his sake!

Waterfowl are next, with a request for the bittern to roar in his memory.
rair = roar

Mourn, clam'ring craiks, at close o' day,
'Mang fields o' flow'ring clover, gay!
And when you wing your annual way
Frae our cauld shore,
Tell thae far warlds, wha lies in clay
Wham we deplore.

At dusk the corncrakes are called to mourn, and, when they leave for warmer climes, to tell the world who they have left buried behind them.

craiks = corncrakes; *cauld* = cold; *warlds* = worlds; *wha* = whom

Ye houlets, frae yer ivy bower
In some auld tree, or eldritch tower,
What time the moon, wi' silent glow'r
Sets up her horn,
Wail thro' the dreary midnight hour,
Till waukrife morn!

He begs the owls, perched in an old tree or haunted tower, to wail from the rise of the moon until the sleepless dawn.

houlets = owls; *eldritch* = haunted; *glow'r* = stare; *horn* = the crescent moon; *waukrife* = wakeful

O, rivers, forests, hills and plains!
Oft have ye heard my canty strains;
But now, what else for me remains
But tales of woe?
And frae my een the drapping rains
Maun ever flow.

The countryside has often heard him in joyful song, but now there is nothing left but the shedding of tears.

canty strains = joyful songs; *frae my een* = from my eyes; *drappin rains* = teardrops; *maun* = must

Mourn, Spring, thou darling of the year!
Ilk cowslip cup shall keep a tear;
Thou, Simmer, while each corny spear
Shoots up its head,
Thy gay, green, flowery tresses shear,
For him that's dead!

In Spring, that favourite season, cowslips will each catch a tear, and Summer should cut back on its beauty in respect of he who is dead.

ilk = each; *Simmer* = Summer

Thou, Autumn, wi' thy yellow hair,
In grief thy sallow mantle tear!
Thou, Winter, hurling thro' the air
The roaring blast,
Wide o'er the naked world declare
The worth we've lost!

Autumn should show its grief, while Winter can send her roaring winds round a desolate world to declare just what a worthy man we've lost.

Mourn him, thou Sun, great source of light!
Mourn, Empress of the silent night!
And you twinkling starnies bright,
My Matthew mourn!
For through your orbs he's ta'en his flight,
Ne'er to return.

The sun, the night, the stars should mourn, as he's never to return.

starnies = stars

O Henderson, the man! the brother!
And art thou gone, and gone forever?
And hast thou crost that unknown river,
Life's dreary bound?
Like thee, where shall I find another,
The world around?

Now that Henderson has gone into the next life, the distraught poet begs to know where he will find such a true friend anywhere in the world.

crost = crossed

Go to your sculpter'd tombs, ye Great,
In a' the tinsel trash o' state!
But by thy honest turf I'll wait,
Thou man o' worth!
And weep the ae best fellow's fate
E'er lay in earth!

Finally, the poet scorns those who are buried ceremoniously in great tombs, as the best man he ever knew lies under honest turf.

THE EPITAPH

Stop, passenger! my story's brief,
And truth I shall relate, man:
I tell nae common tale o' grief,
For Matthew was a great man.

If thou uncommon merit hast,
Yet spurn'd at Fortune's door, man;
A look of pity hither cast,
For Matthew was a poor man.

If thou a noble sodger art,
That passest by this grave, man;
There moulders here a gallant heart.
For Matthew was a brave man.

sodger = soldier

If thou on men, their works and ways,
Canst throw uncommon light, man;
Here lies wha weel had won thy praise,   *wha weel* = who well
For Matthew was a bright man.

If thou, at friendship's sacred ca',
Wad life itself resign, man;
Thy sympathetic tear maun fa',   *maun fa'* = must fall
For Matthew was a kind man,

If thou art staunch, without a stain,   *art staunch* = are trusty
Like the unchanging blue, man;
This was a kinsman o' thy ain,
For Matthew was a true man.

If thou hast wit, and fun, and fire,
And ne'er guid wine did fear, man;
This was thy billie, dam, and sire,   *billie, dam and sire* = brother, mother and
For Matthew was a queer man.   father

If onie whiggish, whingin' sot,   *onie whiggish, whingin' sot* = any prudish,
To blame poor Matthew dare, man;   complaining fool; *dool* = misery
May dool and sorrow be his lot!
For Matthew was a rare man.

A Mother's Lament

A short poem written to commemorate a young man who died while attending a military academy in Strasbourg. This gives an insight into the hardship Robert Burns endured. When he wrote these lines he was on horseback, having left home at 3am to ride 46 miles to his farm, while holding down a job as an excise officer at the same time.

Fate gave the word – the arrow sped,
And pierc'd my darling's heart,
And with him all the joys are fled
Life can to me impart.

By cruel hands the sapling drops,
In dust dishonor'd laid:
So fell the pride of all my hopes,
My age's future shade.

The mother linnet in the brake
Bewails her ravish'd young;
So I, for my lost darling's sake,
Lament the live-day long.

Death, oft I've fear'd thy fatal blow!
Now fond I bare my breast;
O, do thou kindly lay me low
With him I love at rest!

Auld Lang Syne

This is certainly the most famous song to come from the pen of Robert Burns, the inspiration coming from an old Scots ballad. Sung at gatherings throughout the world, particularly at the beginning of each New Year, 'Auld Lang Syne' has become the International Anthem of the world as people of all creeds and colours join hands in celebration. However, unfortunately very few people actually know the words they are singing, and fewer still understand the meaning and relevance of these words. I can only hope that when you have read the words and understand what Burns was really saying, that you will give the song the respect that it truly deserves.

Chorus
For auld lang syne, my dear,
For auld lang syne,
We'll tak a cup o' kindness yet,
For auld lang syne.

Should auld acquaintance be forgot,
And never brought to min'?
Should auld acquaintance be forgot,
And auld lang syne?

The message is that we should never forget old friends.
auld = old; *min'* = mind; *o' lang syne* = of long ago

And surely ye'll be your pint stowp!
And surely I'll be mine!
And we'll tak a cup o' kindness yet,
For auld lang syne.

Let us raise our glasses to toast their memories.
stowp =drinking vessel; *tak* = take

We twa hae run about the braes
And pu'd the gowans fine;
But we've wandered mony a weary fit
Sin' auld lang syne.

We played together, but grew up and went our independent ways.
twa = two; *hae* = have; *braes* = hills; *pu'd the gowans* = pulled the daisies; *mony a weary fit* = travelled great distances

We twa hae paidl't i ' the burn,
Frae mornin' sun till dine;
But seas between us braid hae roar'd
Sin' auld lang syne..

As children, we paddled in the stream, but since then have been separated by the width of the oceans.

paidl't 'i the burn paddled in the burn; *frae mornin' sun till dine* = all day; *braid* = broad

And there's a hand, my trusty fiere!
And gie's a hand o' thine!
And we'll tak a right guid-willie-waught,
For auld lang syne.

Shake my hand my trusted friend and let us share a goodwill drink to the memory of these happy days.

fiere = friend; *a right guid-willie waught* = a goodwill drink

A Sonnet Upon Sonnets

Burns poetry had always flowed in an unrestricted manner, with no great thought given to the length of the finished work, and the fourteen-line sonnet does not sit naturally with his style of writing. However he was aware of how popular William Shakespeare had made sonnets and this was Burns' first attempt to write one.

Fourteen, a sonneteer thy praises sings;
What magic myst'ries in that number lie!
Your hen hath fourteen eggs beneath her wings
That fourteen chickens to the roost may fly.
Fourteen full pounds the jockey's stone must be;
His age fourteen – a horse's prime is past,
Fourteen long hours too oft the Bard must fast;
Fourteen bright bumpers – bliss he ne'er must see!
Before fourteen, a dozen yields the strife
Before fourteen – e'en thirteen's strength is vain.
Fourteen good years – a woman gives us life;
Fourteen good men – we lose that life again.
What lucubrations can be more upon it?
Fourteen good measur'd verses make a sonnet.

The Blue-eyed Lassie

Another lovely short poem extolling the beauty of yet another beautiful young girl. On this occasion the subject was Jean Jaffray, the daughter of a minister, who was in her mid-teens when Burns was enchanted by her eyes.

I gaed a waefu' gate yestreen,
A gate I fear I'll dearly rue,
I gat my death frae twa sweet een,
Twa lovely een o' bonie blue!
'Twas not her golden ringlets bright,
Her lips like roses wat wi' dew,
Her heaving bosom, lily-white:
It was her een sae bonie blue.

gaed a waefu gate yestreen =
went a miserable route yesterday;
een = eyes; *wat* = wet

She talk'd, she smil'd, my heart she wyl'd,
She charm'd my soul I wist na how;
And ay the stound, the deadly wound,
Cam frae her een sae bonie blue.
But 'spare to speak, and spare to speed,'
She'll aiblins listen to my vow
Should she refuse, I'll lay my dead
To her twa een sae bonie blue.

wyl'd = beguiled; *stound* = thrill;
aiblins = perhaps

The Silver Tassie

An old Jacobite ballad rewritten by the Bard. A silver tassie is a silver goblet and the Ferry which is mentioned in the poem is Queensferry, now the site of the two bridges which span the Forth, a short distance from Edinburgh.

Go fetch to me a pint o' wine,
And fill it in a silver tassie;
That I may drink before I go,
A service to my bonie lassie:
The boat rocks at the Pier o' Leith,
Fu' loud the wind blaws frae the Ferry,
The ship rides by the Berwick-Law,
And I maun leave my bonie Mary.   *maun* = must

The trumpets sound, the banners fly,
The glittering spears are ranked ready,
The shouts o' war are heard afar,
The battle closes deep and bloody.
It's not the roar o' sea or shore,
Wad mak me longer wish to tarry;
Nor shouts o' war that's heard afar—
It's leaving thee, my bonie Mary!

Afton Water

This is a particularly lovely piece which is always a great favourite when sung at any Burns gathering. It refers to the River Afton, a small river, whose beauty obviously greatly enchanted the Bard.

Flow gently, sweet Afton, among thy green braes!   braes = banks
Flow gently, I'll sing thee a song in thy praise!
My Mary's asleep by thy murmuring stream –
Flow gently, sweet Afton, disturb not her dream!

Thou stock-dove whose echo resounds thro' the glen, stock dove = a wood pigeon
Ye wild whistling blackbirds in yon thorny den,   yon = yonder
Thou green-crested lapwing, thy screaming forbear,
I charge you, disturb not my slumbering Fair!

How lofty, sweet Afton, thy neighbouring hills,
Far mark'd with the courses of clear, winding rills! rills = small brooks; cot = cottage
There daily I wander, as noon rises high,
My flocks and my Mary's sweet cot in my eye

How pleasant thy banks and green valleys below,
Where wild in the woodlands the primroses blow,
There oft, as mild ev'ning weeps over the lea,
The sweet-scented birk shades my Mary and me   birk = birch

Thy crystal stream, Afton, how lovely it glides,
And winds by the cot where my Mary resides!
How wanton thy waters her snowy feet lave,   wanton = luxurious; lave = wash;
As, gathering sweet flowerets, she stems thy   flowerets = little flowers;   clear
   wave!   stems = checks

Flow gently, sweet Afton, among thy green braes,
Flow gently, sweet river, the theme of my lays!   lays = short narrative poems
My Mary's asleep by thy murmuring stream –
Flow gently, sweet Afton, disturb not her dream!

Kirk and State Excisemen

The Bard is trying to excuse himself for having taken on the duties of the Excise by pointing out that all sorts of people in all sorts of positions are also tax gatherers.

Quite a turn-around from his words in 'Scotch Drink' when he referred to Excisemen as 'curst horse-leeches' and hoped they would suffer Hell and Damnation. However, Burns was in dire straits financially at this juncture and had little choice in his mode of employment.

Ye men of wit and wealth, why all this sneering
'Gainst poor Excisemen? Give the cause a hearing.
What are your Landlord's rent-rolls? Taxing ledgers!
What Premiers? What ev'n Monarchs? Mighty Gaugers!
Nay, what are Priests (those seemingly godly wise-men)?
What are they, pray, but Spiritual Excisemen!

The Wounded Hare

Once again we hear Burns tell of his sympathy towards the plight of a wild creature. In this instance he recalls hearing a shot while out working in the fields at Ellisland, and his anger when shortly afterwards, he sees a badly injured hare limp by. One can imagine his tears of outrage over such an act of violence and destruction.

Inhuman man! curse on thy barb'rous art,
And blasted be thy murder-aiming eye;
May never pity soothe thee with a sigh
Nor never pleasure glad thy cruel heart.

Go live, poor wanderer of the wood and field,
The bitter little that of life remains!
No more the thickening brakes and verdant plains
To thee shall home, or food, or pastime yield.

Seek, mangled wretch, some place of wonted rest,
No more of rest, but now thy dying bed!
The sheltering rushes whistling o'er thy head,
The cold earth with thy bloody bosom prest.

Oft as by winding Nith I, musing, wait
The sober eve, or hail the cheerful dawn,
I'll miss thee sporting o'er the dewy lawn,
And curse the ruffian's aim, and mourn thy
    hapless fate.

The Kirk's Alarm

This satirical poem was written to mock several of Burns' old adversaries in the ministry. A good friend of his, a New-Licht preacher, the Rev. William McGill, was castigated by the General Assembly for having written an essay, 'The Death of Jesus Christ', which did not conform to the church's teachings. McGill was forced to make a grovelling apology to the Presbytery and and denounce his own work. Burns recognised that the old guard, who had been the cause of his own public humiliation, were behind this and attacked them in verse.

Orthodox! orthodox!
Wha believe in John Knox—
Let me sound an alarm to your conscience:
A heretic blast
Has been heard i' the Wast,
That what is not sense must be nonsense—
Orthodox!
That what is not sense must be nonsense.

Burns mocks the clergy for their closed minds and inability to understand any view which differs from their own narrow ideas on religion.
Wast = West

Doctor Mac! Doctor Mac!
You should stretch on a rack,
To strike wicked Writers wi' terror:
To join Faith and Sense
Upon onie pretence,
Was heretic, damnable error.
Doctor Mac!
Twas heretic, damnable error.

McGill will be castigated by the church hierarchy if his revolutionary ideas which encompass common sense and faith are not curbed.

Town of Ayr! Town of Ayr!
It was rash I declare,
To meddle wi' mischief a-brewing:
Provost John is still deaf
To the Church's relief,
And Orator Bob is its ruin—
Town of Ayr!
And orator Bob is its ruin.

John Ballantyne, the provost of Ayr, and Robert Aiken were friends of Burns who also stood against the tyranny of the old church teachings.

D'rymple mild! D'rymple mild
Tho' your heart's like a child!
An' your life like the new-driven snaw,
Yet that winna save ye,
Auld Satan must have ye,
For preaching that three's ane an' twa—
D'rymple mild!
For preaching that three's ane an' twa.

William Dalrymple was the man who baptised Burns, and Burns warns him that his faultless life will fail to save him if he continues to be so straightforward and honest in his teachings.

Calvin's sons! Calvin's sons!
Seize your sp'ritual guns
Ammunition you can never need;
Your hearts are the stuff
Will be powther enough,
And your skulls are storehouses o' lead.
Calvin's sons!
Your skulls are storehouses o' lead.

The Calvinists are vividly described here as unthinking people without love or compassion.

powther = powder

Rumble John! Rumble John!
Mount the steps with a groan,
Cry, 'The Book is wi' heresy cramm'd';
Then lug out your ladle,
Deal brimstone like adle,
And roar ev'ry note of the damn'd—
Rumble John!
And roar ev'ry note of the damn'd.

Rev 'Black Jock' Russell is described as one who preaches with the threat of fire and brimstone to the sinners.

adle = cow's urine

Simper James! Simper James!
Leave the fair Killie dames—
There's a holier chase in your view:
I'll lay on your head
That the pack you'll soon lead,
For puppies like you there's but few—
Simper James!
For puppies like you there's but few.

Rev James McKinlay is portrayed as being more interested in the female sex than in the church, but Burns has has no doubt that he will join the pack in pursuit of McGill.

Singet Sawnie! Singet Sawnie,
Are ye herdin the penny,
Unconscious what evils await?
Wi' a jump, yell and howl!
Alarm ev'ry soul,
For the Foul Fiend is just at your gate,
Singet Sawnie!
The Foul Fiend is just at your gate.

Rev Alexander Moodie, already featured in The Twa Herds, is also painted as a minister who terrifies his congregation with his wild sermonising.

Daddie Auld! Daddie Auld!
There's a tod in the fauld,
A tod meikle waur than the clerk;
Tho ye do little skaith,
Ye'll be in at the death,
And gif ye canna bite, ye may bark,
Daddie Auld!
For gif ye canna bite, ye may bark.

Rev William Auld, an old adversary of the Bard, is warned that there is a fox in the fold who might tempt away his congregation. Burns has no doubt that Auld will be in the kill although he will be at the back shouting.

tod = fox; *skaith* = damage; *gif* = if

Jamie Goose! Jamie Goose!
Ye hae made but toom roose,
In hunting the wicked Lieutenant;
But the Doctor's your mark,
For the Lord's haly ark,
He has cooper'd an' ca'd a wrang pin in't.
Jamie Goose!
He has cooper'd an' ca'd a wrang pin in't.

Rev James Young is accused of producing nothing but empty rhetoric in his preaching, but will no doubt pursue McGill with the others as McGill has introduced doubt into their preaching.

cooper'd an' ca'd a wrang pin in't = knocked a hole in it

Davie Rant! Davie Rant!
Wi' a face like a saunt,
And a heart that wad poison a hog,
Raise an impudent roar,
Like a breaker lee-shore,
Or the kirk will be tint in a bog.
Davie Rant!
Or the kirk will be tint in a bog.

Rev David Grant may have a saintly appearance but is rotten through and through. Another who preaches Hell and damnation.

saunt = saint; *tint* = lost

Poet Willie! Poet Willie!
Gie the Doctor a volley,
Wi' your 'Liberty Chain' and your wit;
O'er Pegasus' side
Ye ne'er laid a stride,
Ye but smelt, man, the place where he shit,
Poet Willie!
Ye but smelt, man, the place where he shit.

Rev William Peebles is obviously not a man admired by Burns as he writes a highly insulting verse to describe his lack of charity.

Andro Gowk! Andro Gowk!
Ye may slander the Book,
An' the Book no the waur, let me tell ye;
Ye are rich, an' look big,
But lay by hat an' wig,
An' ye'll hae a calf's head o' sma' value,
Andro Gowk!
Ye'll hae a calf's head o' sma' value.

Andrew Mitchell is described as being rich and vain, but he at least laughed at Burns' description of him and admitted it may have been correct.

Gowk = fool; *waur* = worse

Barr Steenie! Barr Steenie!
What mean ye? What mean ye?
If ye meddle nae mair wi' the matter,
Ye may hae some pretence,
To havins and sense,
Wi' people wha ken ye nae better,
Barr Steenie!
Wi' people wha ken ye nae better.

Rev Stephen Young is only able to convince those who do not know him that he is a mannerly and sensible person.

havins = manners

Irvine-side! Irvine-side!
Wi' your turkey-cock pride
Of manhhood but sma' is your share:
Ye've the figure 'tis true,
Ev'n your faes maun allow.
An' your friends daurna say ye hae mair,
Irvine-side!
Your friends daurna say ye hae mair.

Rev George Smith is a vain man, but Burns sees him as being a man with no stature.

Muirland Jock! Muirland Jock!
Whom the Lord gave a stock
Wad act up a tinker in brass;
If ill-manners were wit,
There's no mortal so fit
To prove the poor Doctor an ass,
Muirland Jock!
To prove the poor Doctor an ass.

John Sheppard considered himself to be a wit, but Burns saw him as no more than a foul-mouthed lout, no better than a tinker.

Holy Will! Holy Will!
There was wit i' your skull,
When ye pilfer'd the alms o' the poor;
The timmer is scant
When ye're taen for a saunt,
Wha should swing in a rape for an hour,
Holy Will!
Ye should swing in a rape for an hour.

William Fisher, better known to us as Holy Willie, is described as being a thieving scoundrel who deserves to be hanged for his sins.

timmer = wood, material; *rape* = rope

Poet Burns! Poet Burns!
Wi' your priest-skelpin turns,
Why desert ye your auld native shire?
Your Muse is a gypsy,
Yet were she e'en tipsy,
She could ca' us nae waur than we are—
Poet Burns!
Ye could ca' us nae waur than we are.

Burns is obviously pleased with his priest-bashing, but thinks even if his Muse was drunk she could not describe them as being worse than they really are.

skelpin = hitting; *nae waur* = no worse

PRESENTATION STANZAS
TO CORRESPONDENTS

Afton's Laird! Afton's Laird,
When your pen can be spared,
A copy of this I bequeath,
On the same sicker score
As I mentioned before,
To that trusty auld worthy, Clackleith—
Afton's Laird!
To that trusty auld worthy Clackleith.

John Logan, a laird and friend of Burns;
Clackleith, a neighbour of Logan's.

Factor John! Factor John!
Whom the Lord made alone,
And ne'er made anither thy peer,
Thy poor servant, the Bard,
In respectful regard,
He presents thee this token sincere,
Factor John!
He presents thee this token sincere.

Some doubt whether this refers to John
Murdo or John Kennedy

227

Beware of Bonie Ann

This poem was dedicated to a young lady from Edinburgh, named Ann Masterton. Ann's father was a schoolmaster and composer and was a friend of Robert Burns.

It is certainly a poem which any young lass would feel flattered to have written in her honour, but as we read the various tributes which Burns has composed on behalf of the many other young ladies who have caught his eye, we must question just how much poetic licence the Bard allowed himself – or was eighteenth-century Scotland really awash with flawless beauties?

Ye gallants bright, I rede you right,
Beware o' bonie Ann!
Her comely face sae fu' o' grace,
Your heart she will trepan,
Her een sae bright, like stars by night,
Her skin is like the swan;
Sae jimply lac'd her genty waist,
That sweetly ye might span.

Youth, Grace, and Love, attendant move,
And Pleasure leads the van;
In a' their charms, and conquering arms,
They wait on bonie Ann
The captive bands may chain the hands,
But Love enslaves the man:
Ye gallants braw, I rede you a',
Beware o' bonie Ann!

gallant = a splendid man; *rede* = advise;
bonie = beautiful; *comely* = pleasing;
sae fu' o' = so full of; *trepan* = snare;
een = eyes; *jimply lac'd* = neatly corseted;
genty = slender

van = those who lead the way

John Anderson, My Jo

This beautiful simple old song tells the story of two people who have grown old together. It did not start off this way and it was in fact an old, bawdy ballad that the Bard breathed upon and revitalised.

John Anderson, my jo, John,
When we were first acquent;
Your locks were like the raven,
Your bonie brow was brent;
But now your brow is beld, John,
Your locks are like the snaw;
But blessings on your frosty pow,
John Anderson, my jo.

The wife is reminding her husband that when they first met, his hair was as black as a raven and his brow was smooth and unlined. However, now he is almost bald and his few remaining locks are as white as snow.

jo = sweetheart; *acquent* = acquainted; *locks* = hair; *brent* = smooth; *beld* = bald; *snaw* = snow; *frosty pow* = white head

John Anderson, my jo, John,
We clamb the hill thegither;
And mony a cantie day, John,
We've had wi' ane anither;.
Now we maun totter down, John,
And hand in hand we'll go,
And sleep thegither at the foot,
John Anderson, my jo!

They have gone through life together and shared many happy days. Now as they approach the end of their lives, they still have each other.

clamb = climbed; *thegither* = together; *mony* = many; *cantie* = cheerful; *wi' ane anither* = with one another; *maun* = must; *totter* = stagger

Scots Prologue for Mrs Sutherland

ON HER BENEFIT-NIGHT AT THE THEATRE, DUMFRIES, MARCH 3rd, 1790

Burns became involved with a new theatre that was being built in Dumfries around 1790, and he wrote the following lines to the wife of the proprietor. His irritation at the lack of Scottish material for theatregoers is evident.

What needs this din about the
    town o' Lon'on?
How this new play an' that new song is comin'?
Why is outlandish stuff sae meikle courted?
Does nonsense mend, like brandy when
    imported?
Is there nae poet, burning keen for fame,
Will bauldly try to gie us plays at hame?
For comedy abroad he need na toil:
A knave and fool are plants of ev'ry soil.
Nor need to stray as far as Rome or Greece
To gather matter for a serious piece:
There's themes enow in Caledonian story
Would shew the tragic Muse in a' her glory.

In the opinion of Burns, there is little merit in London's influence upon the arts in Scotland. Rubbish will always be rubbish. Surely there is a writer who can recognise that it is unnecessary to look beyond the history of Scotland to find material for a serious drama to equal any Greek or Roman tragedy.

sae meikle = so greatly; *mend* = improve; *bauldly* = boldly; *enow* = enough

Is there no daring Bard will rise and tell
How glorious Wallace stood, how hapless fell?
Where are the Muses fled, that should
    produce
A drama worthy o' the name o' Bruce?
How on this spot, he first unsheath'd the sword
'Gainst mighty England and her guilty lord,
And after monie a bloody, deathless doing,
Wrench'd his dear country from the
    jaws of Ruin!
O! for a Shakespeare, or an Otway scene
To paint he lovely, hapless Scottish Queen!

Is there not a writer who can describe the struggles and dreadful death that became William Wallace, are there no playwrights who can tell of Bruce's great battles against the English tyrant? Oh, for a Scottish Shakespeare who would write of the tribulations which befell Mary Queen of Scots.

Otway = a seventeenth-century dramatist

Vain ev'n th' omnipotence of female charms
'Gainst headlong, ruthless, mad
    Rebellion's arms.
She fell, but fell with spirit truly Roman.
To glut that direst foe, — a vengeful woman;
A woman (tho' the phrase may seem uncivil),
As able — and as wicked as the Devil!
One Douglas lives in Home's immortal page,
But Douglases were heroes every age:
And tho' your fathers, prodigal of life,
A Douglas followed to the martial strife.
Perhaps, if bowls row right, and
    Right succeeds,
Ye may yet follow where a Douglas leads!

Mary was the victim of the evil and jealous Elizabeth I of England, and was condemned to be beheaded by this woman whose cruelty could equal that of the Devil Himself.

Although the Douglases have fought for generations on the side of freedom for Scotland, only one is immortalised in print, yet the opportunity may arise to follow a Douglas in the battle for freedom.

omnipotence = unlimited power; *glut* = satiate; *Home* = Earls of Home, an old border family; *row* = roll

As ye have generous done, if a' the land
Would take the Muses servants by the hand;
Not only hear, but patronise, befriend them,
And where ye justly can commend,
    commend them;
And aiblins, when they winna stand the test,
Wink hard, and say:"The folks hae
    done their best!"
Would a' the land do this, then I'll be caition,
Ye'll soon hae poets o' the Scottish nation
Will gar Fame blaw until her trumpet crack,
And warsle Time, an' lay him on his back!

If only others would follow the example of Mrs Sutherland and encourage writers through patronage and friendship, and understand that not all will attain perfection, then so many poets and writers will emerge from Scotland that the trumpet of fame will blow until it breaks.

aiblins = perhaps; *caition* = guarantee; *gar* = make; *warsle* = wrestle

For us and for our stage, should onie spier:—
'Whase aught thae chiels maks a' this
    bustle here?"
My best leg foremost, I'll set up my brow:—
We have the honour to belong to you!
We're your ain bairns, e'en guide us as ye like,
But like good mothers, shore before
    you strike;
And gratefu' still, I trust ye'll ever find us,
For gen'rous patronage, and meikle kindness
We've got frae a' professions, sorts an' ranks;
God help us! We're but poor
————ye'se get but thanks!

Should anyone ask who these fellows creating such a stir upon the stage are, Burns will bow and tell that we are your children, to be guided by you, but if they are to criticised, then do it gently. You will find them ever grateful for your patronage, but as they have no money, can only repay you with their grateful thanks.

spier = ask; *whase aught thae chiels maks a' this bustle here* = who owns these people making all this activity here; *shore* = threaten; *meikle* = great, *setts* = groups

On the Birth of a Posthumous Child

BORN IN PECULIAR CIRCUMSTANCES OF FAMILY DISTRESS

In 1790 a Swiss-born gentleman named James Henri died suddenly leaving behind a young widow, Susan Dunlop, in an advanced state of pregnancy. The Bard was extremely fond of both Susan and her mother and when Susan gave birth to a son, he wrote the following lines to the new-born boy, sending them to Mrs Dunlop, Senior.

This poem displays clearly how Burns was able to transfer tragedy into a thing of beauty and he once again reveals his high level of sensitivity and compassion.

Sweet flow'ret, pledge o' meikle love,
And ward o' monie a prayer,
What heart o' stane wad thou na move,
Sae helpless, sweet and fair!

Flow'ret = little flower; *pledge o'* = result of;
meikle = great; *monie* = many; *stane* = stone

November hirples o'er the lea,
Chill, on thy lovely form;
And gane, alas! the shelt'ring tree,
Should shield thee frae the storm.

hirples = limps; *lea* = meadow; *gane* = gone

May He who gives the rain to pour,
And wings the blast to blaw,
Protect thee frae the driving show'r
The bitter frost and snaw!

blast to blaw = wind to blow;
frae = from; *snaw* = snow

May He, the friend of Woe and Want,
Who heals life's various stounds,
Protect and guard the mother plant
And heal her cruel wounds!

stounds = times of trouble

But late she flourish'd, rooted fast,
Fair on the summer morn;
Now, feebly bends she, in the blast,
Unshelter'd and forlorn

Blest by thy bloom, thy lovely gem,   *stem* = branch forth, *deck* = grace
Unscath'd by ruffian hand!
And from thee many a parent stem
Arise to deck our land!

The Gowden Locks of Anna

At first glance it would appear that this song is yet another of the Bard's works intended to flatter one of his lady loves. However, written around 1790, it actually relates to a very significant episode in his life.

Although married to Jean Armour at the time, Burns was having an affair with Anne Park, the niece of the landlady of the Globe Inn in Dumfries. This affair ended in Anne giving birth to a daughter, leaving Burns to present his wife with his illegitimate child a mere nine days before she herself gave birth to a son. Jean Armour must have been a truly remarkable woman, as she accepted young Elizabeth into her family and raised her as her own child. The words need no explanation. They speak clearly of Burns' feelings at the time.

Yestreen I had a pint o' wine,
A place where body saw na;
Yestreen lay on this breast o' mine
The gowden locks of Anna.
The hungry Jew in wilderness
Rejoicing o'er his manna,
Was naething to my hiney bliss
Upon the lips of Anna.

Ye Monarchs tak the East and West,
Frae Indus to Savannah!
Gie me within my straining grasp
The melting form of Anna.
There I'll despise Imperial charms,
An Empress or Sultana,
While dying raptures in her arms
I give and take with Anna!

Yestreen = yesterday; *body saw na* = nobody saw anything; *gowden* = golden; *manna* = food of the Israelites in the wilderness; *naething* = nothing; *hiney* = honey

Awa, thou flaunting God o' Day!
Awa, thou pale Diana!
Ilk Star gae hide thy twinkling ray!
When I'm to meet my Anna!
Come in thy raven plumage, Night;
Sun, Moon and Stars withdrawn a';
And bring an angel pen to write
My transports wi' my Anna!

Diana = the moon-goddess; *ilk* = each;
transports = ecstasies

Postscript

The Kirk and State may join and tell,
To do sic things I mauna;
The Kirk and State can go to hell,
And I'll gae to my Anna.
She is the sunshine o' my e'e,
To live but her I canna;
Had I on earth but wishes three,
The first should be my Anna.

kirk = church; *sic* = such; *mauna* = must
not; *to live but her I canna* = I cannot live
without her

Lament of Mary Queen of Scots

ON THE APPROACH OF SPRING

Burns considered Mary Queen of Scots to be a truly tragic heroine, worthy of a place of honour in Scottish history. He imagines her here, imprisoned in Fotheringay Castle, awaiting her execution at the hands of Queen Elizabeth I of England.

Now Nature hangs her mantle green
On every blooming tree,
And spreads her sheets o' daisies white
Out o'er the grassy lea:
Now Phoebus cheers the crystal streams,
And glads the azure skies:
But nought can glad the weary wight
That fast in durance lies.

The sun may be shining down through clear blue skies but nothing can lighten the despair which is weighing Mary down.

Now laverocks wake the merry morn,
Aloft on dewy wing;
The merle, in his noontide bow'r,
Makes woodland echoes ring;
The mavis wild wi' monie a note,
Sings drowsy day to rest:
In love and freedom they rejoice,
Wi' care nor thrall opprest.

She envies the birds as they sing with no care to burden them.
laverocks = larks; *merle* = hawk

Now blooms the lily by the bank,
The primrose down the brae,
The hawthorn's budding in the glen,
And milk-white is the slae:
The meanest hind in fair Scotland
May rove their sweets amang;
But I, the Queen of a' Scotland,
Maun lie in prison strang.

The flowers may be blooming and the deer running freely, but she must remain in prison.
slae = sloe; *maun* = must; *strang* = strong

I was the Queen o' bonie France,
Where happy I hae been;
Fu' lightly rase I in the morn,
As blythe lay down at e'en:
An' I'm the sov'reign of Scotland,
And monie a traitor there;
Yet here I lie in foreign bands,
And never-ending care.

She was happy in France and could relax without worries, but her foray into Scotland has seen her betrayed and resulted in her being held prisoner in England.

But as for thee, thou false woman,
My sister and my fae,
Grim vengeance, yet, shall whet a sword
That thro' thy soul shall gae!
The weeping blood in woman's breast
Was never known to thee;
Nor th' balm that drops on wounds of woe
Frae woman's pitying e'e.

Elizabet Tudor is a woman with no mercy in her soul and Mary hopes that she will suffer for her cruelty.

My son! My son! may kinder stars
Upon thy fortune shine;
And may these pleasures gild thy reign,
That ne'er would blink on mine!
God keep thee frae thy mother's faes,
Or turn their hearts to thee;
And where thou meet'st thy mother's friend,
Remember him for me!

She hopes that her son, James VI of Scotland, and I of England, will live to have a much happier life than she, and asks him to remember her to the Earl of Bothwell who she married in 1567, should they meet. Bothwell had fled the country and was held prisoner in Denmark until his death.

O! soon, to me, may summer-suns
Nae mair light up the morn!
Nae mair to me, the autumn winds
Wave o'er the yellow corn!
And in the narrow house of death,
Let winter round me rave;
And the next flowers, that deck the spring,
Bloom on my peaceful grave.

She laments that she will never again enjoy the beauties of nature as her death is imminent.

The Selkirk Grace

This is by far the most famous of several graces ascribed to Burns, and is universally given at the start of the traditional Burns' Suppers held in memory of the Bard on the 25th of January each year. Burns was in the presence of the Earl of Selkirk when he stood up and delivered this wonderful piece with no prior preparation.

The following lines are how Burns actually gave the grace, but one will seldom hear it recited in this manner as the temptation to deliver it in the vernacular is now the norm.

Some have meat and cannot eat,
Some cannot eat that want it;
But we have meat and we can eat,
Sae let the Lord be thankit.

The more commonly used version is as follows.

Some hae meat and canna eat,
And some wad eat that want it.
But we hae meat and we can eat,
Sae let the Lord be thankit.

Tam O' Shanter

Here, without doubt, is one of the favourites from the poems of Robert Burns. It features both dark humour and nightmarish images. It tells the story of a country man whose great pleasure in life is drinking with his friends at the local hostelry and goes on to relate what happens one dreadful night when he comes across Satan, with his warlocks and witches, cavorting in wild revelry in a graveyard. All is going well until Tam gets so carried away with the excitement that the creatures of evil become aware that they are being watched and then all hell breaks loose, and Tam o' Shanter is forced to flee for his very life on his old horse. They must cross the river before they are caught, as the creatures cannot cross running water.

Cutty Sark probably means to most readers the name of a well-known brand of Scotch or perhaps the name of the magnificent old tea-clipper which is permanently moored in a dry-dock in Greenwich, England. However, Burns introduces the original meaning when he describes the witches dancing in their 'cutty sarks' or underwear (a 'sark' is generally taken to be a shift or slip or petticoat, and a 'cutty sark' a short version of that garment)..
Author's note: Should you ever be in the vicinity of Greenwich, go and take a look at the *Cutty Sark*. There you will see Nannie, the ship's figurehead, dressed in her cutty sark, and yes, that is poor old Meg's tail she is still clutching.

When chapman billies leave the street,
And drouthy neebors, neebors meet;
As market-days are wearing late
 An' folks begin to tak the gate;
While we sit bousing at the nappy,
An' getting fou and unco happy,
We think na on the lang Scots miles,
The mosses, waters, slaps and styles,
That lie between us and our hame,
Whare sits our sulky, sullen dame,
Gathering her brows like gathering storm,
Nursing her wrath to keep it warm.

The tale opens in the town of Ayr on market day. It is getting late, and the pedlars are leaving and the stallholders are closing. But we find Tam in the local alehouse, having a good time and not even thinking about the long journey home to face an angry wife.
drouthy = thirsty; *neebors* = neighbours /friends; *chapman* = pedlar; *billies* = fellows; *tak the gate* = leave; *bousing at the nappy* = drinking strong ale; *fou* = tipsy; *unco* = very; *slaps* = gaps in fences

This truth fand honest Tam o' Shanter,
As he frae Ayr ae night did canter:
(Auld Ayr, wham ne'er a town surpasses,
For honest men and bonie lasses.)

fand = found; *frae* = from; *wham* = whom

O Tam! had'st thou but been sae wise,
As ta'en thy ain wife Kate's advice!
She tauld thee weel thou was a skellum
A blethering, blustering, drunken blellum;
That frae November till October,
Ae market-day thou was nae sober;
That ilka melder wi' the miller
Thou sat as lang as thou had siller;
That ev'ry naig was ca'd a shoe on
The smith and thee gat roarin fou on;
That at the Lord's house, even on Sunday,
Thou drank wi' Kirkton Jean till Monday.
She prophesied that, late or soon,
Thou would be found, deep drown'd in Doon,
Or catch'd wi' warlocks in the mirk
By Alloways' auld haunted kirk.

Tam's wife, Kate, had told him that he was a good-for-nothing loud-mouth who had never been sober on market-day throughout the year; she told him that he would drink as long as he had money – getting drunk with the miller and with the blacksmith – and even on a Sunday, with Kirkton Jean. She warned him that, one of those days, sooner or later, he would be found drowned in the River Doon, or caught in the dark by the demons that lurked around the old haunted church in Alloway. *tauld* = told; *weel* – well; *skellum* = scoundrel; *bletherin'* = talking nonsense; *blellum* = a babbler; *ilka melder* = every grinding day at the mill; *lang* = long; *siller* = money; *naig* = a horse; *ca'd a shoe on* = put a horseshoe on; *gat roarin fou* = got drunk; *warlocks* = demons; *mirk* = dark; *kirk* =church

Ah! gentle dames, it gars me greet
To think how monie counsels sweet,
How monie lengthen'd, sage advices
The husband frae the wife despises!

But sad to say, Tam, like so many other husbands, paid no attention to his wife's advice.
gars me greet = makes me cry; *monie* = many

But to our tale: – Ae market-night
Tam had got planted unco right,
Fast by an ingle, bleezing finely,
Wi' reaming swats, that drank divinely;
And at his elbow, Souter Johnie,
His ancient, trusty, drouthy cronie:
Tam lo'ed him like a vera brither,
They had been fou for weeks thegither.
The night drave on wi' sangs and clatter;
And ay the ale was growing better:
The landlady and Tam grew gracious,
Wi' favours, secret, sweet and precious:
The Souter tauld his queerest stories;
The Landlord's laugh was ready chorus:
The storm without might rair and rustle,
Tam did na mind the storm a whistle

On this particular night Tam was in his element – he was sitting by the blazing fire drinking foaming pints of beer that tasted better with each drink. By his side was Souter Johnie, the cobbler. They were old friends and drinking buddies and got drunk together every week. They passed the evening with songs and small-talk and while Tam flirted with the landlady, Souter Johnie had the landlord laughing at his stories. All this time the storm outside was raging, but Tam paid it no attention.

planted unco right = made himself comfortable; *fast by an ingle* = beside a fireplace; *bleezing* = blazing; *reaming swats* = foaming ale; *souter* = cobbler; *cronie* = comrade; *lo'ed* = loved; *vera* = very; *brither* = brother; *thegitter* = together; *drave on* = rolled on; *sangs and clatter* = songs and loud chatter; *rair* = roar

Care, mad to see a man sae happy,:
E'en drown'd himself amang the nappy:
As bees flee hame wi' lades o' treasure,
The minutes wing'd their way wi' pleasure:
Kings may be blest, but Tam was glorious,
O'er a' the ills o' life victorious!

Oh life felt just so good for Tam that night. As the time flew by, he was gloriously happy.

sae = so; *hame* = home; *lades* = loads

But pleasures are like poppies spread:
You seize the flow'r, its bloom is shed;
Or like the snow falls in the river,
A moment white – then melts for ever;
Or like the borealis race,
That flit ere you can point their place;
Or like the rainbow's lovely form
Evanishing amid the storm
Nae man can tether time or tide;.
The hour approaches Tam maun ride:
That hour, o' night's black arch the key-stane,
That dreary hour he mounts his beast in;
And sic a night he taks the road in,
As ne'er poor sinner was abroad in.

In the first eight lines of this verse, Burns uses poetry which is incredibly beautiful and moving to demonstrate that all good things must come to an end.

It was now time for Tam to get on his horse and head for home through the terrible storm.

flow'r = flower; *borealis race* = the aurora borealis or northern lights; *flit ere* =move before; *maun* = must; *key-stane* = key-one; *sic* = such; *taks* = takes

The wind blew as 'twad blawn its last;
The rattling showers rose on the blast;
The speedy gleams the darkness swallow'd
Loud, deep, and lang the thunder bellow'd:
That night, a child might understand,
The Deil had business on his hand.

This was the kind of night when even a child might be aware that the devil was around.

twad blawn = was blowing; *Deil* = Devil

Weel mounted on his gray mare, Meg,
A better never lifted leg.
Tam skelpit on thro' dub and mire,
Despising wind, and rain, and fire;
Whiles holding fast his guid blue bonnet,
Whiles crooning o'er some auld Scots sonnet,
Whiles glow'ring round wi' prudent cares,
Lest bogles catch him unawares:
Kirk-Alloway was drawing nigh,
Whare ghaists and houlets nightly cry.

Mounted on his grey mare, Meg, Tam rode on through the storm, holding onto his hat and all the time singing to himself to bolster his courage as he kept glancing about him, just in case some goblin would catch him by surprise. But he was getting close to the church at Alloway, where he knew that the nights were filled with the cries of ghosts and owls.

ghaists and houlets = ghosts and owls; *meare* = mare; *skelpit on* = hurried on; *thro' dub and mire* = through puddles and mud

By this time he was cross the ford,
Whare in the snaw the chapman smoor'd;
And past the birks and meikle stane,
Whare drunken Charlie brak's neck-bane;
And thro' the whins, and by the cairn,
 Whare hunters fand the murder'd bairn;
And near the thorn, aboon the well,
Whare Mungo's mither hang'd hersel'.
Before him Doon pours all his floods;
The doubling storm roars thro' the woods;
The lightnings flash from pole to pole,
Near and more near the thunders roll:
When, glimmering thro' the groaning trees,
Kirk-Alloway seem'd in a bleeze,
Thro' ilka bore the beams were glancing,
And loud resounded mirth and dancing.

Now he was at the scary part of his journey. After he crossed the ford he was in the area where several frightening events had taken place: where a pedlar had been smothered in the snow; where drunken Charlie had fallen and broken his neck at the big stone; where some hunters had found the body of a murdered child; where Mungo's mother had hanged herself. And all the time the storm raged on! Tam could see that the church was brightly lit and there was the sound of laughter and dancing.

whare = where; *snaw* = snow; *chapman;* = pedlar; *smoor'd* = smothered; *birks* = birch trees; *meikle stane* = big stone; *brak's neck-bane;* = broke his neck; *whins* = gorse; *cairn* = a heap of stones; *fand* = found; *bairn* = child; *aboon* = above; *bleeze* = blaze; *thro' ilka bore* = through the trees

Inspiring bold John Barleycorn,
What dangers thou canst make us scorn!
Wi' tipenny, we fear nae evil;
Wi' usquabae, we'll face the Devil!
The swats sae reamed in Tammie's noddle,

It is amazing the courage that drinking can give. With a few beers we fear no evil and add some whisky and we will take on the Devil himself. And so, Tam, his brain addled by his night of imbibing, didn't give a farthing for what he might come across.

Fair play, he car'd na deils a boddle.
But Maggie stood, right sair astonish'd,
Till, by the heel and hand admonished,
She ventur'd forward on the light;
And, vow! Tam saw an unco sight!

But such was not the case with Meg and she had to be given a kick to get her going again. And what a picture they saw!

John Barleycorn = alchohol; *tippenny* = ale; *usquabae* = whisky; *noddle* = head; *he car'd na deils a boddle* = he did not care a farthing for the devils; *sair* = sore; *unco* = strange

Warlocks and witches in a dance:
Nae cotillion brent new frae France,
But hornpipes, jigs, strathspeys, and reels,
Put life and mettle in their heels.
A winnock-bunker in the east,
There sat Auld Nick, in shape o' beast;
A touzie tyke, black, grim, and large,
To gie them music was his charge:

The goblins and witches were dancing –
not a decorous French cotillion but wild
Scottish reels and strathspeys. And there,
in a window-seat in the church, was Satan
himself – he was playing the music for his
terrible horde.

warlocks = demons; brent = brand; winnock-
bunker = window-seat; auld Nick = Satan;
touzie tyke = unkempt dog

He screw'd the pipes and gart them skirl,
Till roof and rafters a' did dirl.
Coffins stood round, like open presses,
That shaw'd the dead in their last dresses;
And by some devilish cantraip slight,
Each in its cauld hand held a light:
By which heroic Tam was able
To note upon the haly table,
A murderer's banes, in gibbet-airns;
Twa span-lang, wee, unchristen'd bairns;
A thief, new-cutted frae a rape –
Wi' his last gasp his gab did gape;
Five tomahawks, wi' bluid red-rusted;
Five scymitars, wi' murder crusted;
A garter which a babe had strangled;
A knife a father's throat had mangled –
Whom his ain son o' life bereft –
The grey-hairs yet stack to the heft;
Three lawyers' tongues, turned inside-out
Wi' lies seamed like a beggar's clout;
Three priests' hearts, rotten, black as muck,
Lay stinking, vile in every neuk.
Wi' mair of horrible and awefu',
Which even to name wad be unlawfu'.

The scene was horrific. While Satan was
making the rafters ring with his pipes,
there were coffins standing around, open
like cupboards and in each one was a
corpse with a candle in its cold hand. On
the altar there were some dreadful relics of
unspeakable events that had taken place –
including hangings and murders!

gart = made; dirl = vibrate; presses =
cupboards; shaw'd = showed; devilish
cantraip sleight = black magic; cauld han' =
cold hand; haly table = altar; banes = bones;
gibbet-airns = gibbet irons; twa span-lang,
wee unchristen'd bairns = two tiny babies;
new cutted frae a rape = just cut down from
a hangman's noose; gab did gape = mouth
wide open; bluid = blood; heft = handle;
clout = ragged clothes; neuk = nook and
cranny

As Tammie glowr'd, amaz'd and curious,
The mirth and fun grew fast and furious;
The piper loud and louder blew,
The dancers quick and quicker flew,
They reel'd, they set, they cross'd, they deekit,
Till ilka carlin swat and reekit,
And coost her duddies to the wark,
And linket at it in her sark!

As Tam stared in fascination, the dancing got even faster and faster until the dancers were soaked in sweat and they threw off their clothes and danced only in their filthy underwear.

glowr'd = stared; *cleekit* = linked together; *ilka carlin swat and reekit* = all the old hags were sweating and breathless; *coost her duddies on the wark* = cast off her rags; *linket at it in her sark* = danced in her slip

Now Tam, O Tam! had thae been queans,
A' plump and strapping in their teens!
Their sarks, instead o' creeshie flannen,
Been snaw-white, seventeen hunder linen!
Thir breeks o' mine, my only pair,
That ance were plush, o' guid blue hair
I wad hae gien them off my hurdies,
For ae blink o' the bonie burdies!

But wither'd beldams, auld and droll,
Rigwoodie hags wad spean a foal,
Louping and flinging on a crummock,
I wonder did na turn thy stomach!

If only they had been young women in clean clothes, then Tam could easily have let his desires get the better of him and shed his trousers, but these wrinkled, ugly old women wearing greasy flannel, who were leaping and capering with their cudgels, should have been enough to make him throw up.

queans = young women; *creeshie flannen* = greasy flannel; *snaw-white* = snow-white; *seventeen hunder linen* = fine-gauge linen; *thir breeks* = these trousers; *ance* = once; *I wad hae gien them off my hurdies* = I would have given them off my behind; *bonie burdies* lovely girls; *beldams* = old hags; *droll* = peculiar; *ringwoodie* = gallows *worthy*; *crummock* = cudgel

But Tam kend what was what fu' brawlie:
There was ae winsome wench and wawlie,
That night enlisted in the core
(Lang after kend on Carrick shore,
For monie a beast to dead she shot,
An' perish'd monie a bonie boat,
And shook baith meikle corn and bear,
And kept the country-side in fear:)
Her cutty sark, o Paisley harn,
That while a lassie she had worn
In longitude tho' sorely scanty,
It was her best, and she was vauntie…
Ah! little kend thy reverend grannie,
That sark she coft for her wee Nannie,
Wi' twa pund Scots (twas a' her riches),
Wad ever grac'd a dance of witches!

But here my Muse her wing maun cour,
Sic flights are far beyond her pow'r;
To sing how Nannie lap and flang,
(A souple jade she was, and strang)
And how Tam stood like ane bewitch'd,
And thought his very een enrich'd;

Even Satan glowr'd and fidg'd fu' fain,
And hotch'd and blew wi' might and main:
'Till first ae caper, syne anither,
Tam tint his reason a' thegither,
And roars out 'Weel done, Cutty-Sark!'
And in an instant all was dark:
And scarcely had he Maggie rallied
When out the hellish legion sallied.

But Tam had spotted the one who was different, a lively attractive girl who had just joined the corp of witches that night (he was not aware of the evil and the deaths she had wrought). She was wearing a petticoat that her grandmother had used all her savings to buy for her when she was a little girl and who had never thought that it would ever be worn in a dance of witches. It was really more than a bit short for her, but it was her best and she was rather vain about it.

kend… fu'brawlie = knew very well; *winsome wench and wawlie* = a jolly, attractive girl; *core* = corp; *lang after kenn'd* = known long after; *Paisley harn* = a coarse cloth; *vauntie* = vain; *coft* = bought; *twa pounds Scots* = two Scottish pounds

This young witch, Nannie, was an incredible dancer and Tam was enthralled just watching her, as was Satan himself who was struggling to keep his music going while watching the dancer. But Tam forgot where he was and in a moment of lunacy, so carried away was he by the spectacle, that he shouted out 'Well done Cutty-sark'. There was instant darkness and he hardly had time to get Maggie moving when the dreadful band came streaming out of the churchyard, intent on catching this interloper.

her wing maun cour = her imagination must be curbed; *lap and flang* = leaped and capered; *souple* = supple; *jade* = an ill-natured woman; *strang* = strong; *fidg'd fu' fain* = fidgeted in excitement; *syne* = then; *tint* = lost

As bees bizz out wi' angry fyke,
When plundering herds assail their byke;
As open pussie's mortal foes,
When, pop! she starts before their nose;
As eager runs the market-crowd,
When 'Catch the thief!' resounds aloud:
So Maggie runs, the witches follow,
Wi' monie an eldritch skriech and hollow.

Just like a swarm of angry bees after an intruder in their hive, so the creatures of evil came storming after Tam and Maggie filling the darkness with their frightening screams and screeches. *bizz* = buzz; *fyke* = fuss; *herds* = shepherds; *byke* = bee-hive; *pussie* = hare; *eldritch skriech and hollow* = unearthly, frightful screams

Ah, Tam! Ah, Tam! thou'll get thy fairing!
In hell they'll roast thee like a herrin'!
In vain thy Kate awaits thy comin'!
Kate soon will be a woefu' woman!
Now, do thy speedy utmost, Meg,
And win the key-stane of the brig;
There, at them thou thy tail may toss,
A running stream they dare na cross!
But ere the key-stane she could make,
The fient a tail she had to shake;
For Nannie, far before the rest,
Hard upon noble Maggie prest,
And flew at Tam w' furious ettle;
But little wist she Maggie's mettle
Ae spring brought off her master hale,
But left behind her ain gray tail:
The carlin claught her by the rump,
And left poor Maggie scarce a stump.

Tam, what have you done? Now you are going to get your just reward. You will finish up in hell, being roasted like a herring. Kate will never see you again, unless Maggie can get across the bridge before the witches catch up with you, because the witches cannot cross running water. Maggie was going well but there was one witch who was away in front of the others – Nannie. She was right at their back and gaining. At the very last moment, Maggie made a surge and brought Tam past the all important key-stone of the bridge. But it was not without cost – the evil Nannie had made a desperate grab for Tam, but missed and caught the horse's rump, catching her by the tail which came off, leaving poor Maggie with only a stump. *fairin'* = reward; *fient* = fiend; *prest* = pressed; *ettle* = intention; *little wist she Maggie's mettle* = little was she aware of Maggie's spirit; *hale* = whole; *claught* = clutched

Now, wha this tale o' truth shall read,
Ilk man, and mother's son, take heed:
Whene'er to drink you are inclin'd,
Or cutty-sarks run in your mind,
Think! ye may buy the joys o'er dear:
Remember Tam o' Shanter's mare.

Now pay attention every man and mother's son who reads this true story Any time you think about having a drink, or if the thought of a girl in a short petticoat crosses your mind, you may have to pay a high price for these pleasures!

To The Memory of The Unfortunate Miss Burns

Burns was constantly at war with both the church and the law over what he considered to be their tyranny and hypocrisy. This poem was dedicated to a celebrated Edinburgh prostitute whose activities had so offended the City Fathers of Edinburgh that they had banished the unfortunate woman to a nearby village where she died within three years of her expulsion.

The woman's name was Margaret Burns and although we know that the poet and Miss Burns were not related by blood, we know nothing of his relationship with the lady herself. Suffice to say that he knew her well enough to write these few lines in her memory, although we also know that he scorned any man who had to use the services of a prostitute.

By this time, Burns was himself a celebrity and a favourite in the drawing rooms of the very people he had held in such contempt in his earlier years. This poem is written with little dialect, therefore it requires no words of explanation but it does indicate once again the Bard's ability to produce verse that is as appropriate in today's society as it was some two hundred years ago.

Like to a fading flower in May,
Which Gardner cannot save,
So Beauty must, sometime, decay
And drop into the grave.

Fair Burns, for long the talk and toast
Of many a gaudy Beau,
That Beauty has forever lost
That made each bosom glow.

Think fellow sisters on her fate!
Think, think how short her days!
Oh! think and e'er it be too late,
Turn from your evil ways.

Beneath this cold, green sod lies dead
That once bewitching dame
That fired Edina's lustful sons,   *Edina* = Edinburgh
And quenched their glowing flame.

249

The Banks O' Doon

More commonly known as *Ye Banks and Braes* this sad, wistful song typifies the elegance and beauty of Burn's words when writing of love. He was never more wistful than when he was saying goodbye to one of his many loves, or when he was describing the misfortunes of someone else's love life. In this case, his tale is of a young lady who has been betrayed by her lover.

Ye banks and braes o' bonie Doon,
How can ye bloom sae fresh and fair?
How can ye chant, ye little birds,
And I sae weary, fu' o' care
sae weary = so tired; *bonie* = beautiful;
Thou'll break my heart, thou warbling bird
That wantons thro' the flowering thorn!
wantons = to move freely
Thou minds me o' departed joys,
Departed – never to return.

Aft hae I rov'd by bonie Doon,
To see the rose and woodbine twine,
And ilka bird sang o' its luve,
ilka = every
And fondly sae did I o' mine.

Wi' lightsome heart I pu'd a rose,
Fu' sweet upon its thorny tree,
And my fause luver staw my rose,
But ah! he left the thorn wi' me.

The girl's lover stole her rose and left her with nothing but the thorn. This could be interpreted as her being left with more than a broken heart. Times haven't changed as much as we may think, women in Burns' day were often left to bring up children alone.
pu'd = pulled; *fause* = false; *staw* = stole

On Genriddell's Fox Breaking His Chain

Captain Robert Riddell was a very good friend of Robert Burns, but to the disgust of the poet, he kept a fox chained to a kennel. Burns was totally against the keeping of any wild animal in captivity, and was inspired to write this poem when the fox managed to break its chain and escape.

Thou, Liberty, thou art my theme:
Not such as idle poets dream,
Who trick thee up a heathen goddess
That a fantastic cap and rod has!
Such stale conceits are poor and silly:
I paint thee out, a Highland filly,
A sturdy, stubborn, handsome dapple,
As sleek's a mouse, as round's an apple,
That when thou pleasest, can do wonders,
But when thy luckless rider blunders,
Or if thy fancy should demur there,
Wilt break thy neck ere thou go further.

Burns refuses to consider the idea of Liberty being represented by some strangely clad goddess. No, he saw her as a beautiful Highland pony that would never allow captivity to break her spirit.
trick thee up = dress you up; *stale conceits* = overused pretences; *demur* = hesitate

These things premis'd, I sing a Fox,
Was caught among his native rocks,
And to a dirty kennel chained,
How he his liberty regained.

He tells of the fox being caught, but also of it eventually regaining its freedom.
premis'd = assumed

Glenriddell! A Whig without a stain,
A Whig in principle and grain,
Coulds't thou enslave a free-born creature,
A native denizen of Nature ?
How coulds't thou with heart so good
(A better ne'er was sluiced with blood),
Nail a poor devil to a tree,
That ne'er did harm to thine or thee ?

He asks his friend, Glenriddell, a man of truth and principle, how such a kind-hearted person could ever hold an animal in captivity, especially as the fox has done no harm to him or his family.
grain = moral fibre

The staunchest Whig Glenriddell was,
Quite frantic in his Country's cause;
And oft was Reynard's prison passing,
And with his brother-Whigs canvassing,
The Rights of Men, the Powers of Women,
With all the dignity of Freemen.

Glenriddell was a staunch Whig,
regularly discussing the rights of men and
women with his political allies as they
passed by the fox's kennel. But they were
free men while the fox was a prisoner.
Reynard = fox; *canvassing* = discussing

Sir Reynard daily heard debates
Of princes', kings', and nations' fates,
With many rueful, bloody stories
Of tyrants, Jacobites, and Tories:
From liberty, how angels fell,
That now art galley-slaves in Hell;
How Nimrod first the trade began
Of binding Slavery's chains on man;
How fell Semiramis, – God damn her!-
Did first with sacreligious hammer
(All ills till then were trivial matters).
For Man dethron'd forge hen-peck fetters;
How Xerxes, that abandon'd Tory,
Thought cutting throats was reaping glory,
Until the stubborn Whigs of Sparta
Taught him great Nature's Magna Charta;
How mighty Rome her fiat hurl'd
Resistless o'er a bowing world,
And, kinder than they did desire,
Polish'd mankind with sword and fire:
With much too tedious to relate
Of ancient and of modern date,
But ending still, how Billy Pitt
(Unlucky boy!) with wicked wit,
Has gagg'd old Britain, drain'd her coffer,
As butchers bind and bleed a heifer.

Each day during his captivity, the fox
heard debates on mans' inhumanity to
man. An incredible range of topics fell
upon his ever attentive ears, ranging from
mythology to historical facts, from the
ravagings of the Roman Empire to the
imposition of income tax by William Pitt.

Thus wily Reynard, by degrees,
In kennel listening at his ease,
Suck'd in a mighty stock of knowledge,
As much as some folks at a college;
Knew Britain's rights and constitution,
Her aggrandizement, diminution;
How Fortune wrought us good from evil;
Let no man then, despise the Devil,
As who should say 'I ne'er can need him.'
Since we to scoundrels owe our freedom.

By the time the fox made his escape, he had absorbed as much information as if he'd been a college graduate, but he also learned that tyrants and other evil people are why the British set such high store on freedom.

suck'd in = absorbed; *aggrandizement* = making great; *diminution* = lessening, *wrought* = fashioned

Hughie Graham

This is an old ballad that the Bard chose to rewrite, adding several lines of his own, as well as including the name of a prominent Ayrshire family.

Our Lords are to the mountains gane,
A hunting o' the fallow deer;
And they hae gripet Hughie Graham
For stealing o' the bishop's mare.

Hughie Graham has been arrested and charged with the theft of the bishop's mare.

gripet = arrested

And they hae tied him hand and foot,
And led him up thro' Stirling town;
The lads and lasses met him there,
Cried, 'Hughie Graham thou art a loun.'

The crowds have yelled abuse at Hughie Graham as he is led through the streets.

oun = fool

'O lowse my right hand free,' he says,
'And put my braid sword in the same;
He's no' in Stirling town this day,
Daur tell the tale to Hughie Graham.'

If his bonds were cut he would challenge anyone who miscalled him, if they dared.

owse = release; *braid* = broad; *daur* = dare

Up then bespake the brave Whitefoord,
As he sat by the bishop's knee;
'Five hundred white stots I'll gie you,
If ye'll let Hughie Graham gae free'.

A friend offered the bishop five-hundred head of cattle to secure Hughie's release.

stots = bullocks

'O haud your tongue, the bishop says,
And wi' your pleading let me be;
For tho' ten Grahams were in his coat,
Hughie Graham this day shall die.'

The bishop tells him to be silent and states that Hughie must die.

Up then bespake the fair Whitefoord,
As she sat by the bishop's knee;
'Five hundred white pence I'll gie you
If ye'll gie Hughie Graham to me.'

The friend's wife then offers a large sum of money to the bishop for Hughie's freedom.

'O haud your tongue now lady fair,
And wi' your pleading let me be;
Altho ten Grahams were in his coat,
It's for my honour he must die.'

The bishop tells her to be silent and states that Hughie must die

They've taen him to the gallows knowe,
He looked to the gallows tree,
Yet never colour left his cheek,
Nor ever did he blin' his e'e.

Hughie is unflinching as he is led to the gallows.

At length he looked round about,
To see whatever he could spy;
And there he saw his auld father,
And he was weeping bitterly.

Looking around, he sees his father weeping.

'O haud your tongue, my father dear,
And wi' your weeping let it be;
Thy weeping's sair upon my heart,
Than a' that they can do to me.'

The father is told that his weeping is harder to bear than any punishment.
sair = sore

And ye may gie my brother John
My sword that's bent in the middle clear,
And let him come at twelve o' clock
And see me pay the bishop's mare.

One brother is to bring his unused sword with him to witness the hanging.

'And ye may gie my brother James
My sword that's bent in the middle brown;
And bid him come at four o' clock,
And see his brother Hugh cut down.'

The other brother, however, is to fetch the one which is stained with blood to cut him down.

'Remember me to Maggy my wife,
The niest time ye gang o'er the moor;
Tell her, she staw the bishop's mare,
Tell her, she was the bishop's whore.'

Hughie then tells his father that it was his wife who stole the mare, and that she was the bishop's mistress.
niest = next; *staw* = stole

'And ye may tell my kith and kin,
I never did disgrace their blood;
And when they meet the bishop's cloak,
To mak it shorter by the hood.'

Assure his kinsmen that he was an honest man, but should the opportunity arise, they should remove the bishop's head with their sword.

255

Thou Gloomy December

This poem shows how Burns was becoming depressed as the departure date for his beloved Clarinda, or Nancy, approached.

Ance mair I hail thee, thou gloomy December!   *hail* = shout at
Ance mair I hail thee, wi' sorrow and care!
Sad was the parting thou makes me remember:
Parting wi' Nancy, Oh, ne'er to meet mair!   *mair* = more

Fond lovers' parting is sweet, painful pleasure,
Hope beaming mild on the soft parting hour;
But the dire feeling, O farewell forever!
Anguish unmingled and agony pure!

Wild as the winter now tearing the forest,
Till the last leaf o' the summer is flown—
Such is the tempest has shaken my bosom,
Till my last hope and last comfort is gone!

Still as I hail thee, thou gloomy December,
Still shall I hail thee wi' sorrow and care;
For sad was the parting thou makes me remember;
Parting wi' Nancy, O, ne'er to meet mair!

Ae Fond Kiss

This, one of the most beautiful songs to be written by Robert Burns, as well as one of the saddest, tells of his heartache when his beloved Nancy McLehose, more famously known as Clarinda, finally set sail for the West Indies in an attempt to retrieve her marriage. This song will live forever.

Ae fond kiss, and then we sever!
Ae fareweel, and then forever,
Deep in heart-wrung tears I'll pledge thee,
Warring sighs and groans I'll wage thee.
Who shall say that Fortune grieves him,
While the star of hope she leaves him?
Me, nae cheerfu' twinkle lights me,
Dark, despair around benights me.

sever = separate; *wage* = pledge; *benights* = clouds with disappointment; *ae* = one

I'll ne'er blame my partial fancy:
Naething could resist my Nancy!
But to see her was to love her.
Love but her, and love for ever.
Had we never lov'd sae kindly,
Had we never lov'd sae blindly,
Never met – or never parted—
We had ne'er been broken-hearted.

naething = nothing

sae = so

Fare-thee-weel, thou first and fairest!
Fare-thee-weel, thou best and dearest!
Thine be ilka joy and treasure,
Peace, Enjoyment, Love, and Pleasure!
Ae fond kiss, and then we sever!
Ae fareweel, alas, for ever!
Deep in heart-wrung tears I'll pledge thee,
Warring sighs and groans I'll wage thee.

fare-thee-weel = farewell

ilka = every

Bonie Wee Thing

As we read the many beautiful poems and songs that Burns composed over the years, we must marvel at his ability to use his verse as a means of flattering whichever young woman had caught his eye. This particular song was dedicated to a lass by the name of Deborah Duff Davies, who was also the recipient of several letters from the Bard. Although I have no idea whether or not Burns was successful in his pursuit of Miss Davies, I do know that this song has become one of his best-loved works, and expect that it will remain so for many years to come.

Bonie wee thing, cannie wee thing,   *bonie* = beautiful; *cannie* = gentle,
Lovely wee thing, wert thou mine,   *wad* = would; *tine* = lose
I wad wear thee in my bosom
Lest my jewel I should tine.

Wistfully I look and languish,
In that bonie face o' thine
And my heart it stounds with anguish.   *stounds* = pains; *na* = not
Lest my wee thing na be mine.

Wit and Grace and Love and Beauty,   *ae* = one
In ae constellation shine;
To adore thee is my duty,
Goddess o' this soul o' mine.

Geordie – An Old Ballad

Another old ballad collected by the Bard. There is some doubt as to whether or not he revised it as he normally would do with such songs, or if this remains the original version. The verses are believed to relate to George Gordon, 4th Earl of Huntly, who was imprisoned in Edinburgh Castle in 1554, although another school of thought considers the 6th Earl to be a more likely candidate. Whatever, it remains a stirring tale that illustrates how justice was dispensed in a summary manner during that period in history.

There was a battle in the north,
And nobles there was many,
And they hae kill'd Sir Charles Hay,
And they laid the wyte on Geordie.

Geordie has been blamed for the murder of another nobleman, Sir Charles Hay.

wyte = blame

O, he has written a lang letter,
He sent it to his lady;
Ye maun cum up to Enbrugh town
To see what words o' Geordie.

He's written a letter to his wife telling her that she must come to Edinburgh to see what has befallen him.
maun cum = must come; *Enbrugh* = Edinburgh

When first she look'd the letter on,
She was baith red and rosy;
But she had na read a word but twa,
Till she wallow't like a lily.

Her colour changed when she read the letter and she went deathly pale.

wallow't = wilted

'Gar get to me my gude grey steed,
My menzie a' gae wi' me;
For I shall neither eat nor drink
Till Enbrugh town shall see me.'

Her retinue were commanded to accompany her to Edinburgh.
gude = good; *menzie* = retinue, armed followers

And she has mountit her gude grey steed,
Her menzie a' gaed wi' her;
And she did neither eat nor drink
Till Enbrugh town did see her.

She got on her horse and left for Edinburgh with her retinue. She didn't eat or drink until she arrived in the city.

And first appear'd the fatal block,
And syne the aix to head him;
And Geordie cumin down the stair,
And bands o' airn upon him.

The block and axe were produced and
Geordie appeared, held in chains.
syne = then; *aix* = axe; *airn* = iron

But tho' he was chain'd in fetters strang,
O' airn and steel sae heavy,
There was na ane in a' the court,
Sae braw a man as Geordie.

Even although he was chained up, there
was no better man in court than Geordie
fetters = shackles

O, she's down on her bended knee,
I wat she's pale and weary,
'O pardon, pardon, noble king,
And gie me back my Dearie!

His wife pleads with the king to spare
him.
wat = pledge

I hae born seven sons to my Geordie dear,
The seventh ne'er saw his daddie:
O pardon, pardon, noble king,
Pity a waefu' lady!'

She has borne seven sons to Geordie, but
the youngest has not yet seen his father.
She begs for pardon.
waefu' = woeful

'Gar bid the headin-man mak haste!'
Our king replied fu lordly:
'O noble king, tak a' that's mine,
But gie me back my Geordie.'

The pleas fell on deaf ears as the king told the
executioner to proceed. The wife then offered
all her worldly goods for Geordies' release.
headin-man = executioner; *gar* = make/compel

The Gordons cam and the Gordons ran,
And they were stark and steady;
And ay the word amang them a'
Was, 'Gordons keep you ready.'

Meanwhile, the Gordon clan were
preparing themselves to do battle for their
chief.
stark = strong; *ay* = all

An aged lord at the king's right hand
Says, 'Noble king, but hear me:
Gar her tell down five thousand pound,
And gie her back her Dearie.'

However, another member of the court
suggested to the king that a ransom might
be more appropriate.

Some gae her marks, some gae her crowns,
Some gae her dollars many;
And she's tell'd down five thousand pound,
And she's gotten again her Dearie.

The clan made up the ransom with currency from all over the world, and Geordie gained his release.

She blinkit blythe in Geordie's face,
Says, 'Dear I've bought thee, Geordie:
But there sud been bluidy bouks on the green,
Or I had tint my laddie.'

She smiled brightly at him and told him that she had paid dearly for his life, but if she had lost him, bodies would be lying on the green.

sud = should; *bouks* = torsos; *tint* = lo

He claspit her by the middle sma',
And he kist her lips sae rosy:
'The sweetest flower o' woman-kind
Is my sweet, bonie Lady!'

He clasped her by her small waist and kissed her, calling her the sweetest flower of all woman kind.

Bessy and her Spinnin'-Wheel

Here we have a poem dedicated to the pleasant simplicity of rural life, and describing the pastoral scenes enjoyed daily by the country woman as she works at her spinning-wheel. The lusciousness of nature, described in both this work and the Elegy on Capt Matthew Henderson, emphasises only too clearly the effects of industrial developments upon the countryside which Robert Burns loved so dearly

O, leeze me on my spinnin'-wheel!
And leeze me on my rock and reel,
Frae tap to tae that cleeds me bien,
And haps me fiel and warm at e'en!
I'll set me down and sing and spin,
While laigh descends the summer sun,
Blest wi' content, and milk and meal—
O, leeze me on my spinnin'-wheel!

Bessy is blessing the good fortune that allows her to be well clothed and well fed at all times.
leeze = blessings; *rock* = distaff; *cleeds* = clothes; *bien* = well; *haps me fiel* = covers me well; *laigh* = low

On ilka hand the burnies trot,
And meet below my theekit cot,
The scented birk and hawthorn white
Across the pool their arms unite,
Alike to screen the birdie's nest,
And little fishes caller rest.
The sun blinks kindly in the biel,
Where blythe I turn my spinnin'-wheel.

This verse describes the thatched cottage and the views enjoyed by Bessy,
ilka = each; *burnies* = streams; *theekit cot* = thatched cottage; *birk* = birch; *caller* = cool; *biel* = shelter

On lofty aiks the cushats wail,
And Echo cons the doolfu' tale,
The lintwhites in the hazel braes,
Delighted, rival ither's lays.
The craik amang the claver hay,
The paitrick whirrin' o'er the ley,
The swallow jinkin' round my shiel,
Amuse me at my spinnin'-wheel.

This time it is the bird-life surrounding the cottage that is described in detail.
aiks = oaks; *cushats* = pigeons; *lintwhites* = linnets; *lays* = songs; *craik* = corncrake; *claver* = clover; *paitrick* = partridge; *ley* = meadow; *jinkin'* = darting; *shiel* = hut; *cons* = returns

Wi' sma' to sell and less to buy,
Aboon distress, below envy,
O, wha wad leave this humble state
For a' the pride of a' the great?
Amid their flarin', idle toys,
Amid their cumbrous, dinsome joys,
Can they the peace and pleasure feel
Of Bessy at her spinnin'-wheel?

Bessy may live humbly but has no envy of the wealthy with their life of rowdy pleasures. Nothing can compare with the simple life which she enjoys and the peace which surrounds her.

Country Lassie

Whether to marry for love or to marry for money was always a favourite subject of the Bard's. This poem, written in 1794, follows that theme and Burns as ever takes the side of love.

In simmer, when the hay was mawn,
And corn wav'd green in ilka field,
While claver blooms white o'er the ley,
And roses blaw in ilka bield;
Blythe Bessie, in the milkin-shiel,
Says, 'I'll be wed come o't what will;'
Outspak a dame in wrinkled eild,
'O' gude advisement comes nae ill.'

Young Bessie was in the milking-shed when she announced that she intended to be married soon, come what may. An old lady advised her to consider the merits of marrying a wealthy suitor.
simmer = summer; *mawn* = mown; *claver* = clover; *ilka bield* = every field; *shiel* = shed; *eild* = old-age

'It's ye hae wooers mony ane,
And lassie ye're but young ye ken;
Then wait a wee and cannie wale,
A routhie butt, a routhie ben:
There's Johnie o' the Buskieglen,
Fu' is his barn, fu' is his byre;
Tak this frae me my bonie hen,
It's plenty beets the luver's fire.'

She points out that Bessie will have many wooers and is still young, and that a well-stocked household can be preferable to love.
mony ane = many-a-one; *wait a wee* = wait a short while; *cannie wale* = carefully select; *routhie* = plentiful; *butt* = kitchen; *ben* = parlour/best room; *byre* = cattle-shed; *beets* = fans; *luver's fire* = passion

'For Johnie o' the Buskieglen,
I dinna care a single flie;
He lo'es sae weel his craps and kye,
He has nae loove to spare for me:
But blythes the blink o' Robie's e'e,
And weel I wat he lo'es me dear;
Ae blink o' him I wadna gie
For Buskieglen and a' his gear.'

But Bessie thinks that Johnie is too fond of his farm and would ignore her, whereas Robie is another matter altogether.
craps = crops; *kye* = cattle; *blithe* = merry; *wat* = know; *gear* = wealth; *faught* = struggle; *fechtin* = fighting

'O thoughtless lassie, life's a faught,
The canniest gate, the strife is sair;
But ay fu'han't is fechtin best,
A hungry care's an unco care;
But some will spend, and some will care
An' wilfu' folk maun hae their will;
Syne as ye brew, my maiden fair,
Keep mind that ye maun drink the yill.'

The old lady states that life is a battle in which one is better to be well-armed and whatever the girl decides is what she will have to live with.

faught = fight; *canniest gate* = most careful path; *fu'-han't* = full-handed; *maun* = must; *craps* = crops; *kye* = cows; *wat* = promise`

'O gear will buy me rigs o' land,
And gear will buy me sheep and kye;
But the tender heart o' leesome loove,
The gowd and siller canna buy:
We may be poor, Robie and I,
Light is the burden loove lays on;
Content and loove brings peace and joy:
What mair hae queens upon a throne?'

Bessie knows that money can keep a farm well-stocked, but it cannot buy the love that she and Robie will share.

rigs = ridges of land; *leesome* = tender; *gowd* = gold; *siller* = silver; *loove* = love

Willie Wastle

SIC A WIFE AS WILLIE'S WIFE

The name Willie Wastle was derived from a children's game similar to 'I'm the King of the Castle'. It is written in *grotesquerie*, a style which was popular in Scotland.

Willie Wastle dwalls on Tweed,
The spot they ca' it Linkumdoddie;
A creeshie wabster till his trade,
Can steal a clue wi' ony body:
He has a wife that's dour and din,
Tinkler Madgie was her mither;
Sic a wife as Willie's wife,
I wad na gie a button for her.—

Willie Wastle lives on the Tweed, in a place called Linkumdoddie. His trade is oily-weaving. His wife is sullen and noisy.
dwalls = dwells; *creeshie wabster* = greasy weaver; *clue* = portion of cloth or yarn; *din* = dingy; *tinkler* = tinker; *wad na gie* = would not give

She has an e'e, she has but ane,
Our cat has twa, the very colour;
Five rusty teeth, forbye a stump,
A clapper-tongue wad deave a miller:
A whiskin beard about her mou,
Her nose and chin, they threaten ither;
Sic a wife as Willie's wife,
I wad na gie a button for her.—

She has only one eye, which is like a cat's, five rotten teeth and a stump, with a beard and huge nose and chin. She talks enough to deafen a miller.
deave = deafen; *mou* = mouth

She's bow-hough'd, she's hem-shin'd,
Ae limping leg a hand-bread shorter;
She's twisted right, she's twisted left,
To balance fair in ilka quarter:
She has a hump upon her breast,
The twin o' that upon her shouther;
Sic a wife as Willie's wife,
I wad na gie a button for her.—

She's bow legged and has shins shaped like horse shoes. One of her legs is shorter than the other. She's all twisted, with twin humps.
bow-hough'd = bow-legged; *hem-shin'd* = the shape of a horse-collar; *shouther* = shoulder

Auld baudrans by the ingle sits,
An' wi' her loof her face a-washin;
But Willie's wife is na sae trig,
She dights her grunzie wi' a hushian;
Her waly nieves like midden-creels,
Her feet wad fyle the Logan-water;
Sic a wife as Willie's wife,
I wad na gie a button for her.—

An old cat sits by the fire, washing her face with a paw. But Willie's wife isn't so clean, she wipes her nose with her old footless sock. Her fists are like manure buckets, and her feet stink.

auld baudrans = old cat; *loof* = paw; *trig* = tidy; *dights her grunzie* = wipes her snout; *hushian* = old footless stocking; *waly nieves* = large fists; *midden-creels* = manure baskets; *fyle* = foul

Such a Parcel of Rogues in a Nation

In common with millions of others throughout the ages, Robert Burns was fervently proud of Scotland and all things Scottish. He despised the Act of Union in 1707 and considered that the thirty-one Scottish commissioners, who sold out to England in return for land and money, were no more than a parcel of rogues who had committed treason. His contempt for their actions is abundantly clear in the following verses.

Fareweel to a' our Scottish fame,
Fareweel our ancient glory!
Fareweel ev'n to the Scottish name,
Sae famed in martial story!
Now Sark rins o'er the Solway sands,
An' Tweed rins to the ocean,
To mark where England's province stands,
Such a parcel of rogues in a nation!

What force or guile could not subdue
Thro' many warlike ages
Is wrought now by a coward few
For hireling traitor's wages.
The English steel we could disdain,
Secure in valour's station;
But English gold has been our bane,
Such a parcel of rogues in a nation!

O, would, or I had seen the day
That Treason thus could sell us,
My auld grey head had lien in clay,
Wi' Bruce and loyal Wallace!
But pith and power, till my last hour,
I'll mak this declaration;
'We're bought and sold for English gold',
Such a parcel of rogues in a nation!

The Slave's Lament

Maya Angelou, the famous Afro-American poet and admirer of Robert Burns, expressed her astonishment that Burns had never been to Africa, yet had written this poem. She felt that this must have been written by someone with first-hand knowledge of slavery – someone who had suffered.

Although not a tied slave, Burns had certainly been a slave to the land and had toiled for many hours for little reward. He had a remarkable ability to highlight injustice, equalled by his ability to empathise with the lot of the persecuted.

It was in sweet Senegal that my foes did me enthral,   *enthral* = enslave
For the lands of Virginia, - ginia O;
Torn from that lovely shore, and must never see it more,
And alas! I am weary, weary O!

All on that charming coast is no bitter snow or frost,
Like the lands of Virginia, - ginia O;
There streams for ever flow, and there flowers forever blow,
And alas! I am weary, weary O!

The burden I must bear, whilst the cruel scourge I fear,
In the lands of Virginia, - ginia O;
And I think on friends most dear, with the bitter, bitter tear,
And alas! I am weary, weary O!

The Deil's Awa Wi' Th' Exciseman

Burns was only too aware of the resentment felt towards himself and his fellow officers who made up the Excise force in Scotland, for at that time smuggling and the illegal distilling of whisky were regarded by the populace as good, honest enterprises. He entertained his fellow officers with this song at an Excise dinner in 1792.

CHORUS
The Deil's awa, the Deil's awa,
The Deil's awa wi' th' Exciseman!
He's danc'd awa, he's danced awa,
He's danced awa wi' th' Exciseman!

The Deil cam fiddlin' thro' the town,
And danced awa wi' th' Exciseman,
An ilka wife cries:— 'Auld Mahoun,
I wish you luck o' the prize man!'

The townswomen are thanking the devil for removing the exciseman, for now they can get on with their home-brewing in peace. *Auld Mahoun* = the devil

'We'll mak our maut, and we'll brew our drink,
We'll laugh, sing, and rejoice, man,
And monie braw thanks to the meikle black Deil,
That danc'd awa wi' th' Exciseman.'

maut = malt; *monie braw thanks* = many good thanks; *meikle* = great;

There's threesome reels, there's foursome reels,
There's hornpipes and strathspeys, man,
But the ae best dance e'er cam to the land
Was *The Deil's awa wi' th' Exciseman.*

Highland Mary

Highland Mary, or Mary Campbell, has been the subject of many Burns researchers through the years. Although the Bard appears to have considered her a saintly being, others have portrayed her in a totally different manner.

Burns' affair with Mary Campbell started after his break-up with Jean Armour, and it certainly appears that he had intended to emigrate with her to the West Indies. However, this was not to be as she died suddenly of either fever, or premature child-birth at the age of twenty-three. No one knows for sure, but what is certain is that Burns was indeed smitten by Mary Campbell, and that his affection for her remained strong long after her untimely death, as this beautiful poem, written six years afterwards, fully illustrates.

Ye banks and braes and streams around,   *braes* = slopes; *drumlie* = muddy;
The castle o' Montgomery,   *unfauld* = unfold
Green be your woods, and fair your flowers,
Your waters never drumlie!
There Simmer first unfauld her robes,
And there the longest tarry!
For there I took the last fareweel,
O' my sweet Highland Mary!

How sweetly bloom'd the gay, green birk,   *birk* = birch
How rich the hawthorn's blossom,
As underneath their fragrant shade,
I clasp'd her to my bosom!
The golden hours on angel wings
Flew o'er me and my dearie;
For dear to me as light and life
Was my sweet Highland Mary.

Wi' monie a vow and lock'd embrace
Our parting was fu' tender;
And pledging aft to meet again,
We tore oursel's asunder.
But O! fell Death's untimely frost,
That nipt my flower sae early!
Now green's the sod, and cauld's the clay,
That wraps my Highland Mary!

wi' monie = with many; *nipt* = nipped;
cauld = cold

O, pale, pale now, those rosy lips
I aft hae kissed sae fondly;
And clos'd for ay, the sparkling glance
That dwalt on me sae kindly;
And mouldering now in silent dust
That heart that lo'ed me dearly!
But still within my bosom's core
Shall live my Highland Mary.

The Rights of Woman

It is an indisputable fact that Burns was a lover of woman. His many documented affairs have earned him the reputation of being a true rake and opportunist who would happily seduce any pretty girl he met. We should note, however, that those with whom he had relationships were willing participants.

There is a side to Burns that is not so well recognised, and that is his strong support for the feminist movement. At a time when few men took women's place in society seriously, Burns felt that woman's rights were important, as the following illustrates.

While Europe's eye is fix'd on might things,
The fate of Empires and the fall of Kings;
While quacks of State must each produce his plan, *quacks* = mere talking pretenders
And even children lisp the Rights of Man;
Amid this mighty fuss, just let me mention,
The Rights of Woman merit some attention.

First, in the sexes' intermix'd connection,
One sacred Right of Woman is Protection.
The tender flower that lifts its head elate,   *elate* = proudly
Helpless must fall before the blasts of Fate,
Sunk on the earth, defac'd its lovely form,
Unless your shelter ward th' impending storm.

Our second Right – but needless here is caution –
To keep that right inviolate's the fashion;
Each man of sense has it so full before him,
He'd die before he'd wrong it – 'tis Decorum!
There was, indeed, in far less polish'd days,
A time, when rough, rude Man had naughty ways;
Would swagger, swear, get drunk, kick up a riot,
Nay, even thus invade a lady's quiet!
Now, thank our stars! These Gothic times are fled;   *gothic* = barbarous
Now, well-bred men – (and you are well-bred) –
Most justly think (and we are much the gainers)   *gainers* = winners
Such conduct neither spirit, wit nor manners.

For Right the third, our last, our best, our dearest
That Right to fluttering Female hearts the nearest,
Which even the Rights of Kings, in low prostration,
Most humbly own – tis dear, dear Admiration!
In that blest sphere alone we live and move;
There taste that life of life – Immortal Love.
Smiles, glances, sighs, tears, fits, flirtations, airs –
'Gainst such an host what flinty savage dares?   *flinty* = cruel
When aweful Beauty joins in all her charms,
Who is so rash as rise in rebel arms?
But truce with kings, and truce with Constitutions,
With bloody armaments and Revolutions;
Let Majesty your first attention summon
Ah! ça ira! THE MAJESTY OF WOMAN !   *ca ira* = it will be (French
revolutionary song)

The Lea-Rig

A delightful old Scottish ballad breathed upon by the Bard, and one which remains a popular choice at any function featuring the songs of Robert Burns.

When o'er the hill the eastern star,
Tells bughtin-time is near, my jo,
And owsen frae the furrow'd field,
Return sae dowf and weary, O,
Down by the burn, where scented birks,
Wi' dew are hanging clear, my jo,
I'll meet thee on the lea-rig,
My ain kind Dearie, O!

Evening descends as the sheep are returned to their folds, and the oxen trudge wearily homewards. The young man looks forward to meeting his sweetheart at a later hour. *bughtin-time* = time to bring in the livestock; *jo* = sweetheart; *owsen* = oxen; *furrow'd* = ploughed; *sae dowf* = so dull; *birks* = birches; *lea-rig* = grassy ridge; *ain* = own

At midnight hour, in mirkest glen,
I'd rove, and ne'er be eerie, O,
If thro' that glen I gaed to thee,
My ain kind Dearie, O!
Altho' the night were ne'er sae wet,
And I were ne'er sae weary, O,
I'd meet thee on the lea-rig,
My ain kind Dearie, O!

Darkness holds no fears for him when he is travelling through the countryside to meet his lover. Even if it had never rained so much, or he'd never been so tired, he'd still go to meet them. *mirkest* = gloomiest; *rove* = wander; *ne'er be eerie* = never be frightened; *thro'* = through; *gaed* = went; *sae* = so

The hunter lo'es the morning sun,
To rouse the mountain deer, my jo;
At noon the fisher takes the glen,
Along the burn to steer, my jo;
Gie me the hour o' gloamin' grey,
It makes my heart sae cheery, O,
To meet thee on the lea-rig,
My ain kind Dearie, O!

The hunter may prefer the morning, and the angler midday, but for him the happiest time is when the sun is going down and he's meeting his sweetheart. *lo'es* = loves; *gie* = give; *gloamin'* = dusk

The Tree of Liberty

Here we have another poem by Burns on one of his favourite topics – Liberty. This poem appears to have been inspired by the French Revolution, but the Bard's sympathies obviously lie toward the Jacobite cause.

Heard ye o' the Tree o' France
I watna what's the name o't,
Around it a' the patriots dance,
Weel Europe kens the fame o't.
It stands where ance the Bastile stood
A prison built by kings, man,
When superstition's hellish brood
Kept France in leading strings, man.

By the use of the term the 'Tree of France', the Bard symbolises liberty and freedom. The storming of the infamous Bastille in Paris, and its subsequent use as a prison for the aristocracy before its destruction, marked the beginning of freedom for the oppressed peasants of France.

watna = don't know; *kens* = knows; *ance* = once; *leading strings* = reins

Upo' this tree there grows sic fruit,
Its virtues I can tell, man;
It raises man aboon the brute,
It maks him ken himsel, man!
Gif ance the peasant taste a a bit,
He's greater than a lord, man,
An' wi' the beggar shares a mit
O' a' he can afford, man.

Freedom is a virtue that raises man above the beast. A peasant who tastes freedom will be better than a lord, for he has known poverty and oppression and will be more inclined to help those who have nothing.

upo' = upon; *sic* = such; *aboon* = above; *gif* = if; *ance* = once

This fruit is worth a' Afric's wealth,
To comfort us 'twas sent, man;
To gie the sweetest blush o' health,
An' mak us a' content, man;
It clears the een, it cheers the heart,
Mak's high and low gude friends, man;
And he wha acts the traitor's part
It to perdition sends, man.

Freedom is worth all the wealth to be found in Africa. A free man has clearness of vision, and with happiness in his heart can befriend people in all levels of society. Only ruination will come to those who oppose freedom.

perdition = hell

My blessings aye attend the chiel
Wha pitied Gallia's slaves, man
And staw a branch, spite o' the deil,
Frae 'yont the western waves, man
Fair Virtue water'd it wi' care,
And now she sees wi' pride, man
How weel it buds and blossoms there,
Its branches spreading wide, man.

Burns blesses the person responsible for the start of the French Revolution, and casts his eye to America where the seeds of discontent concerning the slave trade are growing rapidly.

aye = always; chiel = young man; Gallia = France; staw = stole; frae 'yont = from beyond; weel = well

But vicious folk aye hate to see
The works o' Virtue thrive, man;
The courtly vermin's banned the tree,
And grat to see it thrive, man!
King Loui' thought to cut it down,
When it was unco sma', man;
For this the watchman cracked his crown,
Cut off his head and a', man

Not everyone is enthusiastic about the rights of man. The French ruling classes did their utmost to suppress the peasants when revolt threatened, but the ultimate result was that King Louis XVI was beheaded by the very people whom he'd persecuted.

grat = wept; unco sma' = very small

A wicked crew syne on a time,
Did tak a solemn aith, man,
It ne'er should flourish to its prime,
I wat they pledged their faith, man.
Awa' they gaed wi' mock parade,
Like beagles hunting game, man,
But soon grew weary o' the trad
And wished they'd been at hame ,man

Supporters of the aristocracy attempted in desperation to fight back and reinstate the slave-like conditions to which the peasants had been subjected, but they soon realised that the battle was lost.

syne = once; aith = oath; wat = know; gaed = went; hame = home

For Freedom, standing by the tree,
Her sons did loudly ca' , man;
She sang a song o' liberty,
Which pleased them ane and a', man.
By her inspired, the new-born race
Soon drew the avenging steel, man;
The hirelings ran – her foes gied chase,
And banged the despot weel, man.

Inspired by the stirring words of La Marseillaise, the peasant uprising saw the end of the despotic ruling classes throughout the whole of France.

ca' = call; ane and a' = one and all; gied = gave; banged the despot weel = struck a heavy blow against the tyrant

Let Britain boast her hardy oak,
Her poplar and her pine, man!
Auld Britain ance could crack her joke,
And o'er her neighbours shine, man!
But seek the forest round and round,
And soon 'twill be agreed , man,
That sic a tree can not be found,
'Twixt London and the Tweed, man.

The Bard points out that although many trees grow throughout Britain, there is no Tree of Liberty. Freedom no longer exists and the people are again no more than serfs.
auld = old; *ance* = once; *crack* = tell

Without this tree, alake this life
Is but a vale o' woe, man;
A scene o' sorrow mixed wi' strife,
Nae real joys we know, man.
We labour soon, we labour late,
To feed the titled knave, man;
And a' the comfort we're to get
Is that ayont the grave, man

Life without freedom is a joyless existence, where the working-man knows nothing but endless toil trying to meet the demands of his titled master. Only death will relieve him of his burden.
alake = alas; *ayont* = beyond

Wi' plenty o' sic trees, I trow,
The warld would live in peace, man;
The sword would help to mak a plough,
The din o' war wad cease, man;
Like brethren in a common cause,
We'd on each other smile, man;
And equal rights and equal laws
Wad gladden every isle, ma

If all men were free with equal rights, then war would be a thing of the past.
Weapons could be turned into ploughs and mankind could go forward together.
trow = believe; *warld* = world; *din* = noise;
sic = such

Wae worth the loon wha wadna eat
Sic halesome dainty cheer, man;
I'd gie my shoon frae off my feet,
To taste sic fruit, I swear, man.
Syne let us pray, auld England may
Sure plant this far-famed tree, man;
And blythe we'll sing, and hail the day
That gave us liberty, man.

What worth does the man have who wouldn't eat such wholesome cheer. Burns would give the shoes of his feet to see this happening. He prays for the day when Scotland will be free from the English yoke and Scotland can sing the song of liberty.
wae worth the loon = woe befall the rascal; *wha wadna* = who would not; *shoon* = shoes; *frae aff* = from off; *blythe* = cheerfully

Jessie

Once again we have yet another example of the Bard's amazing ability to flatter young women in verse. On this occasion the subject was Jessie Staig, the daughter of the Provost of Dumfries. She died in 1801 at the age of 26. Jessie must have been seventeen or eighteen when the song was written, and Burns recognised that although she was truly beautiful, she was also an extremely modest young lady.

True-hearted was he, the sad swain o' the Yarrow,   *swain* = lover/suitor
And fair are the maids on the banks o' the Ayr,
But by the sweet side o' the Nith's winding river,
Are lovers as faithful, and maidens as fair;
To equal young Jessie seek Scotland all over;
To equal young Jessie you seek it in vain;
Grace, Beauty and Elegance fetter her lover,
And maidenly modesty fixes the chain.

Fresh is the rose in the gay, dewy morning,
And sweet is the lily at evening close;
But in the fair presence o' lovely young Jessie,
Unseen is the lily, unheeded the rose.
Love sits in her smile, a wizard ensnaring;
Enthron'd in her een he delivers his law;
And still to her charms she alone is a stranger!
Her modest demeanour's the jewel of a'.

On The Commemoration of Rodney's Victory

Admiral George Rodney fought a major battle against the French Navy in the West Indies on the 12ᵗʰ April, 1792. This resulted in Great Britain regaining control over the Atlantic, and the victory was the cause of celebration throughout the British Isles. Burns was sufficiently stirred by the event to pen the following tribute.

Instead of a song, boys, I'll give you a toast:
Here's to the mem'ry of those on the Twelth that we lost!—
That we lost, did I say? nay, by Heav'n that we found!
For their fame it shall last while the world goes round.
The next in succession I'll give you The King!
And who would betray him, on high may he swing!
And here's the grand fabric, the Free Constitution,
As built on the base of our great Revolution!
And, longer with Politics not to be cramm'd,
Be Anarchy curs'd, and be Tyranny damn'd!
And who would to Liberty e'er prove disloyal,
May his son be a hangman, and he his first trial!

The Sodger's Return

WHEN WILD WAR'S DEADLY BLAST WAS BLAWN

Once more we have a bawdy old ballad revised by the Bard. This is the story of a soldier returning after years at war, and the welcome given to him by his lover.

When wild War's deadly blast was blawn,
And gentle Peace returning,
Wi' monie a sweet babe fatherless
And monie a widow mourning.
I left the lines and tented field,
Where lang I'd been a lodger,
My humble knapsack a' my wealth,
A poor and honest sodger.

The long war has ended leaving many children fatherless and women widowed, and the soldier sets off home with nothing but his knapsack.
monie = many; *sodger* = soldier

A leal, light heart was in my breast,
My hand unstain'd wi' plunder,
And for fair Scotia, hame again,
I cheery on did wander:
I thought upon the banks o' Coil,
I thought upon my Nancy,
And ay I mind't the witching smile
That caught my youthful fancy.

His mind was on his Nancy as he walked the long road home in light-hearted mood.
leal = true

At length I reached the bonie glen,
Where early life I sported.
I pass'd the mill and trysting thorn,
Where Nancy aft I courted.
Wha spied I but my ain dear maid,
Down by her mother's dwelling,
And turn'd me round to hide the flood
That in my een was swelling!

Eventually he arrived at the glen where he had lived as a youngster, but became emotional when he saw Nancy in the distance.
trysting thorn = meeting place

Wi' alter'd voice, quoth I – 'Sweet lass,
Sweet as yon hawthorn's blossom,
O, happy, happy may he be,
That's dearest to thy bosom!
My purse is light, I've far to gang,
And fain wad be thy lodger;
I've served my king and country lang,
Take pity on a sodger.'

With husky voice he asked her if she could find him accommodation as he had travelled a distance and had little money.
fain wad be = would like to be

Sae wistfully she gaz'd on me,
And lovelier she than ever.
Quo she, 'A sodger ance I lo'ed,
Forget him shall I never:
Our humble cot, and hamely fare,
Ye freely shall partake it;
That gallant badge, the dear cockade,
Ye're welcome for the sake o't!'

She looked at him sadly without recognising him and told him that she had loved a soldier, therefore he would be welcome in her home.
ance = once; *cot* = cottage; *hamely fare* = simple food; *cockade* = rosette worn as a cap badge

She gaz'd, she redden'd like a rose,
Syne, pale like onie lily,
She sank within my arms and cried,
'Art thou my ain dear Willie?'
'By him who made yon sun and sky,
By whom true love's regarded,
I am the man, and thus may still
True lover's be rewarded!

Sudden recognition came to her and they fell into each others arms.
syne = then

'The wars are o'er, and I'm come hame,
And find thee still true-hearted.
Tho' poor in gear, we're rich in love,
And mair, we'se ne'er be parted'
Quo' she, 'my grandsire left me gowd,
A mailen plenish'd fairly!
And come, my faithfu' sodger lad,
Thou'rt welcome to it dearly!'

He assured that he was home for good, and although they would have little money, they would be rich in love. However her grandfather had left her money and a well stocked farm which she would share with him.
gear = wealth; *grandsire* = grandfather; *mailen* = farm; *plenish'd fairly* = well stocked

For gold the merchant ploughs the main,
The farmer ploughs the manor;
But glory is the sodger's prize,
The sodger's wealth is honour!
The brave poor sodger ne'er despise,
Nor count him as a stranger:
Remember he's his country's stay
In day and hour of danger.

One must never look down on a soldier as
he is the mainstay in times of trouble.

Meg O' The Mill

Anyone entering a loveless marriage for the sake of wealth and possessions could expect nothing but scorn from the Bard as the following verses show.

O ken ye what Meg o' the mill has gotten?
An' ken ye what Meg o' the mill has gotten?
She's gotten a coof wi' a claut o' siller,
And broken the heart o' the barley miller!

Do you know what Meg of the Mill has got? She's married a wealthy laird, breaking the heart of the miller.
ken = know; *coof* = dolt; *claut o' siller* = horde of money

The miller was strappin', the miller was ruddy,
A heart like lord, and a hue like a lady;
The laird was a widdifu', bleerit knurl—-
She's left the good-fellow, and ta'en the churl!

The miller was handsome, but the laird is repulsive.
widdifu' bleerit knurl = gallows-worthy; bleary-eyed dwarf; *churl* = miserable person

The miller, he hecht her a heart leal and luving;
The laird did address her wi' matter
      mair moving,
A fine pacing-horse wi' a clear chained bridle,
A whip by her side, and a bonie side-saddle!

The miller offered love and devotion, but the laird's offer of a fine horse and all the trimmings was more tempting to Meg.
hecht = offered; *leal* = loyal; *mair* = more

O, wae on the siller, it is sae prevailing!
And wae on the luve that is fixed on a mailin!
A tocher's nae word in a true lover's parl,
But gie me my love, and a fig for the warl!

Money may be more attractive to Meg than a life of toiling on a farm, but a dowry should never be part of a lover's vocabulary.
wae = woe; *siller* = silver; *mailin* = farm; *tocher* = dowry; *parl* = speech; *warl* = world

Whistle An' I'll Come To You, My Lad

In this popular song, the lass is concerned that their relationship will be noticed by others, so she instructs the lad to make sure that he does not pay her attention should they meet outside.

CHORUS
O, whistle an' I'll come to ye, my lad!
O, whistle an' I'll come to ye, my lad!
Tho' father an' mither,and a' should gae mad,
O, whistle an' I'll come to ye, my lad!

But warily tent when ye come to court me,   *warily tent = be careful*
And come nae unless the back-yett be a-jee;   *yett = gate; a-jee = ajar*
Syne up the back-style, and let naebody see,
And come as ye were na comin to me,
And come as ye were na comin to me!

At kirk, or at market, whene'er ye meet me,
Gang by me as tho' ye car'd na a flie;   *gang = go*
But steal me a blink o' your bonie black e'e,
Yet look as ye were na lookin at me,
Yet look as ye were na lookin at me!

Ay vow and protest that ye care na for me,
And whyles ye may lightly my beauty a-wee;   *may lightly my beauty a-wee =*
But court nae anither, tho' jokin ye be,   talk about me a little
For fear that she wyle your fancy frae me,
For fear that she wyle your fancy frae me!

Scots, Wha Hae

ROBERT BRUCE'S ADDRESS TO HIS ARMY AT BANNOCKBURN

The verses of this song, guaranteed to make the blood tingle in the veins of any true Scot, were written by Burns after visiting the field of Bannockburn in 1787. In common with most other Scots who have visited the site throughout the years, he appears to have been overwhelmed by the vision of a free Scotland, fired no doubt by the apparent success of the French Revolution which had dominated the news for the past year.

Scots, wha hae wi' Wallace bled,
Scots, wham Bruce has aften led,
Welcome to your gory bed,
Or to victorie!
Now's the day, and now's the hour;
See the front o' battle lour;
See approach proud Edward's power,
Chains and slavery.

As the time for battle draws near, Burns visualises Bruce reminding his men that Scots have already shed their blood alongside William Wallace, and that he, Bruce, has led them before against the enemy. Today however is win or die – or worse – become a slave of King Edward.
wha hae = who have; *wham* = whom; *gory* = bloody; *lour* = threaten

Wha will be a traitor-knave?
Wha can fill a coward's grave?
Wha sae base as be a slave?
Let him turn and flee!
Wha for Scotland's King and Law,
Freedom's sword will strongly draw,
Free-man stand or Free-man fa',
Let him follow me.

He asks if any of his men could be traitors or cowards or willing to accept the life of a slave. If so then turn and flee now or else live or die as free men.
sae base = so worthless

By Oppression's woes and pains!
By your Sons in servile chains!
We will drain your dearest veins,
But they *shall* be free!
Lay the proud usurpers low!
Tyrants fall in every foe!
Liberty's in every blow!
Let us Do – or Die!!!

To fight the oppressor is to fight for the freedom of their own children. They themselves may die in battle but their children will be free. Every blow struck is a blow for liberty. Fight or die!

My Luve is Like a Red, Red Rose

This is one of the most beautiful love-songs ever written. It is not known whether Burns had any lady in mind when he penned the words, but no one could fail to be enthralled by it.

O, my Luve's like a red, red rose.
That's newly sprung in June.   *sprung* = blossomed
O, my Luve's like the melodie
That's sweetly play'd in tune.

As fair art thou, my bonie lass,
So deep in luve am I,
And I will luve thee still, my Dear,
Till a' the seas gang dry.   *till a' the seas gang dry* = until the oceans dry up

Till a' the seas gang dry, my Dear,
And the rocks melt wi' the sun!
And I will luve thee still, my Dear,
While the sands o' life shall run.

And fare thee weel, my only Luve!
And fare thee weel, a while!
And I will come again, my Luve,
Tho' it were ten thousand mile!

Behold The Hour, The Boat Arrive

Second Version

The departure of Nancy McLehose was a major influence in the Bard's life. This is one of several poems written on her leaving.

Behold the hour, the boat arrive!
Thou goest, thou darling of my heart!
Sever'd from thee, can I survive?
But Fate has will'd, and we must part.
I'll often greet this surging swell,
Yon distant Isle will often hail:—
'E'en here, I took the last farewell;
There, latest mark'd her vanish'd sail.'

Along the solitary shore,
While flitting sea-fowl round me cry,
Across the rolling, dashing roar,
I'll westward turn my wistful eye:
'Happy, thou Indian grove' I'll say,
'Where now my Nancy's path may be!
While thro' thy sweets she loves to stray,
O tell me, does she muse on me?'

You're Welcome, Willie Stewart

Another short example of how the friends of the Bard were immortalised through his verse. Willie Stewart was the son of a publican who Burns visited while carrying out his duties as an exciseman. The following lines were engraved onto a glass, much to the annoyance of the landlady. This glass eventually came into the possession of Sir Walter Scott and remains on view at Abbotsford to this day.

CHORUS

You're welcome, Willie Stewart!
You're welcome, Willie Stewart!
There's ne'er a flower that blooms in May,
That's half sae welcome's thou art!

Come, bumpers high! express your joy!
The bowl we maun renew it;
The tappet-hen, gae bring her ben,
To welcome Willie Stewart!

bumper = a glass filled to the brim; *maun* = must; *tappet-hen* = a six-pint jug; *ben* = through

May foes be strang, and friends be slack!
Ilk action may he rue it!
May woman on him turn her back,
That wrangs thee, Willie Stewart!

slack = free and open; *ilk* = each; *wrangs* = wrongs

A Man's a Man Far A' That

In this poem, Burns clearly reveals his contempt for rank and title. It was written in 1795, a year before his death, and it gives the impression that by that time he had developed an intense dislike of the aristocracy. Perhaps his rubbing shoulders with Edinburgh's upper-crust helped.

However, the fact remains that this poem has attained international recognition among those who believe in the equality of man. The Russians honoured Burns by issuing a set of commerative stamps to him during the twentieth-century and his works continue to be part of the school curriculum in that country.

Is there for honest poverty
That hings his head, and a' that?
The coward-slave, we pass him by,
We dare be poor for a' that !
For a' that, and a' that,
Our toils obscure, an' a' that
The rank is but the guinea's stamp,
The Man's the gowd for a' that.

Here Burns is telling us that although a man be poor and a hard worker, he is still a man. Burns has no time for either the servile creature who always hangs his head or for the would-be high and mighty person who bought such power.
hings = hangs; *gowd* = gold

What though on hamely fare we dine,
Wear hoddin grey and a' that.
Gie fools their silks, and knaves their wine,
A Man's a Man for a' that
For a' that and a' that,
Their tinsel show, and a' that,
The honest man, tho' e'er sae poor,
Is king o' men for a' that

Just because a man dines on simple food and wears clothes that may not be considered fashionable, it does not make him any less a man than one whose clothes are made of silk and who drinks wine.
hamely fare = homely food; *hoddin grey* = a coarse grey woollen cloth; *gie* = give

Ye see yon birkie ca'd, 'a lord,'
Wha struts, an stares, and a' that?
Tho' hundreds worship at his word,
He's but a cuif for a' that.
 For a' that, and a' that,
His ribband, star and a' that,
The man o' independent mind,
He looks an' laughs at a' that.

Look at that swaggering fellow who is called 'a lord' with hundreds of people listening to his every word – in actual fact he is nothing but a fool. A real man just looks at all the ribbons and stars being worn and laughs at them.
birkie = a strutting swaggering fellow; *cuif (coof)* = fool; *ribband* = ribbon

A prince can mak a belted knight,
A marquis, duke, and a' that!
But an honest man's aboon his might,
Guid faith he mauna fa' that!
For a' that, and a' that,
Their dignities, and a' that
The pith o' Sense an' pride o' Worth,
Are higher rank than a' that

Then let us pray that come it may,
As come it will for a' that,
That Sense and Worth, o'er a' the earth,
Shall bear the gree, and a' that.
For a' that, and a' that,
It's comin' yet for a' that,
That Man to Man, the world o'er,
Shall brithers be for a' that.

Any man can be given a title by royalty but that does not make him any better than an honest man who has faith in himself. To know one's worth is value in excess of the foolish dignity of these people.

mak = make; *aboon* = above; *gude* = good; *mauna* = must not; *pith* = importance

However, let us pray that one of those days men will see the pointlessness of struggle over rank and power and come to recognise that all men are equal.

bear the gree = win the victory

The Dumfries Volunteers

In sharp contrast to the profoundly Scottish sentiments expressed in *Scots Wha Hae*, here Burns appears to be truly British, although there is a suspicion that this may have been an attempt to satisfy his masters in the Customs and Excise. In 1795 there was great speculation that Emperor Napoleon was set to invade the British Isles and this led to the formation of the Volunteers Movement, an early version of the Home Guard of the Second World War. Burns was heavily involved in the formation of the Dumfries group and certainly appears to have enjoyed this aspect of his life. One can only wonder what Robert Burns would have made of today's squabbles with Britain's so-called European partners?

Does haughty Gaul invasion threat?
Then let the loons beware, Sir!
There's wooden walls upon our seas,
And volunteers on shore, Sir.!
The Nith shall run to Corsincon,
And Criffel sink in Solway,
Ere we permit a foreign foe
On British ground to rally!

He points out that should the French be foolish enough to launch an invasion not only will they have to face the British Navy but if they ever get to land, they will be confronted by the ranks of volunteers. The River Nith and the hills of Corsincon and Criffel will have to perform geographical miracles before any enemy of Britain will rally on British soil. *Gaul* = France; *loons* = rascals; *wooden walls* = ships

O, let us not, like snarling tykes
 In wrangling be divided;
Till, slap! come in an unco loon
And wi' a rung decide it.
Be Britain still to Britain true,
Amang oursels united;
For never but by British hands
Maun British wrangs be righted!

He warns that fighting among ourselves could be fatal, as we are liable to find too late that the enemy has taken over and that they now rule the British with clubs and cudgels. Only by remaining united will the British right the wrongs within Britain.
tykes = dogs; *unco* = fearsome; *rung* = cudgel; *mang* = among; *maun* = must; *wrangs* = wrongs

The kettle o' the Kirk and State
Perhaps a clout may fail in't;
But deil a foreign tinkler-loun
Shall ever ca' a nail in 't!
Our fathers' bluid the kettle bought,
And wha wad dare to spoil it!
By heaven, the sacreligious dog
Shall fuel be to boil it!

There may be differences between Church and State but no foreigner is going to be allowed to interfere. British freedom was bought with the blood of our forefathers so heaven help anyone who attempts to take away that freedom – especially a Frenchman!

kettle = boiling pot; *Kirk* = church; *clout* = piece of cloth; *tinkler* = gypsy; *ca'* = drive; *bluid* = blood; *wha wad* = who would

The wretch that wad a tyrant own,
And the wretch, his true-sworn brother,
Who would set the mob aboon the throne,
May they be damned together!
Who will not sing 'God save the King,'
Shall hang as high's the steeple;
But while we sing 'God save the King,'
We'll ne'er forget the people.

Any despicable person who would help overthrow the King, and refuses to swear allegiance to the throne, will be hanged. But remember, even as we swear loyalty to our King, we must never overlook the rights of the common man.

aboon = above

How Cruel Are The Parents

There is little doubt but that Burns was a womaniser, but could it be that he was also a visionary who had an extraordinary insight into the plight of women?

How cruel are the parents
Who riches only prize,
And to the wealthy booby,   *booby* = stupid fellow
Poor Woman sacrifice.
Meanwhile the hapless daughter
Has but a choice of strife;
To shun a tyrant father's hate,
Become a wretched wife.

The ravening hawk pursuing,
The trembling dove thus flies,
To shun impelling ruin
Awhile her pinions tries;
Till, of escape despairing,
No shelter or retreat,
She trusts the ruthless falconer,
And drops beneath his feet.

Address to The Toothache

Medicine may have been somewhat primitive in the eighteenth century, but dentistry was pure torture. Toothcare was unheard of and toothache was common.

My curse upon your venom'd stang,
That shoots my tortur'd gums alang,
An' thro' my lug gies monie a twang
Wi' gnawing vengeance,
Tearing my nerves wi' bitter pang,
Like racking engines!

He curses the toothache for the pain it is giving him.
stang = sting; *lug* = ear; *twang* = twinge; *alang* = along; *monie* = many

A' down my beard the slavers trickle,
I throw the wee stools o'er the mickle,
While round the fire the giglets keckle,
To see me loup,
An' raving mad, I wish a heckle
Were i' their doup!

Giggling girls watch him dance around his fire like a madman, and he wishes that they had a rough comb up their backsides.
mickle = large; *giglets keckle* = girls giggle; *a heckle* = heckling comb; *doup* = backside.

When fevers burn, or ague freezes,
Rheumatics gnaw, or colic squeezes,
Our neebors sympathise to ease us,
Wi' pitying moan;
But thou!—- the hell o' a' diseases—
They mock our groan!

Neighbours will show sympathy towards other illnesses but will only mock if you have toothache.
neebors = neighbours

Of a' the numerous human dools—
Ill hairsts, daft bargains, cutty-stools,
Or worthy frien's laid i' the mools,
Sad sight to see!
The tricks o' knaves, or fash o' fools—
Thou bear'st the gree!

Of all the woes suffered by humanity, toothache takes the prize.
dools = woes; *ill hairsts* = poor harvests; *daft bargains* = madness; *cutty-stools* = stools of repentance; *mools* = crumbling earth; *fash* = annoyance; *bear'st the gree* = rank highly

Whare'er that place be priests ca' Hell,
Whare a' the tones o' misery yell,
An' ranked plagues their numbers tell,
In dreadfu' raw,
Thou, *Toothache*, surely bear'st the bell
Aboon them a'!

Toothache would be at home in Hell.
raw = row; *bears't the bell* = take the prize;
aboon = above

O! thou grim, mischief-making chiel,
That gars the notes o' discord squeel,
Till human-kind aft dance a reel
In gore a shoe thick,
Gie a' the faes o' Scotland's weal
A Towmond's Toothache!

He hopes that Scotland's foes will suffer a
twelve-month toothache.
chiel = fellow; *faes* = foes; *weal* = well-being;
towmond = twelve months

The Toad-eater

The Toad-eater displays Burns' contempt for those who boasted of their wealth and social standing.

This short tirade was directed at one young man in particular who had made a great deal of money through speculation and who, although born of low rank, considered himself to be in the higher echelons of society.

What of earls with whom you have supt,   *supt* = supped
And of Dukes that you dined with yestreen?   *yestreen* = yesterday evening
Lord! A louse, Sir is still but a louse,
Though it crawl on the curls of a queen.

On Marriage

This verse illustrates Burns' inability to dedicate his life to one woman.

That hackney'd judge of human life,
The Preacher and the King,
Observes: 'The man that gets a wife,
He gets a noble thing.'

That hackney'd judge = King Solomon

But how capricious are mankind,
Now loathing, now desirous!
We married men, how oft we find
The best of things will tire us!

Charlie, He's My Darling

An old bawdy ballad, refined by Burns, referring to Bonny Prince Charlie's romantic escapades.

CHORUS
An' Charlie, he's my darling.
My darling, my darling,
Charlie, he's my darling—
The Young Chevalier!

'Twas on a Monday morning
Right early in the year,
That Charlie came to our town—
The Young Chevalier!

As he was walking up the street
The city for to view,
O, there he spied a bonie lass
The window looking thro'!

Sae light's he jimped up the stair,
And tirl'd at the pin;   *tirl'd on the pin* = rattled the door knob.
And wha sae ready as hersel
To let the laddie in!

He set his Jenny on his knee,
In all his Highland dress;
For brawlie weel he kend the way
To please a bonie lass.

It's up yon heathery mountain
And down the scroggy glen,
We daurna gang a-milking
For Charlie and his men!

The Lass That Made The Bed To Me

This old ballad appears to have originated in the border counties of England, but has been revised by Burns.

When Januar wind was blawin cauld,
As to the North I took my way,
The mirksome night did me enfauld,
I knew na whare to lodge till day.

By my guid luck a maid I met,
Just in the middle o' my care,
And kindly she did me invite
To walk into a chamber fair.

I bow'd fu' low unto this maid,
And thank'd her for her courtesie;
I bow'd fu' low unto this maid,
An' bade her mak a bed for me.

She made the bed baith large and wide,
Wi' twa white hands she spread it down;
She put the cup to her rosy lips,
And drank;— ' Young man, now sleep ye sound.'

She snatch'd the candle in her hand,
And frae the chamber went wi' speed,
But I call'd her quickly back again
To lay some mair below my head.

A cod she laid below my head,   *cod* = pillow
And served me wi' due respect,
And to salute her wi' a kiss,
I put my arms about her neck.

'Haud aff your hands, young man!' she says,   *haud aff* = take off
'And dinna sae uncivil be;
Gif you have onie luve for me,   *gif* = if; *onie* = ony
O, wrang na my virginitie!'

Her hair was like the links o' gowd,   *gowd* = gold
Her teeth were like the ivorie,
Her cheeks like lilies dipt in wine,
The lass that made the bed to me!

Her bosom was the driven snaw,
Twa drifted heaps sae fair to see;
Her limbs the polish'd marble stane,
The lass that made the bed to me!

I kiss'd her o'er and o'er again,
And ay she wist na what to say,   *wist* = wished
I laid her 'tween me and the wa'—
That lassie thocht na long till day.

Upon the morrow, when we raise,
I thank'd her for her courtesie;
But ay she blush'd, and ay she sigh'd,
And said, 'Alas, ye've ruined me!'

I clasp'd her waist, and kiss'd her syne,
While the tear stood twinkling in her e'e,
I said, 'My lassie, dinna cry,
For ye ay shall make the bed to me.'

She took her mither's Holland sheets,
An' made them a' in sarks to me,   *sarks* = shirts
Blythe and merry may she be,
The lass that made the bed to me!

The bonie lass made the bed to me,
The braw lass made the bed to me!
I'll ne'er forget till the day that I die,
The lass that made the bed to me.

Had I The Wyte

A traditional bawdy song, again collected and revised by Burns. It is a story of a battered wife seeking solace with another man.

Had I the wyte? had I the wyte?
Had I the wyte? she bade me!
She watch'd me by the hie-gate side,
And up the loan she shaw'd me,
And when I wadna venture in,
A coward loon she ca'd me!
Had Kirk and State been in the gate,
I lighted when she bade me.

Was it his fault that the lady had invited him into her cottage and taunted him when he appeared reluctant? Had he considered the consequences, he would have rode on.
had I the wyte = was I to blame? *hie-gate* = high-road; *shaw'd* = showed; *loon* = fool; *lighted* = mounted

Sae craftily she took me ben
And bade me mak nae clatter:—
'For our ramgunshoch, glum, guidman
Is o'er ayont the water.'
Whae'er shall say I wanted grace
When I did kiss and dawte her,
Let him be planted in my place,
Syne say I was the fauter!

She led him through the house, telling him to be silent although her surly husband was well out of the way. He felt no guilt as they made love.
ben = through; *clatter* = noise; *ramgunshoch* = bad-tempered; *guidman* = husband; *ayont* = beyond; *dawte* = caress; *syne* = then; *fauter* = wrong-doer

Could I for shame, could I for shame,
Could I for shame refus'd her?
And wadna manhood been to blame
Had I unkindly used her?
He claw'd her wi' the ripplin'-kame,
And blae and bluidy bruis'd her—
When sic a husband was frae hame,
What wife but wad excus'd her?

He felt he could not refuse her, but had to treat her with care as she had suffered brutality at the hands of her husband. Who could blame such a woman for seeking pleasure when her husband was out of the way?
ripplin-kame = wool-comb; *blae* = blue; *bluidy* = bloody

I dighted ay her een sae blue,
An' bann'd the cruel randy,
And, weel I wat her willin mou,
Was e'en as succarcandie.
At gloamin-shot, it was, I wot,
I lighted – on the Monday;
But I cam thro' the Tyeseday's dew,
To wanton Willie's brandy.

He wiped the tears from her eyes and cursed her cruel husband. It was evening when he left, but he was back again the following morning to visit her again.

dighted = wiped; *bann'd* = cursed; *randy* = ruffian; *wat* = know; *mou* = mouth; *gloamin-shot* = sunset; *Tyseday* = Tuesday

For The Sake O' Somebody

These two short verses were not, as we have come to expect, written by the Bard about a very special young lady. In fact they were written by Burns about no less a person than Bonnie Prince Charlie

My heart is sair, I dare na tell,
My heart is sair for Somebody,
I could wake a winter night,
For the sake o' Somebody!
Oh-hon! For Somebody!
Oh-hey! For Somebody!
I could range the warld around
For the sake o' Somebody.

sair = sore; *dare na* = dare not

Ye Powers that smile on virtuous love,
O, sweetly smile on Somebody!
Frae ilka danger keep him free,
And send me safe my Somebody!
Oh-hon! for Somebody!
Oh-hey! for Somebody!
I wad do – what wad I not?
For the sake o' Somebody

frae = from; *ilka* = every

wad = would

Gude Wallace

This is another popular old ballad extolling the heroics of Scotland's most famous warrior, William Wallace. Burns has added seven stanzas of his own to the original but there is a gap of two lines in the poem, lost in the mists of time. This a story in the true 'Braveheart' tradition, full of exaggerated heroism and with blood up to the ankles.

'O for my ain king,' quo gude Wallace,
The rightful king o' fair Scotland;
'Between me and my Sovereign Blude
I think I see some ill seed sawn.'

Wallace wanted to see the English king removed from the Scottish throne.
quo = said; *Blude* = blood; *sawn* = sown

Wallace out over yon river he lap,
And he has lighted low down on yon plain,
And he was aware of a gay ladie,
As she was at the well washing.

As he travelled south he happened upon a lady.
lap = leapt

'What tydins, what tydins, fair lady, he says,
What tydins hast thou to tell unto me;
What tydins, what tydins fair lady,' he says,
'What tydins hae ye in the South Countrie.'

He sought information from her of local activity.
tydins = tidings

'Low down in yon wee Ostler house,
There is fyfteen Englishmen,
And they are seeking for gude Wallace,
It's him to take and him to hang.'

She warned him of a party of redcoats in the local inn asking of his whereabouts as they intend to see him hanged.
Ostler house = inn

'There's nocht in my purse,' quo gude Wallace,
'There's nocht, not even a bare pennie;
But I will go down to yon wee Ostler house,
Thir fyfteen Englishmen to see.'

Wallace apologised to the lady that he was unable to reward her, but declared that he would go and investigate for himself.
nocht = nothing; *yon* = that

And when he cam to yon wee Ostler house
He bad benedicite be there;
(The Englishmen at the table sat
The wine-fac'd captain at him did stare.)

He prayed for good fortune as he reached the inn.

bad = bade; *benedicite* = good fortune

'Where was ye born, auld crookit Carl,
Where was ye born, in what countrie;'
'I am a true Scot born and bred,
And an auld, crookit carl just sic as ye see.'

Disguised as an old man, he was asked by the captain where he was born, and replied that he was a true Scot.

auld crookit carl = bent old man

'I wad gie fyfteen shillings to onie crookit carl,
To onie crookit carl just sic as ye,
If ye will get me gude Wallace,
For he is a man I wad very fain see.'

The captain then offered him a reward if he would help him locate Wallace.

sic = such; *fain* = gladly; *onie* =any

He hit the proud Captain alang the
    chafft-blade,
That never a bit o' meat he ate mair;
And he sticket the rest at the table where
    they sat,
And he left them a' lyin sprawlin there.

Wallace killed the captain with a single blow, then killed the rest of the party as they sat at the table.

chafft-blade = jaw-bone; *sticket* = stabbed

'Get up, get up, gudewife,' he says,
'And get to me some dinner in haste;
For it soon will be three lang days
Sin I a bit o' meat did taste.'

He then asks the innkeeper's wife to pepare him a meal as it is three days since he has eaten.

The dinner was na weel readie,
Nor was it on the table set,
Till other fyfteen Englishmen
Were a' lighted about the yett.

But before it was prepared, another group of fifteen redcoats were at the gate.

yett = gate

'Come out, come out now, gude Wallace,
This is the day that thou maun die;'
'I lippen nae sae little to God,' he says,
'Altho' I be but ill- wordie.'

They called for him to surrender and be hanged, but he has faith in God.

maun = must; *lippen* = trust; *ill-wordie* = ill-worthy.

The gudewife had an auld gudeman,
By gude Wallace he stiffly stood,
Till ten o' the fyfteen Englishmen
Before the door lay in their blude.

The other five to the greenwood ran,
And he hang'd these five upon a grain:
And on the morn wi' his merry men a'
He sat at dine in Lochmaben town.

The innkeeper stood side-by-side with Wallace and soon ten of the redcoats lay dead.

blude = blood

The other five ran to hide in the woods, yet their escape was short-lived as Wallace's men hanged them from a branch before continuing their march south.

grain = branch

The Henpecked Husband

This is a very straightforward, no-holds barred poem by the Bard.

Curs'd be the man, the poorest wretch in life,   *vassal* = slave;
The crouching vassal to the tyrant wife!
Who has no will but by her high permission;
Who has not sixpence but in her possession;
Who must to her his dear friend's secret tell;
Who dreads a curtain-lecture worse than hell.   *curtain-lecture* = a lecture given in bed
Were such the wife had fallen to my part,   by a wife to her husband,
I'd break her spirit, or I'd break her heart.
I'd charm her with the magic of a switch,   *switch* = cane
I'd kiss her maids, and kick the perverse bitch.